MICROBIAL ENVIRONMENT AND BIOREMEDIATION

ENV BOOKS SERIES

MICROBIAL ENVIRONMENT AND BIOREMEDIATION

Editors

Dr. Alka Chauhan

Society for Environment, Health, Awareness of Nutrition & Toxicology (SEHAT)
1775, Sohan Ganj, Near Clock Tower
Delhi - 110 007 (INDIA)

Dr. Ashok K. Rathoure

M/s Vardan EnviroNet, Gurgaon
Formerly, Beehive College of Ad. Studies Dehradun

Dr. Raaz K Maheshwari

Associate Professor
Department of Chemistry
SBRM Govt. PG College
Nagaur, Rajasthan (INDIA)

Series Editor

Dr. Pawan Kumar 'Bharti'

Vice President
Society for Environment, Health, Awareness of Nutrition & Toxicology (SEHAT)
1775, Sohan Ganj, Near Clock Tower
Delhi - 110 007
(INDIA)
E-mail: gurupawanbharti@gmail.com

DPH

DISCOVERY PUBLISHING HOUSE PVT. LTD.

INDIA

Published by:

Namit Wasan

DISCOVERY PUBLISHING HOUSE PVT. LTD.
4383/4B, Ansari Road, Darya Ganj
New Delhi-110 002 (India)
Phone : +91-11-23279245, 43596064-65
Fax : +91-11-23253475
E-mail : discoverypublishinghouse@gmail.com
namitwasan9@gmail.com
sales@discoverypublishinggroup.com
website: www.discoverypublishinggroup.com

***First Edition:* 2017**

ISBN: 978-93-5056-856-9

Microbial Environment and Bioremediation

Printed at:
Infinity Imaging Systems
Delhi

ENV Books Series, (India)

Calls lengthy and error free chapters for further volumes of books on various environmental issues. (Send your manuscripts to envbooks@gmail.com)

Founding Editor (Editor-in-Chief)

Dr. Pawan Kumar 'Bharti'

Society for Environment, Health, Awareness of Nutrition & Toxicology (SEHAT-India)
1775, Sohanganj, Near Clock Tower, Delhi-7, (India)
E-mail:*gurupawanbharti@rediffmail.com*

Other Titles by Editor-in-Chief:

1. **Advances in Biotechnology and Ecological Sciences**
   Bharti, P.K., Chauhan, A. and Ray, J. (eds.)
   (ISBN: 978-93-5056-358-8).
2. **Advances in Agriculture and Ecology**
   Bharti, P.K.; Chauhan, A. and Ezeaku Peter Ikemefuna (eds.)
   (ISBN: 978-93-5056-362-5).
3. **Agriculture and Environmental Biotechnology**
   Bharti, P.K. and Chauhan, A. (eds.)
   (ISBN: 978-93-5056-479-0).
4. **Agriculture Development and Sustainable Environment**
   Ray, J. and Bharti, P. K. (eds.)
   (ISBN: 978-93-5056-759-3)
5. **Agriculture Ecology and Environment**
   Bharti, P.K. and Olubukola O. Babalola (eds.)
   (ISBN: 978-93-5056-480-6).
6. **Agriculture Ecology, Sustainable Development and Agribusiness Management**
   Mehta Piyush; Sharma Pankaj; and 'Bharti' P.K. (eds.)
   (ISBN: 978-93-5056-851-4).
7. **Agriculture, Environment and Nano-science**
   Bharti, Pawan K. (ed.)
   (ISBN: 978-93-5056-760-5).
8. **Agro-biodiversity:** ***Conservation & Sustainable Development***
   Sharma, Pankaj; Singh, Narayan; and Bharti, P.K. (eds.)
   (ISBN: 978-93-505-782-1).
9. **Agro-forestry and Climate Change**
   Bharti, Pawan K. and Singh, Narayan (eds.)
   (ISBN: 978-93-5056-514-8).

10. **Agro-forestry and Sustainable Agriculture**
Sharma, Pankaj; Bharti, P.K. (eds.)
(ISBN: 978-93-5056-786-9).
11. **Aquaculture and Fisheries Environment**
Gupta, S.K. and Pawan K. Bharti (eds.)
(ISBN: 978-93-5056-408-0).
12. **Aquatic Biodiversity and Pollution**
Bharti, P.K.; Chauhan, A. and Kaoud, H.A.H. (eds.)
(ISBN: 978-93-5056-359-5).
13. **Aquatic Ecology and Biotechnology**
Bharti, P.K. and Zaki, M.S.A. (eds.)
(ISBN: 978-93-5056-451-6).
14. **Aquatic Environment and Toxicology**
Bharti, Pawan K. (ed.)
(ISBN: 978-93-5056-236-9).
15. **Biodiversity, Biotechnology and Environmental Conservation**
Bharti, P.K. and Bhandari, G. (eds.)
(ISBN: 978-93-5056-750-0).
16. **Biodiversity of Aquatic Ecosystem: *Significance, Threat and Conservation***
Bharti, P.K. and Kaoud, H.A.H. (eds.)
(ISBN: 978-93-5056-297-0).
17. **Biological Diversity and Ecology**
Arya, M.K.; Bharti, P.K. and Ritesh Joshi (eds.)
(ISBN: 978-93-5056-785-2).
18. **Bioremediation and Microbial Biotechnology**
Gupta, Sandeep; and Bharti, P.K. (eds.)
(ISBN: 978-93-5056-783-8).
19. **Biotechnological Approaches & Water Ecosystem**
Zaki, M.S.A.; and Bharti, P.K. (eds.)
(ISBN: 978-93-5056-779-1).
20. **Biotechnology, Agro-ecology and Environment**
Chauhan, Avnish and Bharti, P.K. (eds.)
(ISBN: 978-93-5056-757-9).
21. **Clean Technologies and Environmental Protection**
Chauhan, A.; Sharma, S. and Bharti, P.K. (eds.)
(ISBN: 978-93-5056-731-9).
22. **Climate Change and Agriculture**
Bharti, P.K. and Chauhan, Avnish (eds.)
(ISBN: 978-93-5056-148-5).
23. **Climate Change and Biodiversity**
Bharti, P.K. and Chauhan, Avnish (eds.)
(ISBN: 978-93-5056-360-1).
24. **Climate Change, Disaster Management and Environment**
Chauhan, Alka; Bharti, P.K. (eds.)
(ISBN: 978-93-5056-784-5).

25. **Conservation and Cultivation of Medicinal Plants**
Bharti, P.K. and Singh Narayan (eds.)
(ISBN: 978-93-5056-740-1).

26. **Crop Productivity and Plant Disease Management**
Chauhan, Alka; Bharti, P.K. and Sadana, Deepti (eds.)
(ISBN: 978-93-5056-791-3).

27. **Eco-toxicology and Eco-technology**
Bharti, P.K. and Zaki, M. (eds.)
(ISBN: 978-93-5056-313-7).

28. **Environmental Biotechnology and Application**
Bharti, P.K. and Chauhan, Avnish (eds.)
(ISBN: 978-93-5056-262-8).

29. **Environmental Conservation and Biotechnology**
Chauhan, A. and P.K. Bharti (eds.)
(ISBN: 978-93-5056-512-4).

30. **Environmental Health and Problems**
Bharti, P.K. and Gajananda, Kh. (eds.)
(ISBN: 978-93-5056-263-5).

31. **Environmental Pollution and Biodiversity**
Bharti, P.K.; Chauhan, Avnish and Kumar, P. (eds.)
(ISBN: 978-93-5056-149-2).

32. **Farming Techniques and Crop Production**
C. Alka; Sharma Anubhuti; Ray Jaswant and 'Bharti' P.K. (eds.)
(ISBN: 978-93-5056-855-2).

33. **Fisheries and Toxicology**
Zaki, M.S.A.; Bharti, P.K. and Chauhan, A. (eds.)
(ISBN: 978-93-5056-452-3).

34. **Fish Habitat and Aquaculture**
Bharti, P.K.; Gupta Kr. Sanjay (eds.)
(ISBN: 978-93-5056-744-9).

35. **Food Processing, Management and Nanotechnology**
Chauhan, Avnish; Bharti, P.K. (eds.)
(ISBN: 978-93-5056-796-8).

36. **Freshwater Ecosystem and Xenobiotics**
Bharti, P.K.; Zaki, M. and Chauhan, A. (eds.)
(ISBN: 978-93-5056-299-4).

37. **Limnology and Aquatic Science**
Sharma, S. and Bharti, P.K. (eds.)
(ISBN: 978-93-5056-735-7).

38. **Medicinal Plants:** ***Distribution, Utilization & Significance***
Sharma, P.; Bharti, P.K. and Narayan Singh (eds.)
(ISBN: 978-93-5056-734-0).

39. **Microbial Applications and Environment**
Bharti, Pawan K. (ed.)
(ISBN: 978-93-5056-515-5).

40. **Microbial Ecology and Habitat**
Bharti, Pawan K. (ed.)
(ISBN: 978-93-5056-514-8).
41. **Natural Ecosystem and Climate Change**
Bharti, P.K., and Kh. Gajananda (ed.)
(ISBN: 978-93-5056-745-6).
42. **Pest Management and Agro-Techniques**
Biswas, Asim; Bharti, P.K., Chauhan, Avnish (eds.)
(ISBN: 978-93-5056-794-4).
43. **Prakriti me Aushadhi (*in Hindi*)**
Singh, J.R.; Bharti, P.K. and Bharti, B.
(ISBN: 978-93-5056-200-0).
44. **Seed Technology, Plant Growth and Cropping System**
Tyagi, P.K. and Bharti, P.K. (eds.)
(ISBN: 978-93-5056-738-8).
45. **Seed Treatment, Plant Heath and Agro-technology**
Chauhan, A. and Bharti, P.K. (eds.)
(ISBN: 978-93-5056-810-1).
46. **Soil Characteristics and Agro-ecology**
Avnish Chauhan and Bharti, P.K. (eds.)
(ISBN: 978-93-5056-758-6)
47. **Soil Contamination and Conservation**
Ezeaku, P.I. and Bharti, P.K. (eds.)
(ISBN: 978-93-5056-737-1).
48. **Soil Quality and Contamination**
Bharti, P.K. and Chauhan, Avnish (eds.)
(ISBN: 978-93-5056-361-8).
49. **Sustainable Aquaculture Management**
Gupta, S.K.; Bharti, P.K (eds.)
(ISBN: 978-93-5056-797-5).
50. **Waste Disposal and Management**
Bharti, P.K.; Tabassum, B. and Bajaj, P. (eds.)
(ISBN: 978-93-5056-729-6).
51. **Waste Generation and Utilization**
Bajaj Priya; Tabassum, B., and Bharti, P.K. (eds.)
(ISBN: 978-93-5056-792-0).
52. **Waste Management and Environmental Health**
Tabassum, B., Bajaj Priya, and Bharti, P.K. (eds.)
(ISBN: 978-93-5056-777-7).
53. **Water Resources and Agriculture**
Bharti, P.K. and Ezeaku Peter Ikemefuna (eds.)
(ISBN: 978-93-5056-481-3).
54. **Waste Resources Management:** ***Monitoring & Assessment***
Gupta, Sandeep and Bharti, P.K. (eds.)
(ISBN: 978-93-5056-799-9).

Preface

Microbial biotechnology is the manipulation of microorganisms at the genetic and molecular level to generate useful products. While some fear microbes due to the association of some microbes with various human illnesses, many microbes are also responsible for numerous beneficial processes such as: industrial fermentation (*e.g.*, the production of alcohol, vinegar and dairy products), antibiotic production and as vehicles for cloning in more complex organisms such as: plants. Scientists have also exploited their knowledge of microbes to produce biotechnologically important enzymes such as: Taq polymerase, reporter genes for use in other genetic systems and novel molecular biology techniques such as: the yeast two-hybrid system.

Bacteria can be used for the industrial production of amino acids. Corynebacterium glutamicum is one of the most important bacterial species with an annual production of more than two million tonnes of amino acids, mainly L-glutamate and L-lysine. Since some bacteria have the ability to synthesize antibiotics, they are used for medicinal purposes, such as: Streptomyces to make aminoglycoside antibiotics.

A variety of biopolymers, such as: polysaccharides, polyesters, and polyamides, are produced by microorganisms. Microorganisms are used for the biotechnological production of biopolymers with tailored properties suitable for high-value medical application such as: tissue engineering and drug delivery. Microorganisms are used for the biosynthesis of xanthan, alginate, cellulose, cyanophycin, poly (gamma-glutamic acid), levan, hyaluronic acid, organic acids, oligosaccharides and polysaccharide, and polyhydroxyalkanoates.

Microorganisms are beneficial for microbial biodegradation or bioremediation of domestic, agricultural and industrial wastes and subsurface pollution in soils, sediments and marine environments. The ability of each microorganism to degrade toxic waste depends on the nature of each contaminant. Since sites typically have multiple pollutant types, the most effective approach to microbial biodegradation is to use a mixture of bacterial and fungal species and strains, each specific to the biodegradation of one or more types of contaminants.

Symbiotic microbial communities are known to confer various benefits to their human and animal hosts health including: aiding digestion, production of beneficial vitamins and amino acids, and suppression of pathogenic microbes. Some benefit may be conferred by consuming fermented foods, probiotics (bacteria potentially beneficial to the digestive system) and/or prebiotics. The ways the microbiome influences human and animal health, as well as methods to influence the microbiome are active areas of research.

Research has suggested that microorganisms could be useful in the treatment of cancer. Various strains of non-pathogenic clostridia can infiltrate and replicate within solid tumors. Clostridial vectors can be safely administered and their potential to deliver therapeutic proteins has been demonstrated in a variety of preclinical models.

Life science research and industry is developing rapidly all over the world. Microbial biotechnology is increasingly being regarded as a core subject in most university and polytechnic life science courses. There already exist a number of excellent general textbooks on microbiology and biotechnology that deal with the basic principles of the field.

Bioremediation is a waste management technique that involves the use of organisms to remove or neutralize pollutants from a contaminated site. According to the United States EPA, bioremediation is a "treatment that uses naturally occurring organisms to break down hazardous substances into less toxic or non-toxic substances". Technologies can be generally classified as in situ or *ex situ*. *In situ* bioremediation involves treating the contaminated material at the site, while *ex situ* involves the removal of the contaminated material to be treated elsewhere. Some examples of bioremediation related technologies are phytoremediation, bioventing, bioleaching, landfarming, bioreactor, composting, bioaugmentation, rhizofiltration, and biostimulation.

Bioremediation may occur on its own (natural attenuation or intrinsic bioremediation) or may only effectively occur through the addition of fertilizers, oxygen, etc., that help in enhancing the growth of the pollution-eating microbes within the medium (biostimulation). Depleted soil nitrogen status may encourage biodegradation of some nitrogenous organic chemicals, and soil materials with a high capacity to adsorb pollutants may slow down biodegradation owing to limited bioavailability of the chemicals to microbes. Recent advancements have also proven successful via the addition of matched microbe strains to the medium to enhance the resident microbe population's ability to break down contaminants. Microorganisms used to perform the function of bioremediation are known as bioremediators.

However, not all contaminants are easily treated by bioremediation using microorganisms. For example, heavy metals such as: cadmium and lead are not readily absorbed or captured by microorganisms. A recent experiment, however, suggests that fish bones have some success absorbing lead from contaminated soil. Bone char has been shown to bioremediate small amounts of cadmium, copper, and zinc. A recent experiment, suggests that the removals of pollutants (nitrate, silicate, chromium and sulphide) from tannery wastewater were studied in batch experiments using marine microalgae. The assimilation of metals such as: mercury into the food chain may worsen matters. Phytoremediation is useful in these circumstances because natural plants or transgenic plants are able to bioaccumulate these toxins in their above-ground parts, which are then harvested for removal. The heavy metals in the harvested biomass may be further concentrated by incineration or even recycled for industrial use. Some damaged artifacts at museums contain microbes which could be specified as bio remediating agents. In contrast to this situation, other contaminants, such as: aromatic hydrocarbons as are common in petroleum, are relatively simple targets for microbial degradation, and some soils may even have some capacity to autoremediate, as it were, owing to the presence of autochthonous microbial communities capable of degrading these compounds.

The elimination of a wide range of pollutants and wastes from the environment requires increasing our understanding of the relative importance of different pathways and regulatory networks to carbon flux in particular environments and for particular compounds, and they will certainly accelerate the development of bioremediation technologies and biotransformation processes.

The present book updates the subject content of microbial ecology, biotechnology, bioremediation, phytoremediation, microbial application, industrial biotechnology and agriculture biotechnology. Thanks are due to the contributors from various organizations and publisher for their interest in the work.

The book will be helpful for the researchers, academia working in the field of microbial ecology, biotechnology, bioremediation, phytoremediation, microbial application, industrial biotechnology and agriculture biotechnology.

– Editors

(envbooks@gmail.com)

Contents

MICROBIAL ENVIRONMENT AND BIOREMEDIATION
Edited by : **Dr. Alka Chauhan; Dr. Ashok K. Rathoure & Dr. Raaz K Maheshwari**
Edition : **2017**
ISBN : 978-93-5056-856-9
Published by : **Discovery Publishing House Pvt. Ltd., New Delhi (India)**

1 Microbial Mediated Degradation of Pyrethroid Insecticides

Anudurga Gajendiran
Jayanthi Abraham*

ABSTRACT

Pyrethroids are synthetic derivates of pyrethrins, which are natural organic insecticides procured from the flowers of Chrysanthemum cinerariaefolium and C. coccineum. These pyrethroids are now found in many synthetic insecticides and are highly specific against insects and are generally used against mosquitoes. Pyrethroids are found to be stable and persist in the environment for longer period of time. Hence, the need for bioremediation of the soil to avoid pollutants from accumulating in the environment is vital. This paper discusses about the classification, structure and insecticidal properties and the toxicity of pyrethroids. The details of molecular basis, the pathway of degradation, the role of carboxylesterase enzyme, genes that are responsible for detoxification of pyrethroids and the various microorganisms capable of biotransformation of pyrethroids has been explored.

Keywords: Pyrethroids, carboxylesterase enzymes, biomineralisation, bacteria.

INTRODUCTION

Pyrethroids and pyrethrins are gradually becoming pre-dominant among insecticides used against insects in agricultural, garden and homes. Pyrethroids insecticides have been developed as a replacement for more toxic or recalcitrant organochlorine and organophosphorus pesticides (Katsuda, 1999). Currently, 16 pyrethroids are registered for use in the United States in a large variety of agricultural products (Bryant and Bite, 2003). Some pyrethroid insecticides have been classified as possible carcinogen to

Microbial Biotechnology Laboratory, School of Biosciences and Technology, VIT University, Vellore - 632 014, Tamil Nadu, India.

human by the US Environmental Protection Agency (EPA) (Tallur *et al.* 2008). The present article focuses on pyrethroids structures and their chemical property, role of carboxylesterases enzymes in degradation of pyrethroids, mechanism of insecticidal action molecular changes which are brought about within the organisms during the process of pyrethroid degradation.

Classes of Pyrethroids and their uses

Natural pyrethrins are organic compounds with insecticidal activity extracted from *Chrysanthemums cinerariaefolium* (Casida and Quistad 1998). Pyrethroids are synthetic analogs of the naturally occurring pyrethrins which, were developed in order to enhance the insecticidal activity of the pyrethrins while increasing stability to light and residence time in the environment (Gosselin, 1984). The pyrethroids are classified into two groups namely class I and class II, based on their toxicity and physical properties. Class I are pyrethroids with basic cyclopropane carboxylic ester structure. Pyrethroids are derivatives of pyrethrin that do not have a cyano group and elicit tumors. Allethrin, Bifenthrin, Permethrin, Phenothrin, Resmethrin, Tefluthrin, Teramethrin are comes compresses of class I pyrethroids. Class II pyrethroids are cyfluthrin, cyhalothrin, cypermethrin, deltamethrin, fenvalerate, fenpropathrin, flucythrinate, flumethrin, fluvalinate and tralomethrin, they have cyano group resulting in salivation and choreoathetosis.

Pyrethroids are efficient against a wide range of insect, pests belonging to the orders of Coleoptera, Hemiptera (Homoptera and Heteroptera), Diptera, Hymenoptera, Lepidoptera, Orthoptera and Thysanoptera. They are also used as household insecticides and grain protectants. Pyrethroids are employed in animal houses, fields, green houses and extensively used in veterinary medicine (Agency for Toxic Substances and Disease Registry 2003), (Table 1.1). The efficacy of the pyrethroids and their selectivity between insect species are based on the factors such as: shape, key structural features like specific chirality and cis or trans stereochemistry across the cyclopropane ring, ester or non-ester and physical properties *e.g.*, volatile compounds are efficient against insects which fly and chemical properties *e.g.*, polar compounds better for knockdown and high lipophilicity which result in reduced fish toxicity (Khambay, 2002).

Chemical Structure of Pyrethroid

Structure of pyrethroid typically consists of one to three asymmetric carbon atoms (chiral centers), so they have high chirality. The chirality of pyrethroids may arise from acid moiety, the alcohol moiety or both (Kurihara and Mayamoto, 1998; Ali *et al.* 2004). All pyrethroids can exist with at least four stereoisomers each with different biological activities. Each pyrethroid structure contains 2 or 4 diastereoisomers or 2 or 4 enantiomer pairs. In general, the isomer selectivity has been extensively observed in insecticidal activity for the isomers of a pyrethroid compound. Recent studies have shown that biodegradation of pyrethroids insecticide also exhibits significant isomer selectivity (Liu *et al.* 2005; Stok, *et al.* 2004). Pyrethroids are persistent compounds with high hydrophobicity (log K_{ow} 5.7-7.6) and very low water solubility.

Most pyrethroids consists of cyclopropane carboxylic acid moieties (or an equivalent group) linked to aromatic alcohols through a central ester (or ether) bond. Alteration to this basic pyrethroid structure are designed to increase insecticidal potency or photostability but may also result in difference in pyrethroid activity in non-target species (Yang *et al.* 1987; Valentine, 1990; Vijverberg and Van den Bercken, 1990; Naumann, 1998; Soderlund, 2002). One such alteration is adding α-cyano group to the alcohol moiety, which significantly increases the insecticidal activity (Zerba, 1999). In addition to the α-cyano group, other alteration to the fundamental acid and alcohol moieties of pyrethroids has been introduced: namely, variations in the identity and position of halogenated and hydrophobic chemical groups and the stereochemical arrangement of these groups. In general, there are about 1000 different structures; some of them are very different from the original structure of the pyrethrins, including structures that lack in dimethylcyclopropane ring.

Toxicity

For increasing the effectiveness of the insecticides, the pyrethroids are formulated with some compounds such as: piperonyl butoxide, piperonyl sulfoxide and sesamex, which act as synergists. Agency for Toxic Substances and Disease Registry, (2003) reported that formulated commercial pyrethroids have a high proportion of other inert ingredients, which are highly toxic. Pyrethroid insecticides are used widely for their high insecticidal activity and with lower levels of acute toxicity for mammals, birds and plants when compared to organochlorine or organophosphate insecticides, however, exposure to high level of pyrethroids insecticides might affect the central nervous system, reproductive toxicity, cause endocrine disruption, suppressive effects on the immune system, lymph node and spleen damage, carcinogenesis, allergic skin reactions and eye irritation (Garey and Wolff 1998; Laskowski, 2002). In addition, it has high acute toxicity to some non target organisms, such as: bees, fish and aquatic invertebrates often at concentrations less than 1 $\mu g\ L^{-1}$ (Bloomquist, 1996; Gan *et al.* 2005; Suchismita and Anilava, 2008; Lutnicka *et al.* 1999 and Kumar *et al.* 2008).

As compared to other pesticides, pyrethroids are more specific towards target species. Organophosphates, organochlorines and carbamates have LD_{50} ratios (*i.e.*, LD_{50} rat/LD50 insect) below 100, while pyrethroids have LD_{50} ratios above 2000 (Katsuda, 1999). But, upon exposure to high level of pyrethroids it may produce evident neurotoxicity in non target species, including mammals. Fishel, (2005) reported that most pyrethroids are non toxic to birds but they can be indirectly affected by pyrethroids through the food chain. Waterfowls which feed mostly on aquatic invertebrates are especially susceptible (Table 1.3). The signs of poisoning in non target species are similar to signs of poisoning observed in insects (Glomot., 1982). These similarities in poisoning may be attributed to similar molecular mechanisms of toxicity at target sites which present across species, such as: voltage sensitive Na^+ channels (VSSCs). Differences in pyrethroid efficiency between species have been attributed to differences in the intrinsic sensitivity of VSSCs to these compounds, body temperature (White *et al.* 1976) and metabolism (Ross *et al.* 2006). The detoxifying efficiency of pyrethroids is dependent on route, and that metabolism and/or limited absorption play a significant protective role against pyrethroid neurotoxicity in mammals (Soderlund *et al.* 2002). Few reports are found on pyrethroid-induced signs of poisoning in larger mammalian species. Some clinical veterinary reports describe the intoxication of dogs and cats by pyrethroids; but these reports are confined mostly to dermal exposures. The component of pyrethroid poisoning is similar across the mammalian species examined. Based on veterinary observations, acute, sub lethal exposure to pyrethroids induces restlessness and hyper-excitability followed by 'drunken movements' (*i.e.*, locomotive ataxia), mydriasis, diarrhea, and general depression. In some cases motor in coordination, paresis, head bobbing, chewing, hyper-salivation, and/or whole-body tremors are being reported (Legath *et al.* 1992).

Mechanism of Insecticidal Action

Pyrethroids are able to change the typical function of insect nerves by altering the kinetics of voltage-sensitive sodium channels (Vssc), which mediate the transient increase in the sodium permeability of the nerve membrane that underlies the nerve action potential (Bloomquist, 1993a). The insecticidal activity of pyrethroids on insect and other invertebrate sodium channels, and their interaction of the effects, has been investigated extensively (Soderlund and Bloomquist, 1989; Narahashi, 1992; Bloomquist, 1993a; Soderlund, 1995; Narahashi, 1996). The prominent site of insecticidal action of pyrethroids is Voltage-sensitive sodium channels (Soderlund, 1997; Soderlund and Knipple, 1999). In the housefly, the super-kdr (enhanced knockdown resistance) and kdr ('knockdown resistance') attribute confer resistance to all pyrethroids by reducing the sensitivity of the fly nervous system to these compounds. Genetic linkage analyses summarized these attributes close to the principal voltage-sensitive sodium channel gene of the housefly (designated Vssc1). In addition, kdr like resistance in other insect species has been mapped to sodium channel genes that are orthologous to Vssc1. The DNA sequence analyses of Vssc1 coding sequences from susceptible and resistant housefly strains identified a single mutation which is common to all resistant strains and a second mutation seen only in the highly-resistant super-kdr strains.

Insertion of these mutations into a susceptible Vssc1 cDNA, followed by functional analysis of the susceptible and point mutation in sodium channels which revealed that these mutations were adequate to account for the resistance caused by the kdr and super-kdr attributes. Therefore, the sodium channels encoded by the Vssc1gene of the housefly and by orthologous genes of other insect species must be the prominent sites of pyrethroid insecticidal action. In another study regarding molecular genetics studies it was demonstrated that sodium channels containing the two mutations associated with the super-kdr resistance were insensitive to pyrethroid (Lee *et al.* 1999; Lee and Soderlund, 2001).

Pathways of Pyrethroid Metabolism

The metabolic pathway of most pyrethroids in animals is illustrated by the generalized pathway shown in Fig. 1.1. 1960'S Casida in Berkeley identified pathways of breakdown of pyrethroids and early pyrethroids. The initial biotransformation of the parent compound product from attack by either esterases at the central ester bond or cytochrome P450-dependent monooxygenases at one or more sites in the acid or alcohol moieties. Although most oxidative pathways yield hydroxyester metabolites, oxidative ester cleavage may be a minor pathway for some pyrethroids. The relative importance of initial hydrolytic or oxidative attack varies from compound to compound and from isomer to isomer for each pyrethroid. Following ester cleavage, primary alcohol moieties (*e.g.* 3-phenoxybenzyl alcohol) undergo additional oxidation via the aldehyde to the corresponding carboxylic acids; whereas -cyano-substituted alcohols lose cyanide non-enzymatically to form the corresponding aldehyde. A portion of these ester cleavage products may be hydroxylated, and a portion of the hydroxylated ester metabolites may be hydrolyzed, thereby producing hydroxylated ester cleavage products. More metabolisms of these initial products of hydrolytic or oxidative attack involve conjugation with amino acids, sugars, sugar acids, or sulfate prior to excretion.

Degradation Methods for Removal of Pyrethroid Residues

Moreover, epidemiological data, clinical reports, and other laboratory studies indicate that pyrethroids possess estrogenic and antiprogestagenic activities as well as other pesticides and they are classified as endocrine disruptors (Garey and Wolff. 1998). Therefore, it is important to develop rapid and efficient degradation processes to eliminate or minimize the contamination in environment. In natural environment, pyrethroid insecticides are degraded by biotic or abiotic pathways, including photo oxidation, chemical oxidation and biodegradation. Degradation of pyrethroids in the soil is mostly done by chemical and microbes.

Microbes play the most important role in degradation of pyrethroids in soils and sediments. The rate of degradation in the soil mainly depends on the type of pyrethroids, soil, climate, the species of microorganisms present and the size of their population. Many pyrethroid-degrading microbes have been isolated from soils (Liang *et al.* 2005; Tallur *et al.* 2008 and Wu *et al.* 2006). Biodegradation has been deemed the most prominent and effective cause of pesticide removal. Microbial degradation is generally considered to be the safest, least disruptive, and reliable, cost-effective technique for pesticide degradation. The microorganisms involved in the degradation of pyrethroids are listed in Table 1.2.

Role of Carboxylesterases Enzymes in Detoxification of Pyrethroids

The Carboxylesterases enzymes (Ces) represent a group of enzymes belonging to α/β hydrolase fold family (Hosokawa *et al.* 2007) that are extremely important in hydrolysis of numerous xenobiotic and endogenous ester containing compounds; they play a consequential role in the detoxification of pyrethroids by the hydrolysis of ester bonds. Carboxylesterase are very efficient at hydrolyzing pyrethroids to their corresponding acid and alcohol and thereby significantly reducing the toxicity. CeS are efficient in rapidly degrading Type I and Type II pyrethroids. It is being recognized as an appropriate tool in removing toxicity of ester containing pyrethroids by scientist. Pyrethroids are a large class of compounds that consists of an ester bond in their molecular structure, which was formed by an alcohol and acid moieties. The major metabolic pathway of pyrethroids residues in resistant insects and degrading microbes involves in oxidation by cytochrome P450s and hydrolysis by esterases (Kasai, 2004). Some pyrethroid carboxylesterases hydrolyzing permethrin into 3-phenoxybenzyl alcohol and 3-(2, 2-dichlorovinyl)-2, 2-dimethylcyclopropane carboxylic acid from pyrethroid-resistant insects have been purified and characterized (Sogorb and Vilanova, 2002), but those enzymes often have a low activity and narrow substrate specificity (Stock, *et al.* 2004).

Hydrolysis of Pyrethroids by Carboxylesterases

The pyrethrins and allethrin are metabolized through oxidation of the side chain of the acid moiety and hydrolysis of the ester bond playing an insignificant role. But for most other pyrethroids, the hydrolysis by CbEs is more essential for degradation and detoxification than oxidation (Lawrence and Casida, 1982). In general, the trans-isomers of the pyrethroids are degraded by CbEs faster when compare to the cis-isomers (WHO, 1989, 1990). The slow degradation of cis-isomers may contribute to a higher toxicity in mammals since this isomer exhibit a higher affinity for the Na + -channel than the trans-isomer and pyrethroids induce their toxic effects through changes in the functions of these channels. (Narahashi, 1992). Truly, it has been described that synergist compounds, through inhibition of CbEs, cause marked increase in the toxicity of pyrethroids (Lawrence and Casida, 1982; Valles *et al.* 2000).

Aspergillus niger ZD11 was found to be efficient in utilizing pyrethroid pesticide as the sole carbon source (Liang et al. (2005). Chen *et al.* 2013 isolated a novel enzyme from *Streptomyces* sp., which could degrade beta cypermethrin. The isolate was found to utilize β cypermethrin as the growth substrate. The enzyme was purified and identified as monooxygenase which was found to be significantly stimulated by Fe^{2+}, and was strongly inhibited by Ag+, Al^{3+} and Cu^{2+}.

Genes Encoding Pyrethroid-hydrolyzing Carboxylesterase

Most of the studies have been focused on detoxification of pyrethroid insecticides and the degrading ability of strains, analysis of metabolites, and purification of some related degrading enzymes. But reports about pyrethroid degrading genes are rare. There are few genes that have been identified for encoding pyrethroid-hydrolyzing carboxylesterase enzymes. To date, only a few pyrethroid-degrading genes, such a sestP, pytH, pye3, and pytZ, are reported (Wu *et al.* 2006; Wang *et al.* 2009; Li *et al.* 2008; Zhai *et al.* 2012).

Pei *et al.* (2006) isolated pyrethroid hydrolyzing esterase (EstP) gene from *Klebsiella* sp., strain ZD 112 and cloned it in *E. coli* which was followed by sequencing the gene. EstP gene has the capability to degrade many pyrethroid pesticides and also organophosphorous pesticide malathion. It could also hydrolyze ρ-nitrophenyl esters of various other fatty acids, which denoted that EstP to be an esterase with broad spectrum substrates.

Wang *et al.* (2009) reported a novel esterase gene, pytH, encoding pyrethroid-hydrolyzing carboxylesterase from *Sphingobium* sp. strain JZ. PytH was able to transform p-nitrophenyl esters of short-chain fatty acids and possess the ability to degrade a wide range of pyrethroid pesticides, and efficient hydrolysis was found to be dependent on the pyrethroid molecular structure. Li *et al.* (2008) identified pyrethroid-hydrolyzing esterase gene (Pye3) a perfect candidate for *in situ* detoxification of pyrethroids and Pye3 gene was cloned successfully using metagenomic DNA. EstP is pyrethroid-hydrolyzing esterase gene from *Klebsiella* sp. strain ZD112 was cloned into *Escherichia coli*. Interestingly, the purified EstP gene has the potency of degrading wide range of pyrethroid pesticides and also organophosphorus insecticide malathion, and also hydrolyzed ρ-nitrophenyl esters of various fatty acids, this suggests that EstP is an esterase with broad substrate utilization (Wu *et al.* 2006).

Fang *et al.* (2013) had done an investigation on fenvalerate degradation with novel strain *Sphingomonas* sp. strain F-7. The organism was found to utilize fenvalerate as the sole carbon source. There was complete degradation of fenvalerate within 72 hrs by hydrolysis of carboxylester linkage yielding 3-phenoxybenzoic acid (3-PBA) as the major metabolite. The scientist further noticed *Sphingomonas* sp., was capable of degrading permethrin, fenpropathrin, beta-cypermethrin, cyhalothrin, deltamethrin, bifenthrin and 3-PBA.

Table 1.1: Molecular structure and application of pyrethroid

Pyrethroid	Molecular Structure	Insects	Crops
Esters Acrinathrin	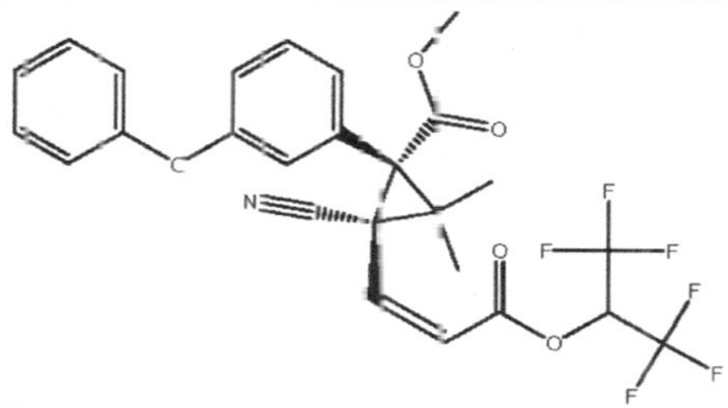	Codling moth, oriental fruit moth, leafhoppers, Red Spider Mite, Two spotted mite, African Red Mite	N/A
Allethrin	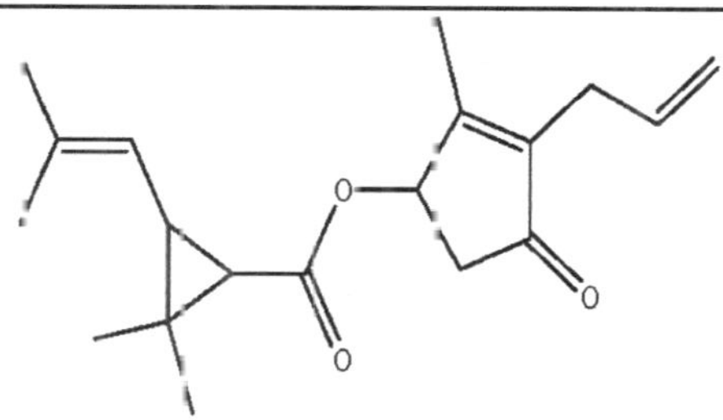	Flies, mosquitoes and ants	N/A
Bifenthrin	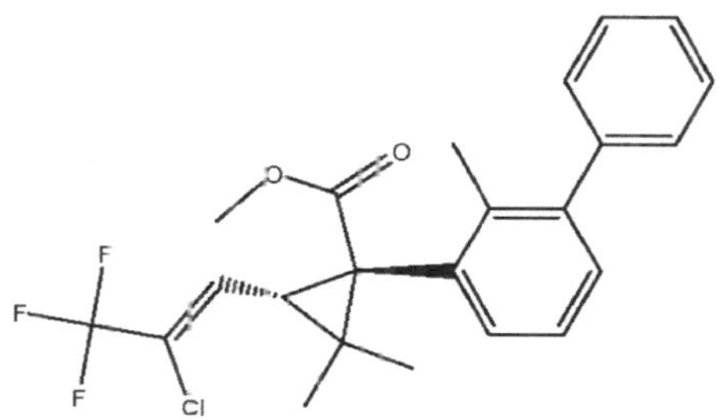	Beetles, weevil, houseflies, mosquitoes, lice, bedbugs, aphids, moths, cockr-oaches and locust	Alfalfa hay, beans, cereals, corn, cotton field and grass seed, hops, melons, oilseed rape, potatoes, peas, watermelons.

Contd...

Pyrethroid	Molecular Structure	Insects	Crops
Cyfluthrin	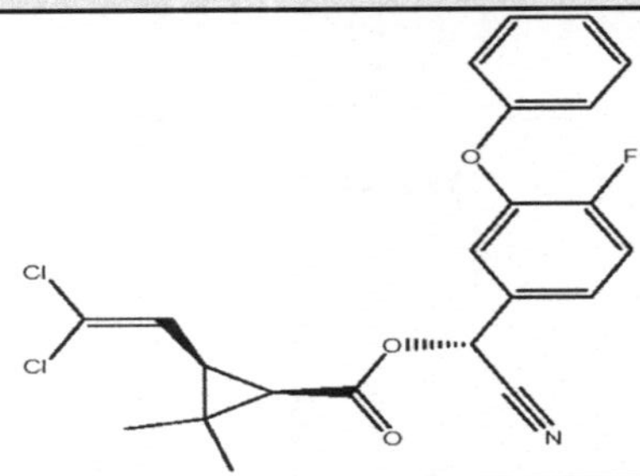	Aphids, cabbage stem flea beetle, cockroaches, houseflies, mosquitoes and rape winter stem weevil	Alfalfa, cereals, cotton, citrus, ground nuts, maize, oilseed rape, potatoes, rice, sugar beet, sugarcane, tobacco, vegetables.
Cyhalothrin	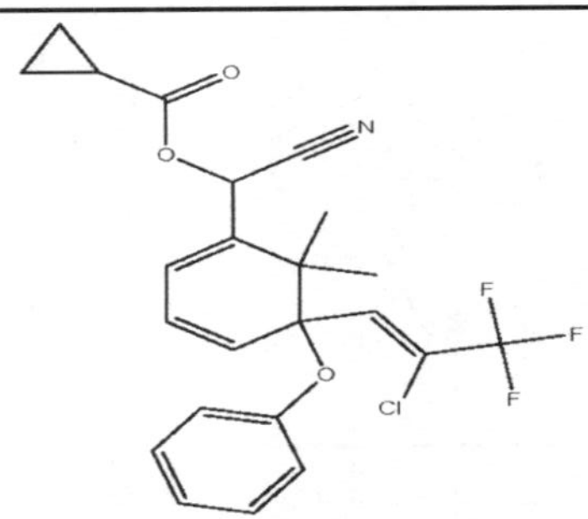	Bedbugs, beetles, houseflies, ked, lice, mosquitoes, moths, weevils	N/A
Cypermethrin	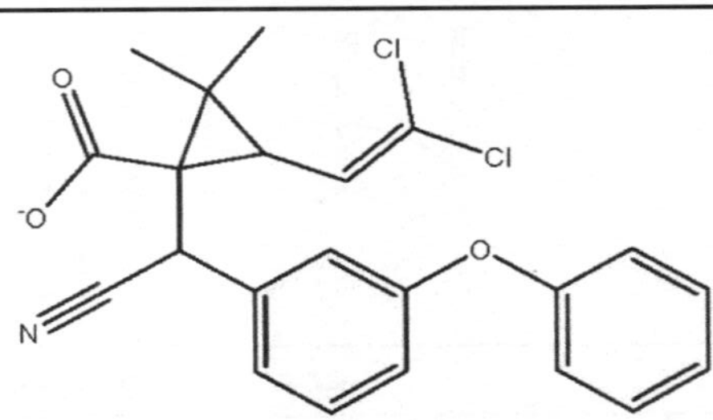	Cockroaches, mosquitoes, moths and flies.	Cotton, onions, pears, peaches, sugar beets.

Contd…

Pyrethroid	Molecular Structure	Insects	Crops
Cyphenothrin	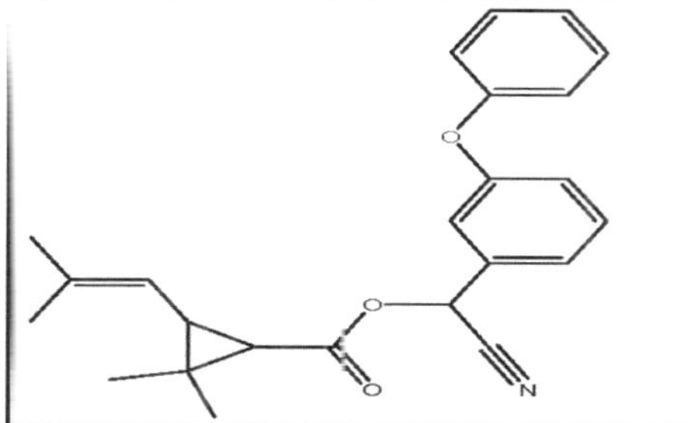	Flies, mosquitoes, cockroaches and also it is used to control insects which attack wood and fabrics	N/A
Deltamethrin	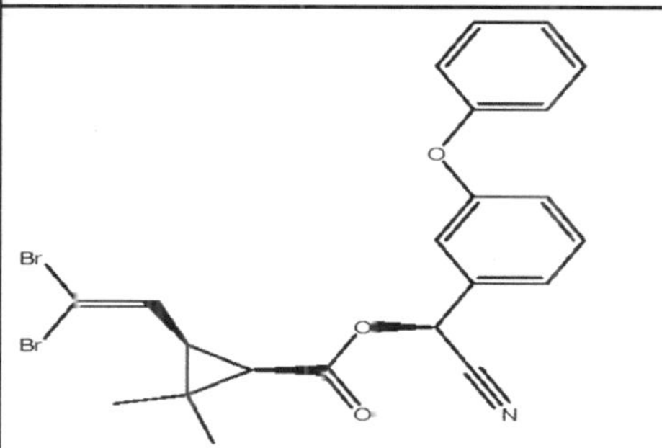	Aphids, beetles, bollworm, budworm, caterpillars cicadas, coding moths, totrix moths, weevils, whitefly and winter moths	Alfalfa, beet, cereals, coffee, cotton, figs, fruit, hops, maize, oilseed rape, olives, oil palms, potatoes, rice, soy-beans, sunflowers, tea, tobacco and vegetables
Fenpropathrin	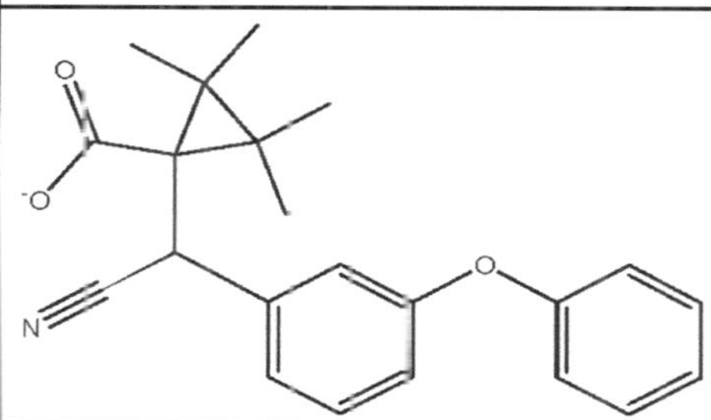	Mites, aphids, beet armyworm, mealybug, potato leafhopper, moths, leafrollers and lacebugs.	Fruits tree, Vegetables, and ornamentals and other fields crops.

Contd...

Pyrethroid	Molecular Structure	Insects	Crops
Fenvalerate	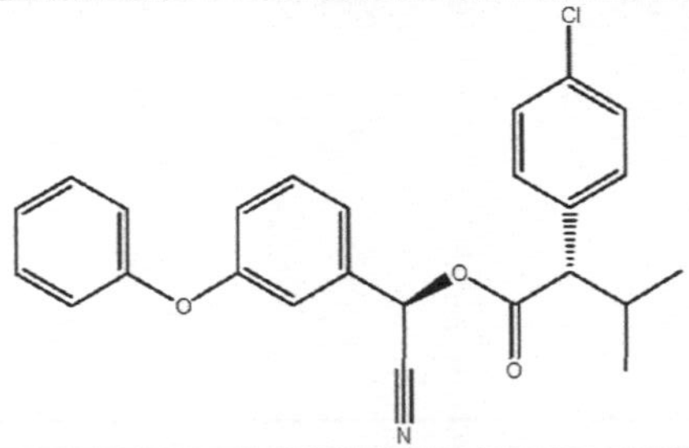	Beetles, cockroaches, flies, locusts, Mosquitoes and moths	Food, feed and cotton products
Flucythrinate	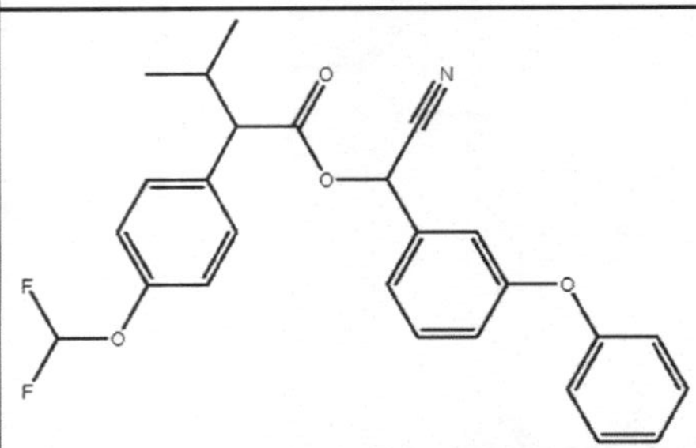	Bollworms, leafworms, sucking insects, whiteflies and beetles	Apple, head cabbage, lettuce, maize and sweet corn.
Fluvalinate	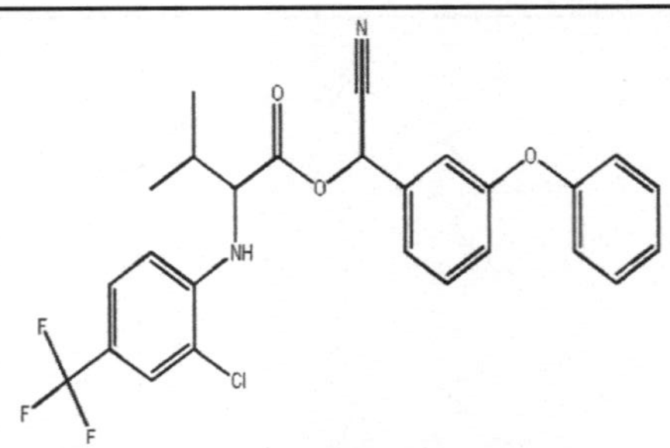	Aphids, leafhoppers, moths, spider mites, thrips and white-flies	Carrots and brassica/cole crops

Contd…

Pyrethroid	Molecular Structure	Insects	Crops
Imiprothrin	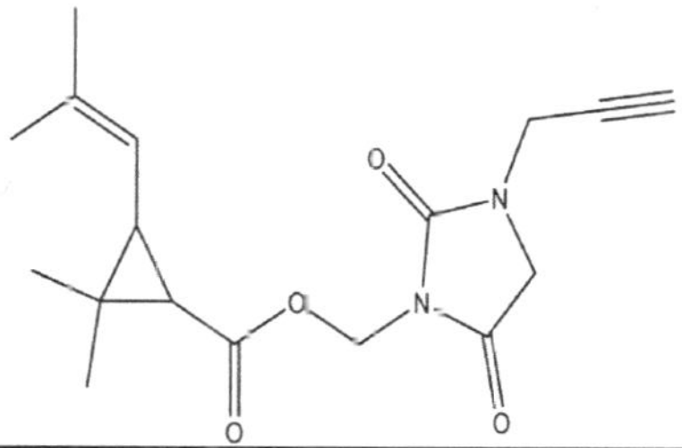	Roaches, Waterbugs, ants, Silverfish, Crickets and Spiders	N/A
Permethrin	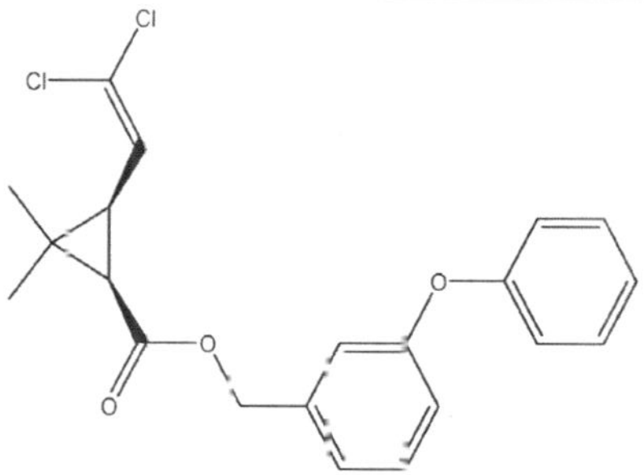	Ants, beetle, bollworm, bud-worm, fleas, flies, lice, moths, mosquitoes, termites, weevils	Alfalfa hay, corn, cotton, grains, lettuce, onion, peaches, potatoes, sweet corn, tomatoes, wheat
Phenothrin	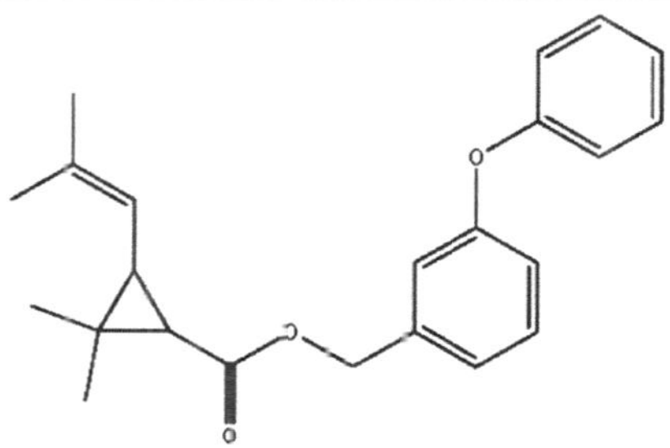	Flies, gnats, and mosquitoes, cockr oaches and lice.	N/A

Contd...

Pyrethroid	Molecular Structure	Insects	Crops
Prallethrin	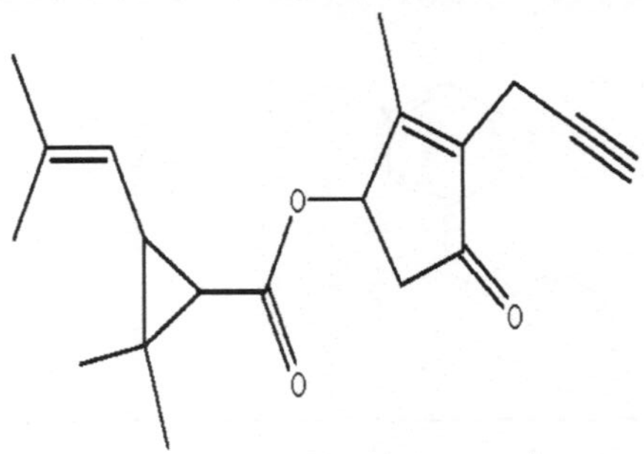	Ants, bees, carpet beetle, clover mite and cockroaches	N/A
Resmethrin	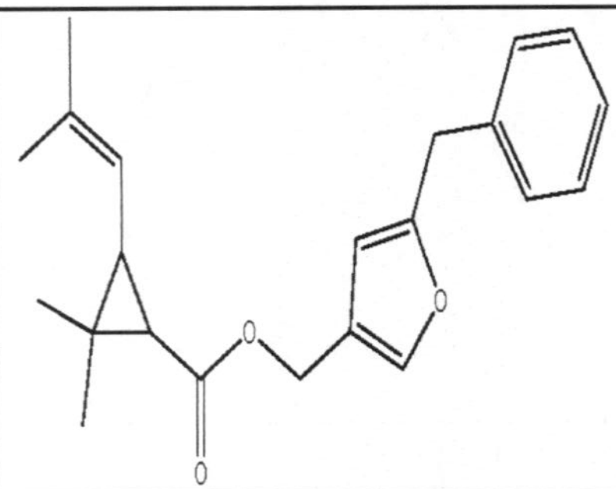	Flies, mosquitoes, gnats, fleas, ticks and black flies	Garden crops

Contd…

Pyrethroid	Molecular Structure	Insects	Crops
Tefluthrin	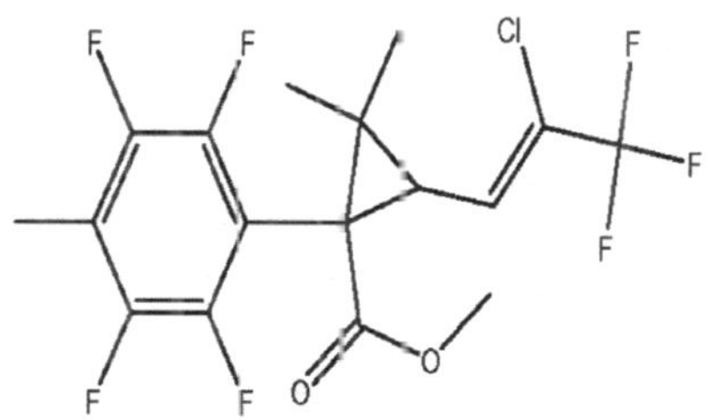	White grub, southern corn leaf beetle, flea beetle, and chinch bug	Maize, sugar beet, corn, grains
Tetramethrin	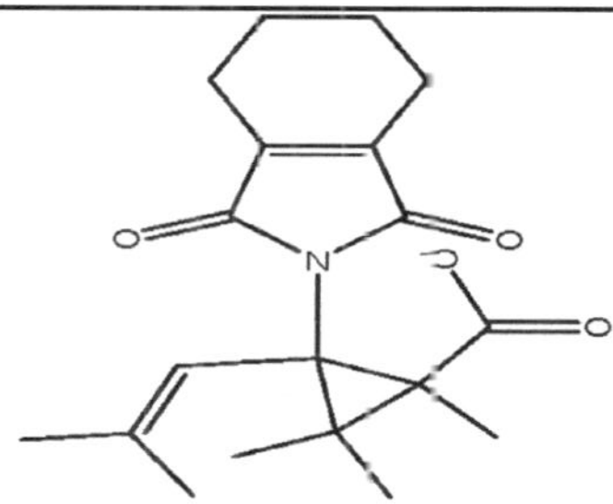	Wasps, hornets, roaches, ants, fleas, and mosquitoes.	Indoor and outdoor plants
Tralomethrin	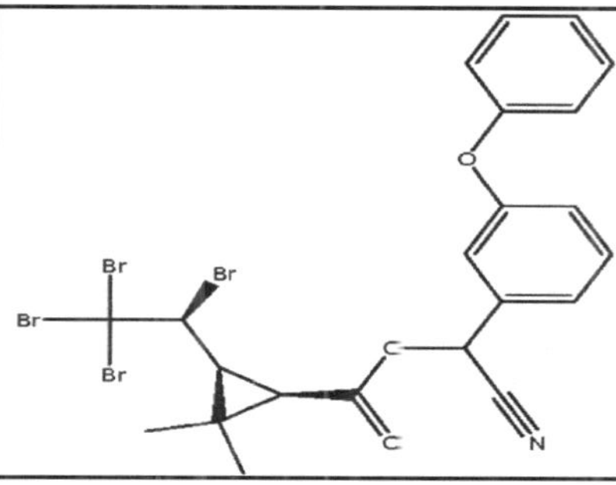	Ants and cockroaches	N/A

Contd...

Pyrethroid	Molecular Structure	Insects	Crops
Transfluthrin	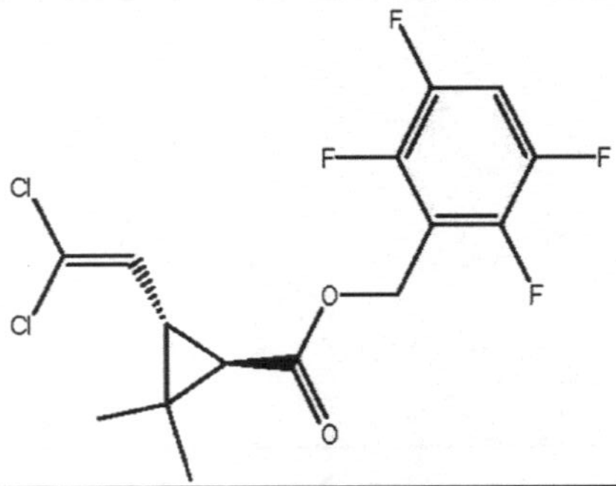	Mosquitoes and flies	N/A
Ethers Halfenprox	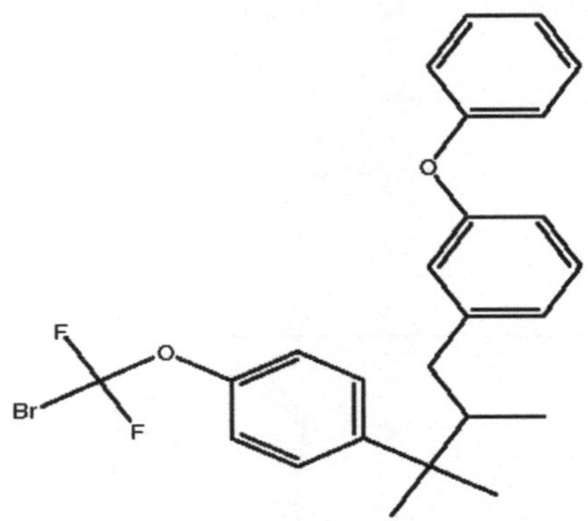	Mites	Fruits such as: apple, pears, papaya, lemons, oranges and other citrus fruits.

In another study, a novel pyrethroid-degrading esterase gene pytY was isolated from the genomic library of *Ochrobactrum anthropi* YZ-1. PytY displayed good degrading ability and stability over a broad range of temperature and pH. The optimal temperature and pH were of 35°C and 7.5. No cofactors were required for enzyme activity (Ruan *et al.* 2013) and so far, reported pyrethroid degrading genes from genomic library are all of single gene. However, pytY is the second degrading gene isolated from the strain of *O. anthropi* YZ-1 making it the first report on two genes from the same strain and both contributing to pyrethroid degradation.

Table 1.2: List of microbes involved in degradation of pyrethroids residues

Pyrethroid degrading bacteria	Referance
Bacillus cereus SM3	Maloney *et al.* 1993
Pseudomonas fluorescens	Grant *et al.* 2002
Pseudomonas sp.	Halden *et al.* 1999
Cladosporium sp.	Chen *et al.* 2011
Rhodococcus sp. CDT3	Xu *et al.* 2007
Vibrio hollisae, Burkholderia picketti, and *Erwinia caroto Vora*	Lee *et al.* 2004
Ochrobactrum anthropi YZ-1	Zhai *et al.* 2012
Aspergillus niger ZD11	Liang *et al.* 2005
Klebsiella sp. ZD112	Wu *et al.* 2006
Sphingobium sp. JZ-2	Guo *et al.* 2009
Achromobacter sp.	Maloney *et al.* 1988
Bacillus cereus and *Serratia plymuthica*	Sakata *et al.* 1992
Pseudomonas sp. YF05	Yu and Fan, 2003
Stenotrophomonas acidaminiphila, Aeromonas sobria and Yersinia frederiksenii	Lee *et al.* 2004
Trichoderma viride	Saikia and Gopal, 2004
Micrococcus sp.	Preeti *et al.* 2008
Serratia sp.	Zhang *et al.* 2010
Streptomyces sp.	Chen *et al.* 2011a
Ochrobactrum sp.	Chen *et al.* 2011b
Stenotrophomonas sp.	Chen *et al.* 2011c

Table 1.3: Acute effects of pyrethroids and pyrethroid formulations on non-target organisms (Mueller-Beilsehmidt, 1990)

Pyrethroids	Birds (mg pyrethroids/ kg body weight)	Fish	Bees
Allethrin	2030	Toxic	-
s-Bioallethrin (Esbiol)	680	Highly Toxic	-
Resmethrin	-	Toxic	Highly Toxic
Bioresmethrin	-	Highly Toxic	Highly Toxic
Tetramethrin	>1000	Toxic	Toxic
Permethrin	>13500	Highly Toxic	Highly Toxic
Fenvalerate	9932	Highly Toxic	Toxic
d-Phenothrin	>2500	Toxic	Toxic
Cypermethrin	-	Extremely Toxic	Toxic
Esfenvalerate	-	Highly Toxic	-
Bifenthrin	>2150	Toxic	-
Fenpropathrin	1089	Toxic	-
Refluthrin	4190	Highly Toxic	-
Cyfluthrin	4450	Toxic	Toxic
Fluvalinate	>5620	Toxic	Non-Toxic
Tralomethrin	7716	Extremely Toxic	Highly Toxic
Deltamethrin	>4640	Toxic	Highly Toxic
Cyhalothrin	>5000	Highly Toxic	-
Kadethrin	-	Toxic	Toxic
Alphacypermethrin	-	Toxic	Toxic
Lambda-cyhalothrin	>3950	Toxic	Toxic

Summary

The ever growing population and ever increasing demand for food depends on pesticide and insecticides to protect the crop field from pest. This comes with a price resulting in environmental pollution which needs to be addressed through cheaper and safer methods. Biodegradation is the only solution which is found to be reliable, eco-friendly and effective in the long run. However, there is more work required in the molecular level for effective implementation of bioremediation of pesticides.

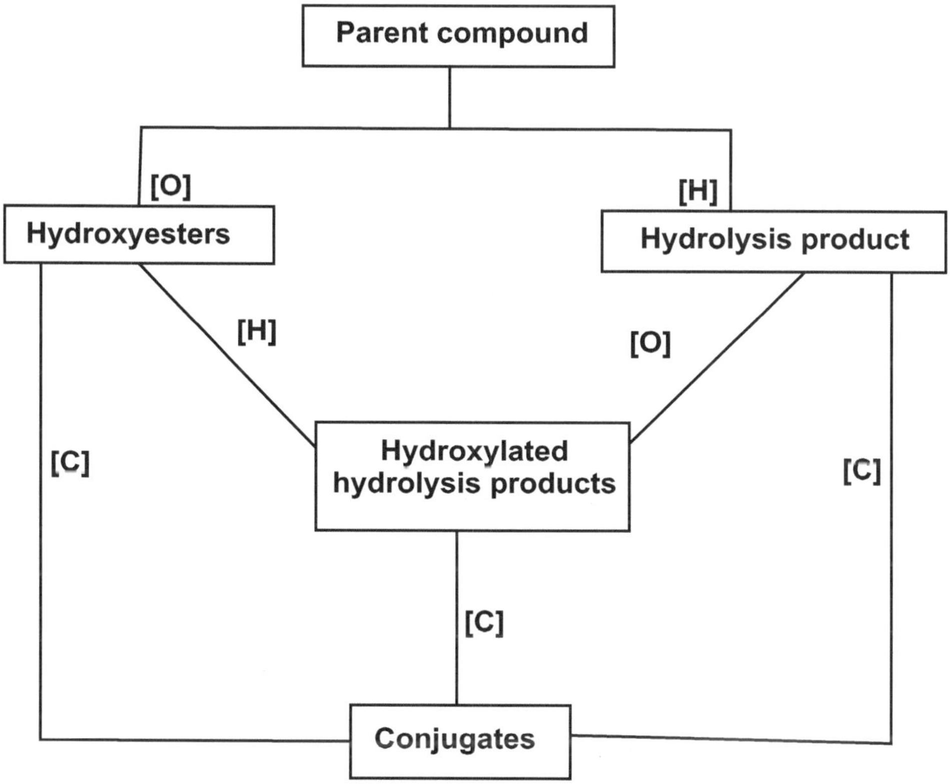

Fig.1.1. Generalized pathway for the metabolism of pyrethroids in mammals by hydrolysis [H], oxidative [O] and conjucation [C] reactions (Soderlund *et al.* 2002)

REFERENCES

Agency for Toxic Substances and Disease Registry, Toxicological Profile for Pyrethrins and Pyrethroids. (2003). US Department of Health and Human Services, pp. 238.

Ali, H.Y, Aboul-Enein (2004). Chiral Pollutants, John Wiley and Sons, Chichester, UK.

Bloomquist, J.R (1996). Ion Channels as Targets for Insecticides, Annual Review of Entomology, 41: pp. 163-190.

Bloomquist, J.R. (1993a). Neuroreceptor Mechanisms in pyrethroid Mode of Action and Resistance. In: Roe, M., Kuhr, R.J. (Eds.), Reviews in Pesticide Toxicology. Toxicology Communications, Raleigh, NC, pp. 81-226.

Bryant, R, Bite, M.G, eds. (2003). Global Insecticide Directory. 3rd ed. Orpington, Kent, UK: Agranova.

Casida, J.E, Quistad, G.B. (1998). Golden Age of Insecticide Research: Past, Present, or Future? *Annu Rev Entomol.* 43 : pp. 1-16.

Chen S, Lin Q, Xiao Y, Deng Y, Chang C, *et al.* (2013). Monooxygenase, A Novel Beta-Cypermethrin Degrading Enzyme from *Streptomyces* sp. PLoS ONE 8(9): e75450. doi:10.1371/journal.pone.0075450

Chen, S.H., Hu, M.Y., Liu, J.J., Zhong, G.H., Yang, L., Rizwan-ul-Haq, M., Han, H.T (2011b). Biodegradation of beta-cypermethrin and 3-phenoxybenzoic acid by a novel *Ochrobactrum lupine* DG-S-01, *J. Hazard. Mater.* 187: pp. 433-440.

Chen, S.H., Lai, K.P., Li, Y.N., Hu, M.Y., Zhang, Y.B., Zeng, Y (2011a). Biodegradation of Deltamethrin and Its Hydrolysis product 3-phenoxybenzaldehyde by a newly isolated *Streptomyces aureusstrain* HP-Ş-01, *Appl. Microbiol. Biotechnol.* 90: pp. 1471-1483.

Chen, S.H., Yang, L., Hu, M.Y., Liu, J.J. (2011c). Biodegradation of fenvalerate and 3-phenoxybenzoic Acid by a Novel *Stenotrophomonas* sp., strain ZS-S-01 and its use in Bioremediation of Contaminated Soils, *Appl. Microbiol. Biotechnol*, 90: pp. 755-767.

Fang B. Yu, Sheng D. Shan, Lin P. Luo, Li B. Guan and Hua Qin (2013). Isolation and Characterization of a *Sphingomonas* sp., strain F-7 degrading fenvalerate and its use in Bioremediation of Contaminated Soil. *Journal of Environmental Science and Health,* Part B: Pesticides, Food Contaminants, and Agricultural Wastes, 48(3): pp. 198-207.

Fishel, F.M (2005). Pesticide Toxicity Profile: Synthetic Pyrethroid Pesticides, University of Florida, Institute of Food and Agricultural Sciences.

Gan, J., Lee, S.J., Liu, W.P., Haver, D.L., Kabashina, J.N. (2005). Effects on Non-target Organisms in Terrestrial and Aquatic Environments. In: Leahey, J.P. (Ed.), The Pyrethroid Insecticides, Taylor and Francis, London, UK.

Garey, J., Wolff, M.S. (1998). Estrogenic and Antiprogestagenic Activities of pyrethroid Insecticides, Biochem. *Biophys. Res. Commun*, 251, pp. 855-859.

Glomot, R. (1982). Toxicity of Deltamethrin to Higher Vertebrates, Deltamethrin (Monograph), Roussel-Uclaf Research Centre, France, 4: pp. 109-136.

Gosselin, R.E. (1984). Clinic Toxicological of Commercial Products, Williams and Wilkins, Baltimore, MD, USA.

Grant, R. J., Daniell, T.J., Betts, W.B. (2002). Isolation and Identification of Synthetic Pyrethroid-degrading Bacteria, *J. Appl. Microbiol*, 92, pp. 534-540.

Guo, P., Wang, B.Z., Hang, B.J., Li, L., Ali, S.W., He, J., Li, S.P. (2009). Pyrethroid Degrading *Sphingobium* sp. JZ-2 and the Purification and Characterization of a Novel pyrethroid hydrolase, *Int. Biodeter. Biodegr*, 63; pp. 1107-1112.

Halden, R.U., Tepp, S.M., Halden, B.G., Dwyer, D.F (1999). Degradation of 3-phenoxybenzoic Acid in Soil by *Pseudomonas pseudoalcaligenes* POB310 (pPOB) and Two Modified *Pseudomonas* strains. *Appl. Environ. Microbiol*, 65: pp. 3354-3359.

Katsuda, Y., (1999). Development of and Future Prospects for pyrethroid Chemistry. Pesticide Science. 55: pp. 775-782.

Khambay, B.P.S. (2002). Pyrethroid Insecticides. The Royal Society of Chemistry.

Kumar, A., Sharma, B., Pandey, R.S. (2008). Cypermethrin and cyhalothrin Induced Alterations in Nucleic Acids and Protein Contents in a Freshwater Fish, Channa Punctatus. *Fish Physiol Biochem.* 34: pp. 331-338.

Kurihara, N. Mayamoto, J. (1998). Chirality in Agrochemicals, John Wiley and Sons, Chichester, UK.

Laskowski, D.A. (2002). Physical and Chemical Properties of Pyrethroids. *Rev. Environ. Contam. Toxicol.* 174: pp. 49-170.

Lawrence, L.J., Casida, J.E. (1982). Pyrethroid Toxicology: Mouse Intracerebral Structure-Toxicity Relationships. *Pestic. Biochem. Physiol.* 18: pp. 9-14.

Lee, S.H., Smith, T.J., Knipple, D.C., Soderlund, D.M. (1999). Mutations in the Housefly Vssc1 Sodium Channel gene associated with super-kdr Resistance abolish the pyrethroid Sensitivity of Vssc1/tipE sodium channels expressed in Xenopusoocytes. *Insect Biochem. Mol. Biol.* 29: pp. 185-194.

Lee, S.H., Soderlund, D.M. (2001). Point Mutations in Homology Domain II Modify the Sensitivity of Rat Nav1.8 sodium Channels to the pyrethroid cismethrin. *Neurotoxicology* (in press).

Lee, S.J., Gan, J., Kim, J.S., Kabashima, J.N., Crowley, D.E. (2004). Microbial Transformation of pyrethroid Insecticides in Aqueous and Sediment Phases. *Environ. Toxicol. Chem.* 23: pp. 1-6.

Legath, J., Neuschl, J., Kacmar, P., Poracova, J., Dudrikova, E., Hlynarcikova, H., Kovac, G., Javorsky, P. (1992). Clinical Signs and Mechanisms of Supermethrin Intoxication in Sheep, *Vet. Hum. Toxicol.* 34 (5): pp. 453-455.

Li, G., Wang, K., Liu, Y.H. (2008). Molecular Cloning and Characterization of a Novel Pyrethroid-hydrolyzing Esterase Originating from the Metagenome. *Microbial Cell Factories* 7, pp. 36.

Liang, W.Q., Wang, Z.Y., Li, H., Wu, P.C., Hu, J.M., Luo, N., Cao, L.X., Liu. Y.H. (2005). Purification and Characterization of a Novel pyrethroid hydrolase from *Aspergillus niger* ZD11. *J. Agric. Food Chem.* 53: pp. 7415-7420.

Liu, W., Gan, J., Schlenk, D., Jury. W.A. (2005). Enantioselectivity in Environmental Safety of Current Chiral Insecticides. *Proc. Natl. Acad. Sci.* 102: pp. 701-706.

Lutnicka, H., Bogacka, T., Wolska, L. (1999). Degradation of pyrethroids in An Aquatic Ecosystem *Model. Wat Res*, 33: pp. 3441-3446.

Maloney, S. E., Maule, A., Smith, A.R.W. (1993). Purification and Pre-liminary Characterization of Permethrinase from a pyrethroid-transforming Strain of *Bacillus cereus, Appl. Environ. Microbiol.* 59: pp. 2007-13.

Maloney, S.E., Maule, A., Smith. A.R.W. (1988). Microbial Transformation of the pyrethroid Insecticides: Permethrin, Deltamethrin, Fastac, Fenvalerate, and Fluvalinate, *Appl. Environ. Microbiol.* 54: pp. 2874-2876.

Mueller-Beilsehmidt, D. (1990). Toxicology and Environmental Fate of Synthetic pyrethroids. *Journal of Pesticide Reform* 10-17.

Narahashi, T. (1996). Neuronal ion Channels as the Target sites of Insecticides. *Pharmacol. Toxicol.* 78: pp. 1-14.

Narahashi, T. (1992). Nerve Membrane Na+ channels as Targets of Insecticides. *Trends in Pharmacological Sciences*, 13: pp. 236-241

Naumann, K. (1998). Research into fluorinated pyrethroid Alcohols: An Episode in the History of Pyrethroid Discovery, *Pestic. Sci*: 52: pp. 3-20.

Pei C. Wu, Yu H. Liu, Zhuo Y. Wang, Xiao Y. Zhang, He Li, Wei Q. Liang, Na Luo, Ji M. Hu, Jia Q. Lu, Tian G. Luan, Li X. Cao (2006). Molecular Cloning, Purification, and Biochemical Characterization of a Novel Pyrethroid-Hydrolyzing Esterase from *Klebsiella* sp., Strain ZD112, *J. Agric. Food Chem*, 54 (3): pp. 836-842.

Preeti, N.T., Veena, B.M., Harichandra, Z.N. (2008). Biodegradation of cypermethrin by *Micrococcus* sp., strain CPN 1. *Biodegradation* 19: pp. 77-82.

Ross, M.K., Borazjani, A., Edwards, C.C., Potter, P.M. (2006). Hydrolytic Metabolism of pyrethroids by Human and other Mammalian carboxylesterases, *Biochem. Pharmacol.* 71 (5): pp. 657-669.

Saikia, N., Gopal, M. (2004). Biodegradation of beta-cyfluthrin by fungi, *Journal of Agricultural Food Chemistry* 5, pp. 1220-1223.

Sakata, S., Mikami, N., Yamada, H. (1992). Degradation of Pyrethroid Optical isomers by Soil Microorganisms, *Journal of Pesticide Science*. 17: pp. 181-189.

Sattelle, D.B., Yamamoto, D. (1988). Molecular Targets of pyrethroid Insecticides, *Adv. Insect Physiol.* 20: pp. 147-213.

Soderlund, D.M. and Knipple, D.C. (1999). Knockdown Resistance to DDT and pyrethroids in the House Fly (Diptera: Muscidae): From Genetic trait to Molecular Mechanism, *Ann. Ent. Soc. Am.* 92: pp. 909-915.

Soderlund, D.M. (1997). Molecular Mechanisms of Insecticide Resistance. In: *Sjut, V.* (Ed.), Molecular Mechanisms of Resistance to Agrochemicals. Springer, Berlin, pp. 21-56.

Soderlund, D.M. Clark, J.M. Sheets, L.P. Mullin, L.S. Picirillo, V.J. Sargent, D. Stevens, J.T., Weiner, M.L. (2002). Mechanisms of pyrethroid Neurotoxicity: Implications for Cumulative Risk Assessment, Toxicology. 171: pp. 3-59.

Soderlund, D.M., Bloomquist, J.R. (1989). Neurotoxic Actions of pyrethroid Insecticides, *Annu. Rev. Entomol*, 34: pp. 77-96.

Sogorb, M.A., Vilanova, E. (2002). Enzymes Involved in the Detoxification of Organophosphorus, Carbamate and Pyrethroid Insecticides through Hydrolysis, *Toxicol. Lett.* 128: pp. 215-228.

Stock J.E., Huang H.Z., Jones P.D., Wheelock C.E., Morisseau C., *et al.* (2004). Identification, Expression, and Purification of a Pyrethroid-hydrolyzing carboxylesterae from mouse liver microsomes. *J. Biol Chem* 279: pp. 29863-29869.

Suchismita, S., Anilava, K. (2008). Acute Toxicity of Synthetic pyrethroid cypermethrin to some Freshwater Organisms. *Bulletin of Environmental Contamination and Toxicology* 80: pp. 49-52.

Tallur, P.N., V.B. Megadi, and H.Z. Ninnekar. (2008). Biodegradation of cypermethrin by *Micrococcus* sp. strain CPN 1. *Biodegradation* 19: pp. 77-82.

Valentine, W.M. (1990). Pyrethrin and Pyrethroid Insecticides, *Vet. Clin. North Am., Large Anim. Pract.* 20: pp. 375-385.

Valles, S.M., Dong, K., Brenner, R.J. (2000). Mechanism Responsible for cypermethrin Resistance in a Strain of German Cockroach germanica, *Pest. Biochem. Physiol*, 66: pp. 195-205.

Vijverberg, H.P.M., Van den Bercken, J. (1990). Neurotoxicological Effects and the Mode of Action of Pyrethroid Insecticides, *Crit. Rev. Toxicol.* 21 (2): pp. 105-126.

Wang B.Z., Guo P., Hang B.J., Li L., He J., *et al.* (2009). Cloning of a Novel Pyrethroid-Hydrolyzing Carboxylesteras gene from *Sphingobium* sp. JZ-1 and Characterization of the gene Product. *Appl Environ Microbiol.* 75: pp. 5496-5500.

WHO, World Health Organization, (1990). Permethrin. In: Environmental Health Criteria, Vol. 94. WHO, Geneva.

WHO, (1989). Task Group on Environmental Health Criteria for Cypermethrin. Environmental Health Criteria 82. Geneva, World Health Organization.

Wu P.C., Liu Y.H., Wang Z.Y., Zhang X.Y., Li H., *et al.* (2006). Molecular Cloning, Purification, and Biochemical Characterization of A Novel Pyrethroid-hydrolyzing Esterase from *Klebsiella* sp., strain ZD112. *J. Agric Food Chem* 54, pp. 836-842.

Xu, Y.X., Sun, J.Q., Li, X.H., Li, S.P., Chen, Y. (2007). Study on Co-operating Degradation of Cypermethrin and 3-phenoxybenzoic Acid by Two Bacteria Strains. *Acta Microbiol. Sin.* 47: pp. 834-837.

Yang, Z.H. Mishimura, M. Nishimura, K. Kuroda, S. Fujita, T (1987). Quantitative Structure – Activity Studies of Pyrethroids. Ch. 12: Physicochemical Substituent Effects of meta-phenoxybenzyl disubstituted Acetates on Insecticidal Activity, *Pestic. Biochem. Physiol.* 29: pp. 217-232.

Yu, Y., Fan, D. (2003). Pre-liminary Study of An Enzyme Extracted from *Alcaligenes* sp., strain YF11 Capable of Degrading Pesticides. *Bulletin of Environmental Contamination and Toxicology* 70: pp. 367-371.

Zerba, E.N. (1999). Susceptibility and Resistance to Insecticides of Chagas Disease Vectors, *Medicina (B. Aires)*. 59 (Suppl. II), 41-46.

Zhai Y., Li K., Song JL., Shi YH., Yan YC. (2012). Molecular Cloning, Purification and Biochemical Characterization of A Novel pyrethroid-hydrolyzing carboxylesterase gene from *Ochrobactrum anthropi* YZ-1. *J. Hazard Mater* 221: pp. 206-212.

Zhang, C., Jia, L., Wang, S.H., Qu, J., Xu, L.L., Shi, H.H., Yan, Y.C. (2010). Biodegradation of Beta-cypermethrin by two *Serratia* sp., with different cell surface Hydrophobicity. *Bioresour. Technol.* 101: pp. 3423-3429.

Zhiyong Ruan, Z., Yi Zhai., Jinlong Song, Yanhua Shi, Kang Li, Bin Zhao, Yanchun Yan (2013). Molecular Cloning and Characterization of a Newly Isolated Pyrethroid-Degrading Esterase Gene from a Genomic Library of *Ochrobactrum anthropi* YZ-1. PLoS ONE 8(10): e77329. doi:10.1371/journal.pone.0077329.

Page 23-36

MICROBIAL ENVIRONMENT AND BIOREMEDIATION
Edited by : **Dr. Alka Chauhan; Dr. Ashok K. Rathoure & Dr. Raaz K Maheshwari**
Edition : **2017**
ISBN : 978-93-5056-856-9
Published by : **Discovery Publishing House Pvt. Ltd., New Delhi (India)**

2 Optimization of Cellulase and Amylase Production by *Bacillus* Strain Isolated from Cultured Fish Intestine

Ariole* C.N.
Igwe U.M.

ABSTRACT

The optimization of some culture conditions for cellulase and amylase production by Bacillus sp., previously isolated from the gut of a farmed freshwater fish (Clarias gariepinus) was carried out. The varied culture parameters assessed were incubation temperature (28, 30, 37, 40 and 45°C), medium pH (4, 5, 6, 7, 8, 9 and 10), additional carbon sources (fructose, sucrose, lactose, glucose, cellulose and starch) and nitrogen sources (yeast extract, urea, ammonium sulphate and peptone). The cellulase and amylase activities of each culture were measured by determining the amount of reducing sugars liberated by using a Dinitrosalicyclic acid (DNS) method and carboxymethyl cellulose and starch as substrate respectively. The optimum conditions observed for cellulase production were incubation temperature 40°C, medium pH 7.0, 1.0 per cent glucose as additional carbon source and yeast extract as nitrogen source. The maximum incubation temperature, medium pH, additional carbon source and nitrogen source observed for amylase production were 37°C, 7.0, glucose and urea respectively. This bacterial isolate has potential that could be commercially exploited to assist in cellulose and starch degradation in various biotechnological applications.

Keywords: Fish intestine, bacteria, enzyme production, optimization.

INTRODUCTION

Cellulose is a polymer of glucose residues connected by β 1, 4 linkages. It is the primary structural material of plant cell wall and the most abundant

Department of Microbiology, University of Port Harcourt, P.M.B. 5323, Port Harcourt, Rivers State, Nigeria. *E-mail: cnariole@yahoo.com carbohydrate in nature (Saha *et al.* 2006). The enzyme that hydrolyses the beta 1, 4 glycosidic bonds in the polymer to release glucose units is called cellulase (Nishida *et al.* 2007). Cellulolytic enzymes play an important role in natural biodegradation processes in which cellulolytic bacteria, fungi, actinomycetes and protozoa efficiently degrade materials. Cellulases have a wide range of enormous potential applications in biotechnology. They are used in the production of fermentable sugars and ethanol (Levy *et al.* 2002; Vanlwyk and Mohulatsi, 2003), organic acids (Luo *et al.* 1997), detergents and other chemicals (Oksanen *et al.* 2000).

They are also used in pulp and paper industry (Oksanen *et al.* 2000), in texile industry (Cavaco-Paulo and Gubitz, 2003; Miettinen-Oinonen *et al.* 2004; Nierstrasz and Warmoeskerken, 2003), in improving digestibility of animal feeds (Ishikuro, 1993) and in food industry (Penttila *et al.* 2004; Urlaub, 2002). Bacteria present an attractive potential for the exploitation of cellulases due to their rapid growth rate, enzyme complexity and extreme habitat variability (Maki *et al.* 2009). Bacteria inhibit a wide variety of environmental niches which produce cellulolytic strains that are extremely resistant to environmental stresses (Maki *et al.* 2009).

Starch is one of the most widely available plant polysaccharides and a major ingredient of the feed for fishes. It is hydrolyzed to its constituent sugar and oligosaccharides in the digestive tract of the fish (Sugita *et al.* 1997). The enzyme amylase is widely distributed in the intestinal tract of freshwater fish and plays an important role in the digestion of starch (Sugita *et al.* 1997; Ariole *et al.* 2014). Alpha-amylase (EC3.2.1.1) cleaves internal α-1, 4-glycosidic linkages in starch to produce glucose, maltose or dextrins and glucoamylase (EC3. 2.1.3) and α-1, 6-glycosidic linkages to release glucose from the non-reducing ends of starch (Xiao *et al.* 2006). Amylases can be obtained from several sources such as: plant, animal and microorganisms (Kathiresan and Manivannan, 2006). Microbial production of amylase is more efficient than that of other sources as the technique is easy, fast and cost effective. It can be modified to obtain enzymes of desired characteristics (Ashwini *et al.* 2011).

The potential of using microorganisms as biotechnological sources of industrially relevant enzymes has stimulated interest in the exploration of extracellular enzymatic activity in several microorganisms (Akpan *et al.* 1999; Pandey *et al.* 2000; Abu *et al.* 2005). With the advent of new frontiers in biotechnology, amylases have wide potential application in a number of industrial processes such as: in the food, paper, textiles, detergent, baking, brewing, pharmaceuticals, fruit juices, sweeteners and spot remover in dry cleaning (Qader *et al.* 2006; Alva *et al.* 2007; Kammoun *et al.* 2008; Bairagi *et al.* 2002; Arikan, 2008; Al Tameemi, 2010; Akpa *et al.* 2004). These uses have placed greater stress on increasing indigenous amylase production and search for more efficient processes (Aiyer, 2005).

The bacterial flora within the GI tract of fish shows very broad and variable enzymatic potential and these enzymatic masses may interfere positively in the digestive process of fish. Fish gut bacterial isolates have been demonstrated to break down cellulose (Saha and Ray, 1998; Bairagi *et al.* 2002; Ghosh *et al.* 2002a; 2010; Saha *et al.* 2006; Mondal *et al.* 2008;) and starch (Banerjee and Ray, 2013; Ariole *et al.* 2014). These intestinal bacterial isolates have potentials that could be exploited to assist in cellulose and starch degradation in various industrial processes. The search for extracellular enzyme-producing beneficial gut bacteria to be used as probiotics for the culturable freshwater fish species and for other industrial purposes will continue to be of interest.

Although a large number of microorganisms can degrade cellulose, only a few of them produce significant quantities of free enzymes capable of completely hydrolyzing crystalline cellulose (Koomnok, 2005). Cellulase yields appear to depend upon a complex relationship involving a variety of factors such as: temperature, carbon sources, medium additives, aeration, presence of inducers, incubation period, cellulose quality and pH of the medium (Immanuel *et al.* 2006). The demands for more stable, highly active and specific enzymes will continue to grow (Sethi *et al.* 2013) and hence, isolation and characterization of cellulase producing bacteria will continue to be an important aspect of biofuel research (Hirasawa *et al.* 2006).

Several physical and chemical parameters such as: pH, temperature, incubation time, carbon source and nitrogen source affect the enzyme production and the enzyme activity (Sudharhsan *et al.* 2007). Optimization of growth condition is a prime step in using microorganisms in fermentation technology (Kathiresan and Manivannan, 2006). The high cost of enzyme production (due to use of pure chemical in production) coupled with low enzyme activities, limits its industrial use. Therefore, efforts are needed to economize cellulase and amylase production by media optimization (Kalra *et al.* 2008). Furthermore, enzyme production is closely controlled in microorganisms and to improve its productivity, these controls can be ameliorated. Therefore, the aim of the present work was to optimize the culture conditions for cellulase and amylase production from *Bacillus* sp., previously isolated from cultured *Clarias gariepinus* intestine (Ariole *et al.* 2014).

Materials and Methods

*Source of Cellulolytic and Amylolytic Bacterium (***Bacillus** *sp.):*

Bacillus sp., was previously isolated from fish, *Clarias gariepinus*, intestine (Ariole *et al.* 2014) and maintained as part of culture collection in Microbiology Laboratory, University of Port Harcourt, Nigeria.

Cellulase and Amylase Production

The production medium of Sethi *et al.* (2013) containing (g/L): cellulose 10.0, peptone 0.75, $FeSO_4$ 0.1, KH_2PO_4 0.5, $MgSO_4$ 0.5 and pH 7.0 was used for cellulase production while the production medium of Ashwini *et al.* (2011) containing (g/L): starch 10, peptone 10, yeast extract 20, KH_2PO_4 0.05, $MnCl_2.4H_2O$ 0.015, MgSO4.$7H_2O$ 0.25, $CaCl_2.2H_2O$ 0.05, $FeSO_4.7H_2O$ 0.01 and pH 7.0 was used for amylase production. One millilitre of a 24 h nutrient broth culture of the *Bacillus* sp., was inoculated into 100ml of production medium in 500 ml Erlenmeyer flask. The inoculated flasks were then incubated for a period of 48 h at 37°C. The culture medium was centrifuged at 5000 rpm for 15 min to obtain the crude extract which was used as enzyme source.

Cellulase Assay

The amount of reducing sugar released by the cellulolytic bacterium was measured by Dinitrosalicyclic acid (DNS) method of Miller (1972) described by Otajevwo and Aluyi, (2011). A reaction mixture which consisted of 0.2 ml of crude enzyme solution and 1.8 ml of 0.5 per cent carboxymethyl cellulose (CMC) in 50 mM sodium phosphate buffer (pH 7) was incubated at 37°C in a shaking water bath for 30 min. The reaction was terminated by adding 3 ml of DNS reagent. The colour was then development by boiling the mixture for 5 min. The optical density (OD) was measured at 540 nm against a blank containing all the reagents except the crude enzyme using spectrophotometer. A unit (U) of cellulase activity was defined as the amount of cellulase required to catalyse the liberation of reducing sugar equivalent to 1µmol of D-glucose per minute under the assay conditions.

Amylase Assay

The amount of reducing sugar released by the amylolytic bacterium was measured by Dinitrosalicyclic acid (DNS) method of Miller (1972) described by Otajevwo and Aluyi (2011). Amylase assay was done by using mixture consisting of one millilitre substrate solution (1% soluble starch in 50 mM phosphate buffer, pH 7) and 0.1 ml enzyme solution. The mixture was then incubated for 10 min at 37°C. The reaction in the mixture was stopped by adding 2.0 ml of DNS reagent and then kept in boiling water bath for 5 min. After cooling at room temperature, the optical density (OD) was measured at 540 nm against a blank containing all the reagents minus the crude enzyme using spectrophotometer (Spectronic N21). One unit (U) of amylase activity was defined as the amount of amylase required to catalyse the liberation of reducing sugar equivalent to 1µmol of D-glucose per minute under the assay conditions.

Optimization of Culture Conditions for Catalase and Amylase Production

Effect of Temperature

Bacillus sp., was cultured at temperatures ranging from 25 to 45°C to select the optimum temperature for maximum cellulase and amylase production using cellulase production medium and amylase production medium respectively while the other parameters were unaltered. Incubation was for 48 h. Each culture broth was harvested by centrifugation at 5000 rpm for 15 min. The supernatant collected from each culture was used as crude enzyme and was assayed for the respective enzyme activity.

Effect of Medium pH

The effect of pH of the cellulase production medium and amylase production medium on cellulase and amylase production respectively was performed by varying pH of each medium from 5 to 10 while keeping the remaining parameters constant. Incubation was for 48 h at 37°C and each crude enzyme obtained after harvesting each culture broth was assayed for the respective enzyme activity.

Effect of Carbon Sources

The effect of additional carbon sources on enzyme production by *Bacillus* sp., was analysed by supplementing the cellulase production medium with different carbon sources (fructose, starch, sucrose, lactose and glucose) at a concentration of 1 per cent (w/v). Fructose, cellulose, glucose, lactose and sucrose at a concentration of 1 per cent (w/v) were added into amylase production medium in 500 ml Erlenmeyer flasks containing 100 ml of liquid medium. Incubation was for 48 h at 37°C and each crude enzyme obtained after harvesting each culture broth was assayed for the respective enzyme activity.

Effect of Nitrogen Sources

The effect of nitrogen sources on cellulase and amylase production was studied by incorporating different nitrogen sources (urea, ammonium sulphate, peptone and yeast extract) in each production medium at a concentration of 1 per cent (w/v). Incubation was for 48 h at 37°C and each crude enzyme obtained after harvesting each culture broth was assayed for the respective enzyme activity.

Statistical Analysis

Standard deviations for each of the experimental results were calculated using Excel Spreadsheets, with Microsoft excel software. Differences between treatments were examined for significance by one-way ANOVA and $P = 0.05$ was considered to be statistically significant.

Results and Discussion

In this study, we assessed the effects of culture conditions on cellulase and amylase producing ability of *Bacillus* sp., previously isolated from the intestine of a freshwater fish (*Clarias gariepinus*) (Ariole *et al.* 2014). Many microorganisms such as: bacteria and fungi are known as potential producers of extracellular cellulase and amylase (Irfan *et al.* 2012; Sethi *et al.* 2013; Otajevwo and Aluyi, 2011; Shahriarinour *et al.* 2011; Fossi *et al.* 2009; Ibatsam *et al.* 2011; Ashwini *et al.* 2011; Sidkey *et al.* 2010). Furthermore, bacteria in the digestive tract of aquatic animals participate with their enzymes in the process of degradation of nutrients (Banerjee and Ray, 2013); Ariole and Kalu, 2014; Sugita *et al.* 1997).

The effect of incubation temperature on cellulase production is shown in Fig. 2.1. The temperature of 40°C was found to be optimum with maximum of 0.53 U/ml cellulase activity.

The enzyme production decreased beyond 40°C. Similarly, the maximum cellulase production by *Serratia marscens, E. coli, Bacillus subtilis* and *Pseudomonas fluorescens* (Sethi *et al.* 2013) and *Bacillus subtilis* and *Bacillus circulans* (Ray *et al.* 2007), was at 40°C. These results are different from the finding of Otajevwo and Aluyi (2011) who recorded 35°C as optimal for cellulolytic activities of *Serratia* spp., *Bacillus subtilis* and *Bacillus circulans*. Also different are the reports of Li *et al.* (2008) and Hirasawa *et al.* (2006) who recorded 50°C as optimal for cellulase production by *Bacillus subtilis* and *Bacillus agaradherens* JAM- Ku-23. These observed differences in optimal temperature for cellulase production may be as a result of differences in source, type and species of the cellulolytic organisms.

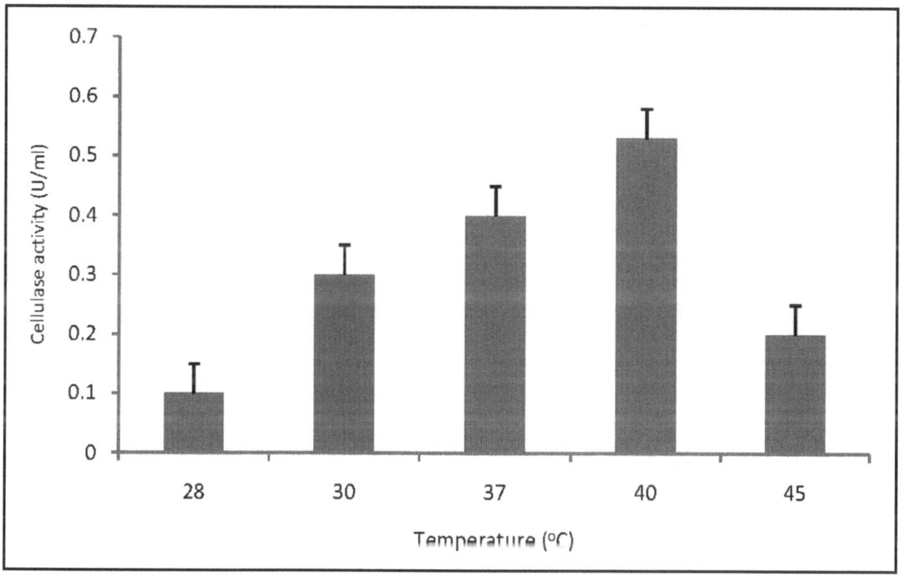

Fig. 2.1: **Effect of incubation temperature on cellulase production by *Bacillus* sp.**

The effect of incubation temperature on amylase production is shown in Fig. 2.2. The temperature of 37°C was found to be optimum with maximum of 0.52 U/ml amylase activity. The enzyme production decreased beyond 37°C. This finding is contrary to that of Ashwini *et al.* (2011) who reported that amylase production by *Bacillus* sp., *marini* was optimum at 40°C. The decrease in enzyme production beyond certain temperature plays a major role in enzyme production. It has been reported that temperature influences secretion of extracellular enzymes by changing the physical properties of the cell membrane (Sahu and Martin, 2011). The effects of pH on cellulase and amylase production are presented in Figs. 2.3 and 2.4 respectively. Maximum cellulase and amylase activities of 0.79 U/ml and 0.42 U/ml respectively, were observed at pH 7.0. Cellulase and amylase activities declined beyond pH 7.0. Similarly, maximum cellulase activity was observed at pH 7.0 for *Serratia marscens, E. coli, Bacillus subtilis* and *Pseudomonas fluorescens* (Sethi *et al.* 2013) and *Bacillus* sp., *marini* (Ashwini *et al.* 2011). These results imply that initial pH of culture medium affects the rate of enzyme production.

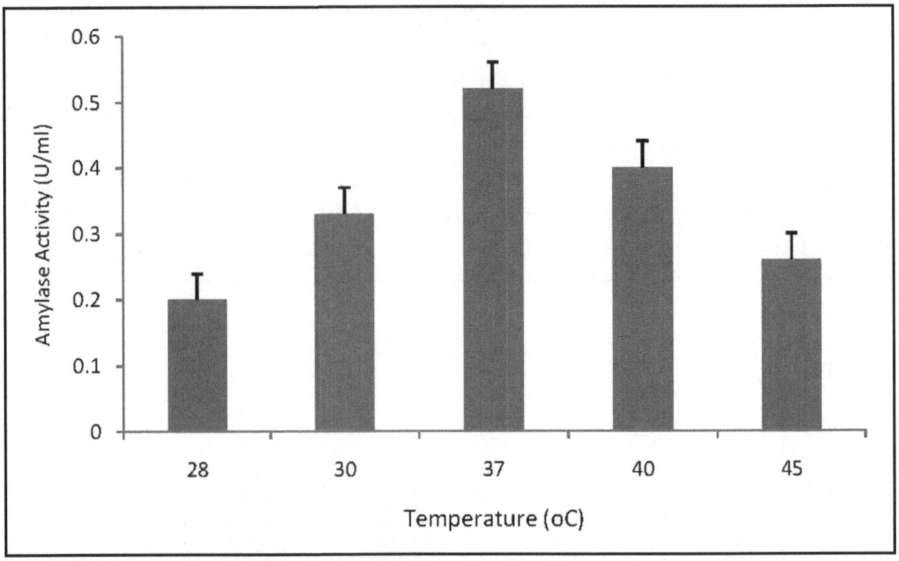

Fig. 2.2: **Effect of incubation temperature on amylase production by *Bacillus* sp.**

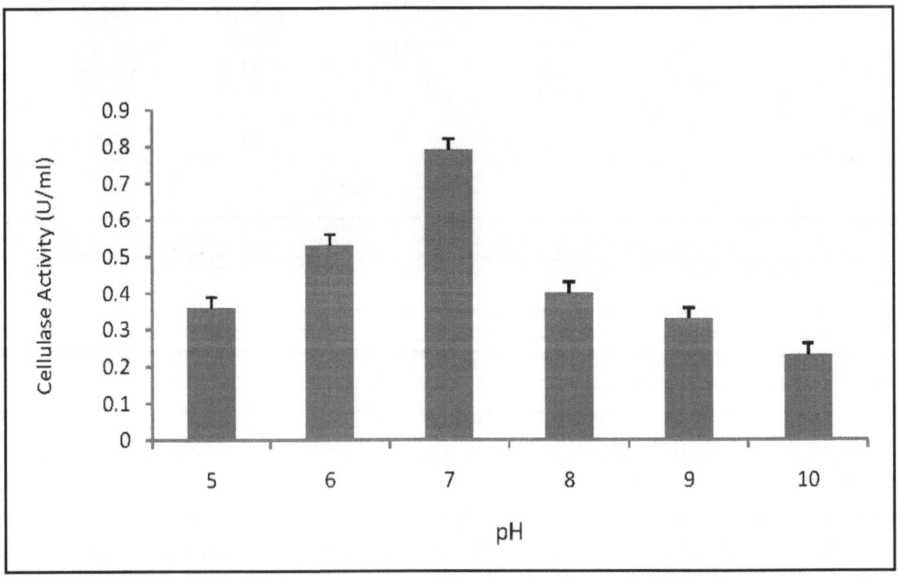

Fig. 2.3: **Effect of medium pH on cellulase production by *Bacillus* sp.**

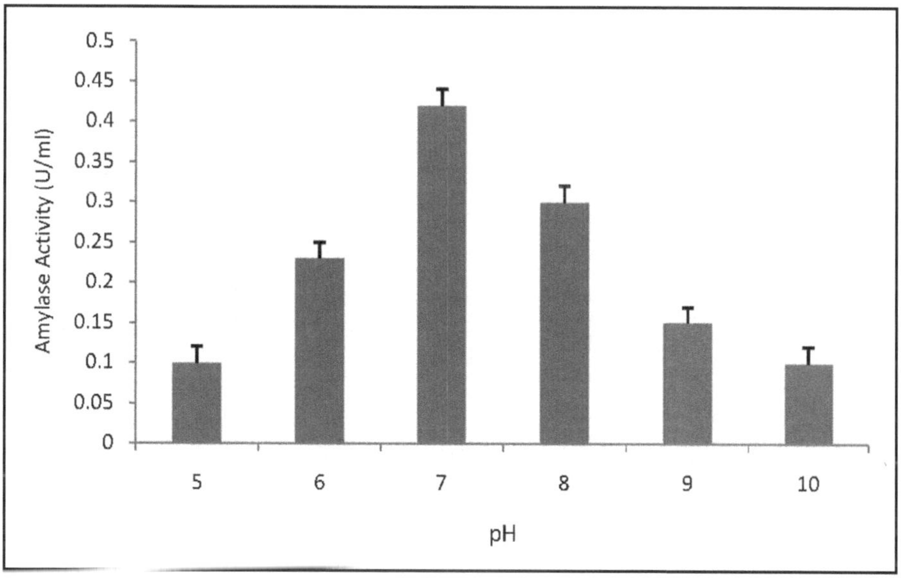

Fig. 2.4: **Effect of medium pH on amylase production by *Bacillus* sp.**

The effects of additional carbon sources on cellulase and amylase production are shown in Figs. 2.5 and 2.6 respectively. The use of fructose, starch, sucrose, lactose or glucose as additional carbon source positively affected cellulase production. The maximum cellulase activity (0.92 U/ml) was observed when glucose was used as additional carbon source. Fructose and glucose also influenced amylase production. The maximum amylase activity (0.71 U/ml) occurred when glucose was used as additional carbon source. However, cellulase, lactose and sucrose caused a reduction in amylase production in comparison with the control (Fig. 2.6). This reduction in enzyme production in the presence of sugars as carbon sources could be due to catabolite repression by readily available carbon sources in the medium (Kiran *et al.* 2008).

The effects of nitrogen sources on cellulase and amylase production are shown in Figs 2.7 and 2.8 respectively. Among the various nitrogen sources tested, yeast extract was found to be the best nitrogen source for cellulase production while urea was the best for amylase production. However, the maximum cellulase and amylase activities were observed when ammonium sulphate was employed as nitrogen source for cellulase production (Sethi *et al.* 2013) and yeast extract for amylase production (Ashwini *et al.* 2011). Production of extracellular enzyme has been reported to be sensitive to repression by different carbohydrate and nitrogen sources (Sethi *et al.* 2013). The results obtained in this study suggest that cellulase and amylase production by *Bacillus* sp., is strongly influenced by medium components as well as cultural parameters.

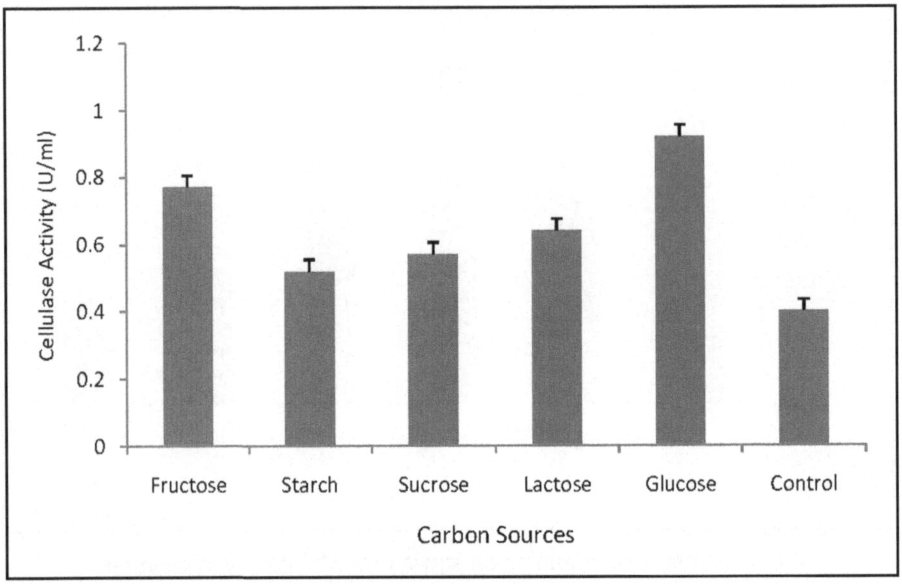

Fig. 2.5: **Effect of additional carbon sources on cellulase production by *Bacillus* sp.**

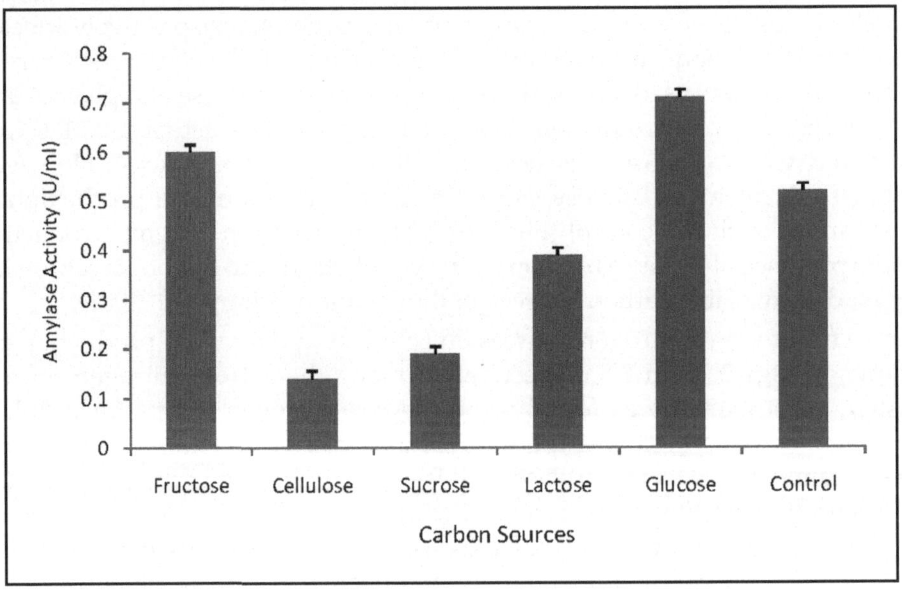

Fig. 2.6: **Effect of additional carbon sources on amylase production by *Bacillus* sp.**

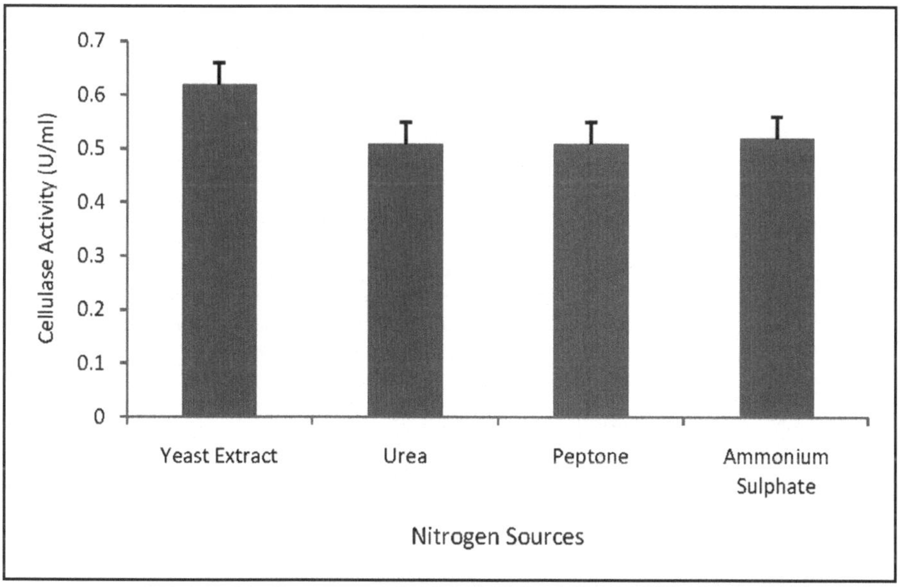

Fig. 2.7: **Effect of nitrogen sources on cellulase production by *Bacillus* sp.**

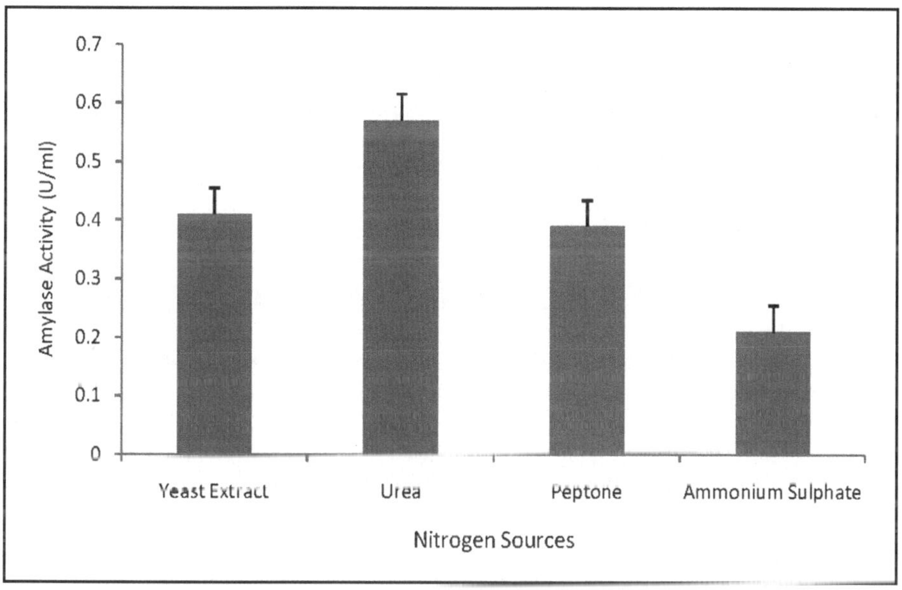

Fig. 2.8: **Effect of nitrogen sources on amylase production by *Bacillus* sp.**

Conclusion

This study reports the optimization of some culture conditions for production of cellulase and amylase by *Bacillus* sp., previously isolated from a freshwater fish (*Clarias gariepinus*) intestine. Cellulase production was found to be optimal in the presence of glucose as additional carbon source and yeast extract as nitrogen source. The optimal temperature and pH for cellulase production were 40°C and 7.0 respectively. The optimum conditions observed for amylase production were temperature 37°C, pH 7.0, glucose as additional carbon source and urea as nitrogen source. This indigenous bacterial isolate has potential that could be commercially exploited to assist in cellulose and starch degradation in various industrial processes.

REFERENCES

Abu, E.A., Ado, S.A. and James, D.B. (2005). Raw Starch Degrading Amylase Production by Mixed Culture of *Aspergillus niger* and *Saccharomyces cerevisiae* Grown on *Sorghum pomace*. *Afr. J. Biotechnol.*, 4(8):785-790.

Aiyer, P.V. (2005). Amylases and their Applications. *Afr. J. Biotechnol.*, 4(13): 1525-1529.

Akpan, I., Bankole, M.O., Adesemowo, A.M. and Latunde-Dada, G.O. (1999). Production of Amylase by *A. niger* in a Cheap Solid Medium Using Rice Band and Agricultural Materials. *Trop. Sci.*, 39: 77-79.

Akpan, T., Kawak, Y.S. and Kudo, T. (2004). Production and Stabilization of Alpha Amylase Preparation from Rice Bran Solid Medium. *World Journal Microbiology Biotechnology*, 20: 47-50.

Al Tameemi, R., Aldubaikul, A. and Salman, N.A. (2010). Comparative Study of α-Amylase Activity in Three Cyprinid Species of Different Feeding Habits from Southern Iraq. *Journal of Fisheries and Aquatic Sciences* 10: 411-414.

Alva, S., Anupama, J., Savla, J., Chiu, Y.Y., Vyshali, P., Shruti, M., Yogeetha, B.S., Bhavya, D., Purvi, J., Ruchi, K., Kumudini, B.S. and Varalakshmi, K.N. (2007). Production and Characterization of Fungal Amylase Enzyme Isolated from *Aspergillus* sp. JGI 12 in Solid State Culture. *Afr. J. Biotecnol.*, 6(5): 576-581.

Arikan, B. (2008). Highly Thermostable, Thermophilic, Alkaline, SDS and Chelator Resistant Amylase from a Thermophilic Bacillus sp. Isolate A3-15. *Bioresource Technology* 99(8): 3071-3076.

Ariole, C.N. and Kanu, N.A. (2014). Bacterial Flora Associated with Intestine of Tropical Estuarine Fish Species. *J. Chem. Biol. Phy. Sci.* 4(1): 209-215.

Ariole, C.N., Nwogu, H.A. and Chuku, P.W. (2014). Enzymatic Activities of Intestinal Bacteria Isolated from Farmed *Clarias gariepinus*. *International Journal of Aquaculture*, 4(18): 108-112.

Ashwini, K., Gaurav, K., Karthik, L., Bhaskara, R.K.V. (2011). Optimization, Production and Partial Purification of Extracellular α-Amylase from *Bacillus* sp. marini. *Archives of Applied Science Research* 3(1): 33-42.

Bairagi, A., Ghosh, K. and Sen, S.K. and Ray, A.K. (2002). Enzyme Producing Bacterial Flora Isolated from Fish Digestive Tracts. *Aquaculture International* 10: 109-121.

Banerjee, G. and Ray, A. K. (2013). Characterization and Identification of Protease and Amylase-producing Bacteria Isolated from the Gastrointestinal Tract of Climbing Perch, *Anabas testudineus* (Bloch). *DCSI*, 9(1): 150-159.

Cavaco-Paulo, A. and Gubitz, G.M. (2003). Catalysis and Processing. In: *Textile Processing with Enzyme*, Cavaco-Paulo, A. and Gubitz, G.M. (Eds.). CRC Press, Boca Raton, FL, USA.

Fossi, B.T., Tavea, F., Jiwoua, C. and Ndjouenkeu, R. (2009). Screening and phenotypic Characterization of thermostable Amylases producing Yeasts and Bacteria Strains from some Cameroonian Soils. *Afr. J. Microbiol. Res.*, 3 (9): 504-514.

Ghosh, K., Roy, M., Kar, N. and Ringø, E. (2010). Gastrointestinal Bacteria in Rohu, *Labeo rohita* (Actinopterygii: Cypriniformes: Cyprinidae): Scanning Electron Microscopy and Bacteriological Study. *Acta Ichthyol. Piscatoria* 40(2): 129-135.

Ghosh, K., Sen, S.K. and Ray, A.K. (2002). Characterization of Bacilli Isolated from the Gut of Rohu, *Labeo rohita*, Fingerlings and its Significance in Digestion. *J. Appl. Aquacult.* 12(3): 33-42.

Hirasawa, K., Uchimura, K., Kashima, M., Grant, W.D., Ito, S., Kobayashi, T. and Horikoshi, K. (2006). Salt Activated endoglucanase of a Strain of Alkaliphilic *Bacillus agaradhaerens*. *Antonie Van Leuwenhoek*, 89(2): 211-219.

Ibatsam, K., Irum, M. and Sobia, M. (2011). Isolation and Screening of Amylolytic Filamentous Fungi. *J. Appl. Sci. Environ. Manage.* 15(1): 203-206.

Immanuel, G., Dhanusha, R., Prema, P. and Palavesam, A. (2006). Effect of Different Growth Parameters on Endoglucanase Enzyme Activity by Bacteria Isolated from Coir Retting Effluents of Estuarine Environment. *Int. J. Environ. Sci. Tech.*, 3:25-34.

Irfan, M., Safdar, A., Syed, Q. and Nadeem, M. (2012). Isolation and Screening of Cellulolytic Bacteria from Soil and Optimization of Cellulase Production and Activity. *Turk. J. Biochem.*, 37 (3): 287-293.

Ishikuro, E. (1993). Feed Additives. *Modern Media*, 46: 289-296.

Kalra, K.L., Kocher, G. and Banta, G. (2008). Optimization of Cellulose Production by Submerged Fermentation of Rice Straw by *Trichoderma harzianum* RUT-C. 8230. *The Internet Journal of Microbiology*. 5(2): 1-7.

Kammoun, R., Naili, B. and Bejar, S. (2008). Application of a Statistical Design to the Optimization of Parameters and Culture Medium for α-Amylase Production by *Aspergillus oryzae* CBS 819.72 Grown on Gruel (Wheat Grinding by-Product). *Bioresource Technol.* 99: 5602-5609.

Kathiresan, K. and Manivannan, S. (2006). Alpha-Amylase Production by *Penicillium fellutanum* Isolated from Mangrove Rhizosphere Soil. *Afr. J. Biotechnol.*, 5: 829-832.

Kiran, G.S., Shanmughapriya, S., Jayalakshmi, J., Selvin, J., Gandhimathi, R., Sivaramakrishnan, S., Arunkumar, M., Thangavelu, T., Natarajaseenivasan, K. (2008). Optimization of Extracellular Psychrophilic Alkaline Lipase Produced by Marine *Pseudomonas* sp. (MSI057). *Bioprocess Biosyst. Eng.* 31: 483-492.

Koomnok, C. (2005). "Selection of Cellulase Producing Thermophilic Fungi," In *Proceedings of the 31st Congress on Science and Technology of Thailand of Technology*, Suranaree University.

Levy, I., Shani, Z. and Shoseyov, O. (2002). Modification of Polysaccharides and Plant Cell Wall by Endo-1, 4-β-Glucanase and Cellulose-Binding Domains. *Biomol. Eng.*, 19: 17-30.

Li, W., Zhang, W.W., Yang, M.M. and Chen, Y.L. (2008). Cloning of the Thermostable Cellulase Gene from Newly Isolated *Bacillus subtilis* and its Expression in *Escherichia coli*. *Mol. Biotechnol.* 2: 195-201.

Luo, J., Xia, L., Lin, J. and Cen, P. (1997). Kinetics of Simultaneous Saccharification and Lactic Acid Fermentation Processes. *Biotechnol. Prog.*, 13:762-767.

Maki, M., Leung, K.T. and Qin, W. (2009). The Prospects of Cellulase_Producing Bacteria for the Bioconversion of Lignocellulosic Biomass, *Int. J. Biol. Sci.*, 5: 500-516.

Miettinen-Oinonen, A., Londesborough, J., Joutsjoki, V., Lantto, R. and Vehmaanper, J. (2004). Three Cellulases from *Melanocarpus albomyces* for Textile Treatment at neutral pH. *Enzyme Microb. Technol.*, 34: 332-341.

Miller, G.L. (1972). Use of Dinitrosalicylic Acid Reagent for Determination of Reducing Sugar. *Biotechnol. Bioeng. Sympo.*, 5: 193-219.

Mondal, S., Roy, T., Sen, S.K. and Ray, A.K. (2008). Distribution of Enzyme-Producing Bacteria in the Digestive Tracts of Some Freshwater Fish. *Acta. Ichthyol. Piscat.*, 38: 1-8.

Nierstrasz, V.A. and Warmoeskerken, M.M.C.G. (2003). Process Engineering and Industrial Enzyme Applications. In: *Textile Processing with Enzymes*, Cavaco-Paulo, A. and Gubitz, G.M. (Eds.). CRC Press, Boca Raton, FL, USA.

Nishida, Y., Suzuki, K.I., Kumagai, Y., Tanaka, H., Inoue, A and Ojima, T. (2007). "Isolation and Primary Structure of a Cellulase from the Japanese Sea Urchin *Strongylocentrotus nudus*," *Biochimie*, 89(8): 1002-1011.

Oksanen, T., Pere, J., Paavilainen, L., Buchert, J. and Viikari, L. (2000). Treatment of Recycled Kraft Pulps with *Trichoderma reesei* Hemicellulases and Cellulases. *J. Biotechnol.*, 78: 39-48.

Otajevwo, F.D. and Aluyi, H.S.A. (2010). Cultural Conditions Necessary for Optimal Cellulase Yield by Cellulolytic Bacterial Organisms as they Relate to Residual Sugars Released in Broth Medium. *Modern Applied Science*, 5(3): 141-151.

Pandey, A., Nigam, P., Soccol, C.R., Soccol, V.T., Singh, D. and Mohan, R. (2000). Advances in Microbial Amylases. *Biotechnol. Applied Biochemistry* 31: 135-152.

Penttila, M., Limon, C. and Nevalainen, H. (2004). Molecular Biology of *Trichoderma* and Biotechnological Applications. In: *Handbook of Fungal Biotechnology*, Arora, D.K., Bridge, P.D. and Bhatnagar, D. (Eds.). Marcel Dekker, New York.

Qader, S.A.U., Bano, S., Aman, A., Syed, N. and Azhar, A. (2006). Enhanced Production and Extracellular Activity of Commercially Important Amylolytic Enzyme by a Newly Isolated Strain of *Bacillus* sp. AS-1. *Turk. J. Biochem.*, 31: 135-140.

Ray, A.K., Bairagi, K.S., Ghosh, A. and Sen, S.K. (2007). Optimization of Fermentation Conditions for Cellulase Production by *Bacillus subtilis* CY5 and *Bacillus circulans* TP3 Isolated from Fish Gut. *Acat. Icht. Et. Pist.*, 37:47-53.

Saha, A. and Ray, A.K. (1998). Cellulase Activity in Rohu Fingerlings. *Aquacult. Int.* 6: 281-291.

Saha, S., Roy, R.N., Sen, S.K. and Ray, A.K. (2006). Characterization of Cellulase-Producing Bacteria from the Digestive Tract of Tilapia, *Oreochromis mossambica* (P) and Grass Carp, *Ctenopharyngodon idella* (V). *Aquacult. Res.* 37: 380-388.

Sethi, S., Datta, A., Gupta, B.L. and Gupta, S. (2013). Optimization of Cellulase Production from Bacteria Isolated from Soil. *ISRN Biotechnology*. 1: 1-7.

Sahu, G.K. and Martin, M. (2011). Optimization of Growth Conditions for the Production of Extracellular Lipase by Bacterial Strains from Dairy Industry Effluents. *Biotechnol. Bioinf. Bioeng.* 1(3): 305-311.

Sahu, G.K. and Martin, M. (2011). Optimization of Growth Conditions for the Production of Extracellular Lipase by Bacterial Strains from Dairy Industry Effluents. *Biotechnol. Bioinf. Bioeng.* 1(3): 305-311.

Shahriarinour, M., Wahab, M.N.A., Ariff, A. and Mohamad, R. (2011). Screening, Isolation and Selection of Cellulolytic Fungi from Oil Palm Empty Fruit Bunch Fibre. *Biotechnology* 10(1): 108-113.

Sidkey, N.M., Abo-Shadi, M.A.A., Al-Mutrafy, A.M., Sefergy, F. and Al-Reheily, N. (2010). Screening of Microorganisms Isolated from some Enviro-Agro-Industrial Wastes in Saudi Arabia for Amylase Production. *Journal of American Science* 6(10): 926-939.

Sudharshan, R.K., Dutt, L. and Nayyar, R. (2007). A Highly Thermostable and Alkaline Amylase from a *Bacillus* sp. PN5. *Bioresour. Technol.*, 21: 25-29.

Sugita, H., Shibuya, K., Harada, H. and Deguchi, Y. (1997). Antibacterial Abilities of Intestinal Microflora of the River Fish. *Fisheries Sci.* 63: 378-383.

Urlaub, R. (2002). Enzymes in Fruit and Vegetable Juice Extraction: Enzymes in Food Technology. Sheffield Academic Press, England, 145-183.

Van Wyk, J.P.H. and Mohulatsi, M. (2003). Biodegradation of Wastepaper by Cellulase from *Trichoderma viride*. *Bioresour. Technol.*, 86: 21-23.

Xiao, Z., Storms, R. and Tsang, A. (2006). A Quantitative Starch-Iodine Method for Measuring Alpha-Amylase and Glucoamylase Activities. *Anal. Biochem.*, 351: 146-148.

Page 37-63

MICROBIAL ENVIRONMENT AND BIOREMEDIATION
Edited by : **Dr. Alka Chauhan; Dr. Ashok K. Rathoure & Dr. Raaz K Maheshwari**
Edition : **2017**
ISBN : 978-93-5056-856-9
Published by : **Discovery Publishing House Pvt. Ltd., New Delhi (India)**

3 Fluoride Intoxication and Possible Altered Biochemistry, Clinical Changes and Organ Histology of Rats

Arpita Samanta[1]
Bidyut Bandyopadhyay[1]
Nirmalendu Das[2*]

ABSTRACT

Fluoride exposure to rats can alter system physiology and biochemistry and results in abnormal organ function. Male albino rats were fed with 5 ppm, 10 ppm, 15 ppm and 20 ppm sodium fluoridated water to create different modes of fluoride toxicity in rats to observe the serum and tissue parameters and organ histology alteration compared to control. Protein, cholesterol, endogeneous antioxidants showed marked changes in fluoride treatment as compare to control. The fluoridated rats showed continuous increase in deposition level in liver, kidney, brain and testis. 20 ppm NaF exposure showed significant (P<0.001) decrease in mitochondrial membrane viscosity leading to alteration of energy production system. Necrotic haemolytic damages and presence of inflammatory cells were observed upon NaF exposure in rat liver and kidney tissues respectively. Similarly neuronal and spermatogonial degenerations were observed in rats brain and testicular cells exposed to fluoride intoxication. All these above result describe the adverse effect of groundwater contaminants fluoride be an environmental threat to animal kingdom.

***Keywords*:** Fluoride, Mitochondrial membrane microviscosities, Fluoride burden, Tissue histological alteration.

1. Department of Biotechnology, Oriental Institute of Science and Technology (Vidyasagar University), Dewandighi, Burdwan - 02, India.
2. Drug Development Diagnostics and Biotechnology, CSIR-Indian Institute of Chemical Biology, 4, Raja S.C. Mullick Road, Jadavpur, Kolkata 700 032, India.

INTRODUCTION

The chemical element fluorine (atomic number: 9) when combines with other chemical substances, it forms fluorides. Fluoride is a ubiquitous substance found naturally in soil, water, plants, and animals in trace quantities and is also a common air pollutant in some industrial productions (WHO, 1984).

Underground water sources are more likely to have higher levels of fluoride, whereas the concentration in seawater averages 1.3 ppm and fresh water supplies generally contain between 0.01-0.3 ppm. According to World Health Organization (1984), the permissible limit of fluoride in drinking water is 1.5 ppm. Over 50 per cent of the groundwater sources in India have been contaminated by fluoride. The problem of fluorosis has been reported in various states in India, where the fluoride concentration in groundwater reaches some times up to 25 ppm, affecting more than 150,000 villages seriously (Teotia and Teotia, 1991). In India there is an essential relation between poverty and fluorosis as malnutrition is found to play an aggressive role in its severity. The fluoride in soil (55-399 mg/kg) was detected to be significantly correlated with the fluoride content in deep tube wells and soil pH (*r*□=□0.56 and 0.71, respectively) (Samal AC *et al.* 2015). There is a high possibility of bio-accumulation of fluoride from contaminated soil and water to cultivated land, which will enhance the quantity of fluoride intake into human food chain.

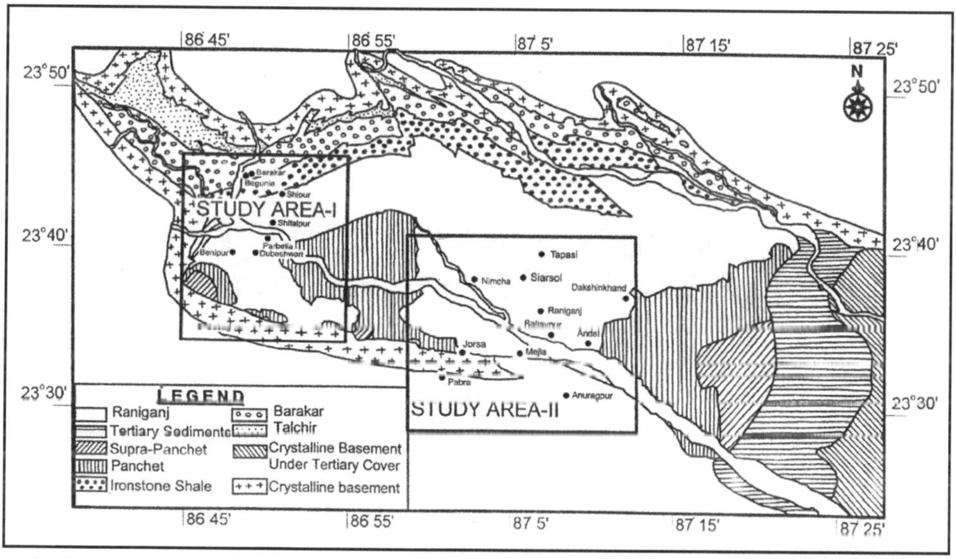

Fig. 3.1: The geological map showing the fluoride status of Raniganj, West-Bengal (Bam Deo Pandey, 2007)

Like other soluble materials, fluoride compounds are readily absorbed by the stomach and intestines, and the excess is excreted through the urine (Baez RJ *et al.* 2007). Ingested fluoride initially acts locally on the gastric mucosa, where it forms hydrofluoric acid in the stomach (Whitford GM,

2000 and Shivarajashankara YM, 2002). Urine tests have been used to ascertain rates of excretion in order to set upper limits in exposure to fluoride compounds and associated detrimental health effects. Excessive ingestion of fluoride causes fluoride intoxication or fluorosis. Endemic fluorosis remains one of the most important water-borne diseases in our country (Piillai KS, 1985). The impact of fluoride on various human and animal tissues and organs has been studied extensively (Whitford GM, 2000 and Shivarajashankara YM *et al.* 2002). The adverse effects of fluoride on hematological parameters including hematopoietic organs have also been reported (Eren E *et al.* 2005 and Machalinska A *et al.* 2002). Prolonged ingestion of drinking water containing 1-3 ppm of fluoride ions causes deleterious effects on skeletal, dental (Choubisa SL, 1999) and soft tissues (Patel PD and Chinoy NJ, 1998). Consumption of fluoride at levels beyond 2 ppm used in fluoridated water for a long period of time causes skeletal fluorosis. In some areas, particularly the Asian subcontinent, skeletal fluorosis is endemic. It is known to cause irritable-bowel syndrome and joint pain (Gupta R *et al.* 2007).

Inorganic fluoride inhibits adenylate cyclase activity which is required for antidiuretic hormone effect on the kidney tubules. Fluoride again stimulates vasodilatation, leading to increased medullary blood flow, which interferes with the counter current mechanism in the kidney required to regulate urine concentration. In blood, brain, and liver of animals, various changes occur after chronic administration of fluoride. These include abnormal behavioural patterns (Mullenix PJ *et al.* 1995) altered neuronal and cerebrovascular integrity (Mullenix PJ *et al.* 1995), and formation of metabolic lesions (Vani ML and Reddy KP, 2000) in brain. Generation of free radicals, lipid peroxidation, and altered antioxidant defence systems are considered to play an important role in the toxic effects of fluoride (Rzeuski R *et al.* 1998).

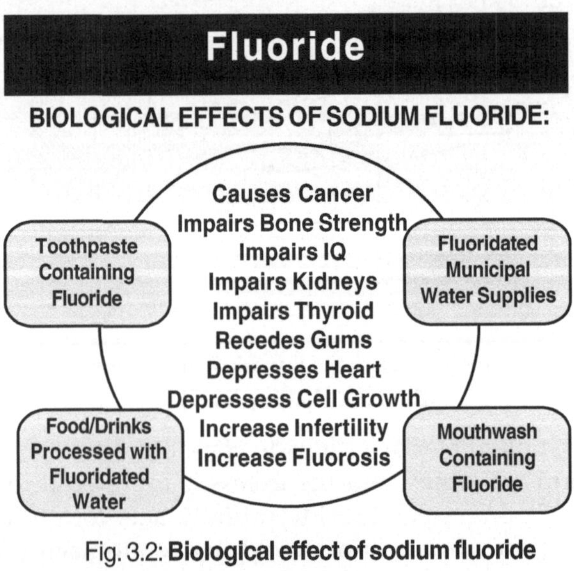

Fig. 3.2: **Biological effect of sodium fluoride**

Fluorosis is linked to:

1. Fluoride exposure disrupts the synthesis of collagen and leads to the breakdown of collagen in bone, tendon, muscle, skin, cartilage, lungs, kidney and trachea. (A.K. Susheela, *et al.* 1981).
2. Fluoride stimulates granule formation and oxygen consumption in white blood cells, but inhibits these processes when the white blood cell is challenged by a foreign agent in the blood. (Robert A. Clark *et al.* 1981).
3. Fluoride depletes the energy reserves and the ability of white blood cells to properly destroy foreign agents by the process of phagocytosis. As little as 0.2 ppm fluoride stimulates superoxide production in resting white blood cells, virtually abolishing phagocytosis. Even micro-molar amounts of fluoride, below 1 ppm, may seriously depress the ability of white blood cells to destroy pathogenic agents. (John Curnette, *et al.* 1979).
4. Fluoride confuses the immune system and causes it to attack the body's own tissues, and increases the tumour growth rate in cancer prone individuals. (John Curnette, *et al.* 1979).
5. Fluoride inhibits antibody formation in the blood. (A.K. Susheela, *et al.* 1981).
6. Fluoride depresses thyroid activity. (A. Benagiano, *et al.* 1965).
7. Fluorides have a disruptive effect on various tissues in the body (T. Takamorim, 1962).
8. Fluoride promotes development of bone cancer. (J.K. Mauer, *et al.* 1990).
9. Fluorides cause premature aging of the human body. (Nicholas Leone, *et al.* 1954).
10. Fluoride ingestion from mouth rinses and dentifrices in children is extremely hazardous to biological development, life span and general health. (Yngve Ericsson, *et al.* 1969).

In the light of above data, the present investigation has been undertaken to focus on the effects of chronic sodium fluoride toxicity on some biochemical, physiological and clinical parameters of albino rats.

Review of Literature

Water is now polluted with various toxic substances specially the underground water and is contaminated by many hazardous pollutants like colored dyes, heavy metals, pesticides, arsenic and fluoride. Out of this, fluoride pollution has now becoming a threat in health related issues.

Children may experience gastrointestinal distress upon ingesting excessive amounts of flavoured fluoridated toothpaste. While the outcomes were generally not serious, gastrointestinal symptoms appear to be the most common problem reported to them (Jay D. Shulman and Linda M. Wells, 1997). Another study described that fluoride stimulates granule formation and oxygen consumption in white blood cells, but inhibits these processes when the white blood cell is challenged by a foreign agent in the blood (Curnette *et al.* 1979). Fluoride depletes the energy reserves and the ability of white blood cells to properly destroy foreign agents by the process of phagocytosis. As little as 0.2 ppm fluorides in blood stimulate superoxide production in resting white blood cells, virtually abolishing phagocytosis. Even micro-molar amounts of fluoride, below 1 ppm, may seriously depress the ability of white blood cells to destroy pathogenic agents (Curnette *et al.* 1979). Fluoride confuses the immune system and causes it to attack the body's own tissues, and increases the tumor growth rate in cancer prone individuals (Curnette *et al.* 1979). The chromosomal breaks and apoptosis observed in the study, (Podder S. *et al.* 2008) could be mediated by reactive oxygen species generated during F-induced oxidative stress. Another important study showed that fluoride inhibits antibody formation in the blood (Susheela and Jha, 1981). Fluoride depresses thyroid activity (Benagiano, 1965), damages various tissues in the body (Takamorim, 1962), causes premature aging (Leone *et al.* 1954) and even promotes development of bone cancer (Mauer *et al.* 1990) in human body. Fluoride ingestion, through mouth rinses and dentifrices in children is extremely hazardous to biological development, life span and general health (Ericsson and Forsman, 1969). Another study showed that fluoride increased quickly in the blood and concentrated in various tissues, especially in the thyroid, bone, and teeth (Cheng-Chun Lee, 1968).

Accumulation of fluoride causes to reduce aerobic metabolism and altered free radical metabolism in liver (Chouhan S and Flora SJ, 2010). Fluoride causes degenerative and inflammatory changes like: dilation, hepatic hyperplasia and accumulation of crystalline bodies in liver cells (Chinoy NJ *et al.* 1993 and Kapoor V *et al.* 1993).

Kidney is the major route for fluoride removal from body (Harrison PT, 2005) and may cause renal damage (Shashi A *et al.* 2002). Fluoride toxicity causes pathological changes in glomeruli at its proximal and distal tubules (Bouaziz *et al.* 2007). Fluoride induces renal toxicity through apoptosis (Xu H *et al.* 20026).

Fluoride is known to cause brain damage and reduce mental accuracy and impairs memory (Waldbott GL, 1955 and Waldbott GL, 1956) observed adverse neurological effects on human brain upon F intoxication. They also suggested that children with dental fluorosis are in high risk of brain damage. The development of children's intelligence is adversely affected with the increasing level of fluoride exposer and accumulation (Xiang Q *et al.* 2003). Fluoride can pass through blood brain barrier (BBB) (Mullienix PJ 1995) to facilitate ROS generation, induce oxidative damage to brain (Ames BN *et al.* 1993).

Fluoride exposer potentially affects male fertility. NaF intoxication changes spermatogenesis pattern and behaviour with altered and disturbed hormonal changes. F toxicity decreases sperm count and altered epididymis and accessory reproductive glands (Pushpalatha T *et al.* 2005) and finally affect fertility. It was also studied the presence of apoptotic spermatogenic cells when fluoride is administered (Kumar AR, Susheela AK, 1995).

Materials and Methods

Materials

(i) Albino rats (Rattus norvegicus).

(ii) The reagents used in these experiments were purchased from MERCK (INDIA) and SRL and were of analytical grade.

Methods

Animal Experiment

Healthy male albino rats of age groups (10 months) weighting 150-200g, were used. The animals were kept in a temperature and humidity-controlled housing with 12-h light and dark cycles. They were acclimatized (26-28°C, 60-80% relative humidity) for 3-5 days to the new environment before use and allowed free access to food and water.

Rats were divided into five groups and each group contained 5 animals. 1st group was used for control experiments. 2nd, 3rd, 4th and 5th groups were ingested with 5 ppm, 10 ppm, 15 ppm and 20 ppm of fluoride water respectively for 60 days. Animal handling and experimental procedures were approved by the Institutional Animal Ethics Committee, OIST, Vidyasagar University and the animals were cared in accordance with the 'Guide for the care and use of laboratory animals' and 'Committee for the purpose of control and supervision on experimental animals.

Hematological Assay

RBC and WBC were counted by the haemocytometric method in which total erythrocytes and total leukocytes count (Wintrobe, 1930), per cent haemoglobin (Crossby *et al.* 1954) values were studied in this experiment.

Biochemical Assay

The total protein (Lowry *et al.* 1951), cholesterol (Zlatkins *et al.* 1953), phospholipid (Zilversmit *et al.* 1950) SGPT (Serum gluterate pyruvate transferase) and SGOT (Serum glutamate oxaloacetate transaminase) were estimated from serum using kit from span diagnostic limited, India. The estimation of cholesterol (Wilson JD and Lindsey Jr CA, 1965), glycogen (Montgomery, 1957) and ascorbic acid (Roe and Kuther, 1943) were done from liver, kidney, brain, heart and testicular tissues separately.

Preparation of Cytosolic Fraction of Isolated Tissue (liver, kidney, brain, heart and testicular cells) Homogenate for the Determination of Antioxidant Enzymes Level

The isolated individual tissues were rinsed with ice-cold saline and were homogenized seperately in 20ml phosphate buffer saline with teflon coated homogenizer. Individual tissue homogenate was rehomogenised in 0.25M sucrose with a teflon coated homogenizer and centrifuged at 10,000 * g for 15 minutes. The supernatant from the second centrifugation contains the cytosolic fraction of isolated tissues (Sarkar *et al.* 1995) and were used for enzymatic assay.

The Estimation of Antioxidant Enzymes Activity from the cytosolic Fraction of Tissue Homogenate

The catalase activity in tissue homogenate was measured spectrophotometrically by calculating the rate of degradation of H_2O_2 (Aebi, 1984). Superoxide dismutase (SOD) activity was assayed according to the method of Beyer and Fridovich (1987). Glutathione transferase (GST) activity was estimated by using the substrate, 1-chloro-2,4-dinitrobenzene (CDNB) by the method devised by Habig *et al.* 1974.

Histological Examination of Liver, Brain, Kidney, Heart and Testicular Tissue of Experimental Animals

Liver, brain, kidney and testicular portions of experimental animals were removed quickly at the time of sacrifice and further fixed overnight in 4 per cent paraformaldehyde at 4°C. Post fixed portions were embedded in paraffin, and 5-μm sections were cut on a microtome. The sections were stained with hematoxylin and eosin (HE) and examined under a light microscope.

Statistical Analysis

A maximum of five replicates were taken for each tissue and treatment. The mean and standard deviation were calculated for all data using MS excel and GRAPHPAD INSTAT software. Significant differences between means were evaluated by one way post hoc analysis of variances comparing all pairs of column by students new man keulis test. All the values were expressed as means ± S.E.M, and $p < 0.05$ was considered as statistically significant.

Results

Fluoride is widely distributed in nature in many forms and its compounds were used extensively. Fluoride is absorbed completely and quickly from GI tract and attack important organs (Hall SK, 1996).

The data revealed from Table 3.1 that different concentration of fluoride treatment to rats did not show any significant change in the body weight but the weight of the vital organs *viz*; kidney, liver, heart and brain weights were declined in the entire group studied. The significant reduction of kidney weight was noticed with 10 ppm and 20 ppm treatment for 60 days. As compared to control value, the weight of heart was also significantly reduced following 10 ppm and 20 ppm fluoride water treatment (Table 3.1).

Table 3.1: Body (g) and Organ weight (mg/100 g body wt.) of control and fluoride contaminated drinking water treated rats for 60 days

Group	Treatment		Body Weight (g)		Vital Organ (mg)			
			Initial	Final	Kidney	Liver	Heart	Brain
I	Control		160.83 ±0.58	180.90 ±6.86	537.26 ±15.23	2241.39 ±69.98	257.16 ±07.79	19540 ±190.76
II	Fluoride contaminated drinking water for 60 days	5 ppm	171.91 ±1.38	192.78 ±6.63	525.71 ±10.06	2287.25 ±103.13	259.42 ±12.13	19271 ±146.23
III		10 ppm	182.17 ±1.79	181.83 ±15.58	452. 41[a] ±09.13	2122.05 ±61.49	166.47[c] ±16.12	19006 ±178.16
IV		15 ppm	179.20 ±1.63	186.75 ±6.23	542.15 ±8.79	2247.14 ±46.78	223.76 ±09.69	18875 ±145.26
V		20 ppm	163.13 ±7.14	192.56 ±9.22	584.18[b] ±6.63	2050.50 ±64.25	201.08 ±50.37	18654 ±195.23

Values are mean±SEM

c = $p \leq 0.05$ almost significant b = $p \leq 0.01$ significant a = $p \leq 0.001$ Highly significant

In the present study, the content of serum protein, cholesterol, phospholipids, SGPT (Serum gluterate pyruvate transferase) and SGOT (Serum glutamate oxaloacetate transaminase) were studied following fluoride water treatment in group II to group V. All the parameters showed significant reduction ($p \leq 0.001$) following different fluoride water treatment (Table 3.2).

Table 3.2: Total Protein, cholesterol, phospholipid, SGPT and SGOT in serum of control and fluoride contaminated drinking water treated rats for 60 days

Group	Treatment		Total Protein	Cholesterol (mg/dl)	Phospholipid (mg/dl)	SGPT (IU/L)	SGOT (IU/L)
I	Control		17686.36 ±312.12	122.02 ±0.23	124.60 ±4.19	40.06 ±0.33	66.43 ±1.23
II	Fluoride Contaminated Drinking Water For 60 Days	5 ppm	15755.92[a] ±29.31	134.13[a] ±0.19	173.23 ±2.98	43.12 ±1.13	72.67 ±3.36
III		10 ppm	14985.23[a] ±29.66	145.05[a] ±1.23	185.37[b] ±8.32	49.23[a] ±2.36	78.33 ±0.49
IV		15 ppm	13918.37[a] ±199.16	158.89[a] ±1.69	196.33[a] ±1.26	56.44 ±3.33	82.09 ±2.61
V		20 ppm	13405.20[a] ±19.36	169.56[a] ±0.98	241.85[a] ±0.36	59. 09[a] ±1.25	87.65 ±1.19

Values are mean±SEM

c = $p \leq 0.05$ almost significant b = $p \leq 0.01$ significant a = $p \leq 0.001$ Highly significant

From Table 3.3, it was observed that the glycogen concentration of liver reduces almost significantly ($p \leq 0.05$) with higher dose of fluoride water content as compared to control but no significant change was observed in heart muscle in all the group studied. Cholesterol content in liver and heart muscle was also significantly reduced in group II to group V of fluoride water exposer to rat as compared to control. Significant reduction ($p \leq 0.001$) was also observed in ascorbic acid content of both liver and heart in the entire group tested (Table 3.3).

Table 3.3A: Glycogen, cholesterol and ascorbic acid in liver and heart tissues of control and fluoride drinking water treated rats for 60 days

Group	Treatment		Glycogen (mg/gm)		Cholesterol (mg/gm)		Ascorbic Acid (mg/gm)	
			Liver	Heart	Liver	Heart	Liver	Heart
I	Control		0.55 ±0.69	6.85 ±0.02	7.48 ±0.59	09.76 ±0.06	0.16 ±1.33	0.14 ±0.33
II	Fluoride Contaminated Drinking Water For 60 Days	5 ppm	0.56 ±0.06	6.87 ±0.05	7.62 ±0.01	10.38 ±0.07	0.22 ±0.11	0.18[a] ±1.09
III		10 ppm	0.59 ±0.66	6.96 ±0.02	7.86 ±0.01	10.71[a] ±0.06	0.26[a] ±0.03	0.19[a] ±1.63
IV		15 ppm	0.61[c] ±0.06	7. 01 ±0.03	8.09[b] ±0.63	10.92[a] ±0.11	0.27[a] ±0.01	0.16[b] ±0.01
V		20 ppm	0.62[c] ±0.03	7.24 ±0.01	8.52[b] ±0.08	11.75[a] ±0.33	0.21 ±0.01	0.12 ±0.02

Values are mean±SEM

c = $p \leq 0.05$ almost significant b = $p \leq 0.01$ significant a = $p \leq 0.001$ Highly significant

Table 3.3B: Glycogen, cholesterol and ascorbic acid in kidney, brain and testicular tissues of control and fluoride drinking water treated rats for 60 days

Group	Treat-ment		Glycogen (mg/gm)			Cholesterol (mg/gm)			Ascorbic Acid (mg/gm)		
			Kidney	Brain	Testi-cular Cells	Kidney	Brain	Testi cular Cells	Kindey	Brain	Testi cular Cells
I	Control		0.62 ±0.14	0.75 ±0.34	0.85 ±0.02	11.48 ±0.59	6.24 ±0.16	5.06 ±0.05	0.15 ±0.33	0.21 ±0.03	0.12 ±0.33
II	Fluoride Contam-inated Drinking Water For 60 Days	5 ppm	0.65 ±0.16	0.78 ±0.19	0.87 ±0.05	11.22 ±0.01	6.38 ±0.08	5.18 ±0.17	0.19 ±0.11	0.24 ±0.05	0.14 ±1.09
III		10 ppm	0.68 ±0.34	0.81 ±0.16	0.88 ±0.02	11.06 ±0.01	6.53[b] ±0.02	5.27[b] ±0.26	0.22[a] ±0.03	0.25 ±0.09	0.15 ±1.63
IV		15 ppm	0.69[c] ±0.06	0.85[b] ±0.28	0. 91 ±0.03	10.89[c] ±0.63	6.87[b] ±0.28	5.42[b] ±0.14	0.22[a] ±0.01	0.22 ±0.03	0.16[b] ±0.01
V		20 ppm	0.74[c] ±0.33	0.90[b] ±0.17	1.25[c] ±0.01	9.22[c] ±0.08	7.06[b] ±0.31	5.75[b] ±0.23	0.15 ±0.01	0.20 ±0.02	0.14 ±0.02

Haematological parameters of the five groups of mice (group I to group V) are shown in Table 3.4, 3.5 and Table 3.6. After 60 days of treatment, the lymphocyte count was reduced with higher levels of fluoride water content. The total R.B.C count showed a significant decrease ($p \leq 0.001$) compared to control group I. Total count of W.B.C were declined significantly following higher doses of fluoride water treatment as compared to control. Haemoglobin percentage also showed a significant decrease ($p \leq 0.001$) compared to the control group I. Effect of fluoride toxicity in blood cells of albino rats with different types of abnormal erythrocytes *viz;* poikilocytes, Schistocytes, elliptical cells etc., were presented in Table 3.5 and Figure 3.3.

Table 3.4: Differential count of different types of white blood cells

Group	Treatment		Blood Count (Differential)				
			Neutrophil	Lymphocyte	Eosinophil	Monocyte	Basophil
I	Control		68	30	01	01	00
II		5ppm	68	30	01	01	00
III		10ppm	69	26	02	03	00
IV		15ppm	69	25	02	03	01
V		20ppm	69	23	03	03	02

Table 3.5: Total count of blood with erythrocyte character

Group	Treatment	Erythrocyte Character
I	Control	Normal healthy blood cells (Normocytic, normochromic)
II	5 ppm	Normocytic, normochromic
III	10 ppm	Poikilocytes
IV	15 ppm	Schistocytes
V	20 ppm	Fragmented RBC, Elliptical cells

Table 3.6: R.B.C., W.B.C., Haemoglobin values of control and fluoride contaminated drinking water treated rats for 60 days

Group	Treatment		Blood		
			R.B.C. (million/mm^3)	W.B.C. (per mm^3)	Haemoglobin (gm%)
I	Control		5.55±0.33	8566.55±169.91	13.99±1.05
II	Fluoride Contaminated Drinking Water For 60 Days	5 ppm	3.65^a±0.31	8732.26±63.12	13.44±0.13
III		10 ppm	2.99^a±0.02	8974.36±21.16	11.26^b±0.09
IV		15 ppm	2.98^a±0.01	9165.06^b±36.36	9.89^a±0.04
V		20 ppm	2.1^a±0.04	10644.03^a±155.36	9.27^a±0.08

Values are mean±SEM

c = $p \leq 0.05$ almost significant b = $p \leq 0.01$ significant a = $p \leq 0.001$ Highly significant

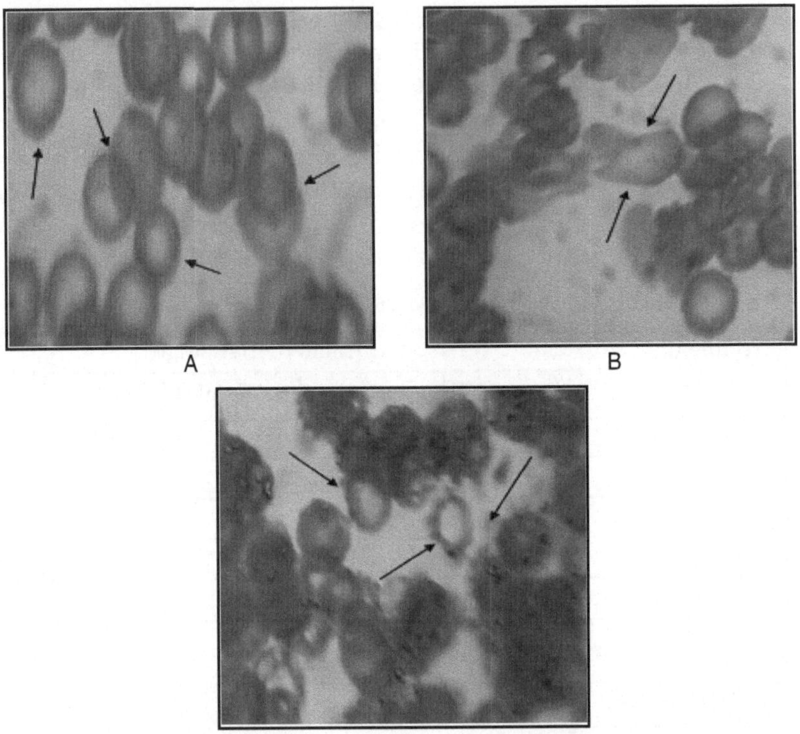

A B C

Fig. 3.3: **Effect of fluoride toxicity in blood cells of albino rats**

A Healthy blood cells showing normocytic and normochromic cells (control)

B Healthy and small number of abnormal shaped RBCs by the effect of fluoride (5 and 10 ppm concentration)

C Blood cells showing Schistocytes and ruptured RBCs by the effect of fluoride (20 ppm concentration)

As shown in Table 3.7, the Superoxide dismutase (SOD), Glutathione transferase (GST) and catalase activity was significantly decreased ($p \leq 0.001$) with higher doses of fluoride content in group II to group V as compared to control in all organs.

Table 3.7A: Effect of Fluoride on Antioxidant Enzymes of liver and kidney tissues

Group	Treatment	SOD (U/mg protein)		Catalase (U/mg protein)		Glutathionenmol formed/mg protein/min.	
		Liver	Kidney	Liver	Kidney	Liver	Kidney
I	Control	9.43±0.13	8.56±0.52	0.745±0.26	0.574±0.52	78.23±1.42	64.52±1.36
II	5 PPM	8.78±0.24	7.63±0.35	0.723±0.42	0.526±0.16	69.32±2.14	59.65±2.43
III	10 PPM	7.45±0.63[a]	6.58±0.17[c]	0.685±0.65[b]	0.482±0.35[a]	61.57±1.37[b]	54.33±2.11[a]
IV	15 PPM	6.28±0.16[a]	5.62±0.38[a]	0.621±0.21[a]	0.425±0.71[a]	54.35±0.84	48.50±145[a]
V	20 PPM	5.59±0.32[a]	5.15±0.23[a]	0.605±0.14[a]	0.392±0.67	51.37±1.53[a]	44.11±1.26[a]

Values are mean±SEM

c = $p \leq 0.05$ almost significant b = $p \leq 0.01$ significant a = $p \leq 0.001$ Highly significant

Table 3.7B: Effect of fluoride on antioxidant enzymes of brain tissues

Group	Treatment	SOD (U/mg protein)	Catalase (U/mg protein)	Glutathionenmol formed/mg protein/min
I	Control	6.01±0.24	0.235±0.32	53.83±2.11
II	5 ppm	5.96±0.42	0.226±0.26	51.35±2.72
III	10 ppm	4.17±0.59[a]	0.185±0.41[a]	44.72±1.92[a]
IV	15 ppm	3.11±0.38[a]	0.140±0.68[a]	40.22±1.39[a]
V	20 ppm	3.04±1.24[b]	0.138±0.20[c]	39.26±1.67

c = $p \leq 0.05$ almost significant b = $p \leq 0.01$ significant a = $p \leq 0.001$ Highly significant

Histopathological Study

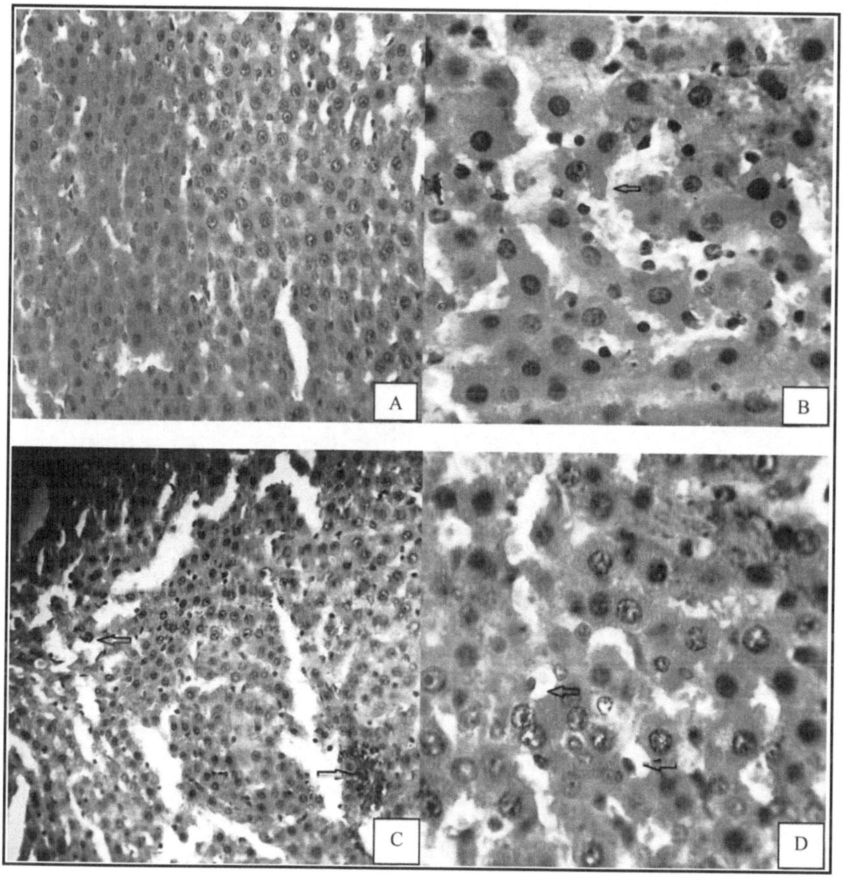

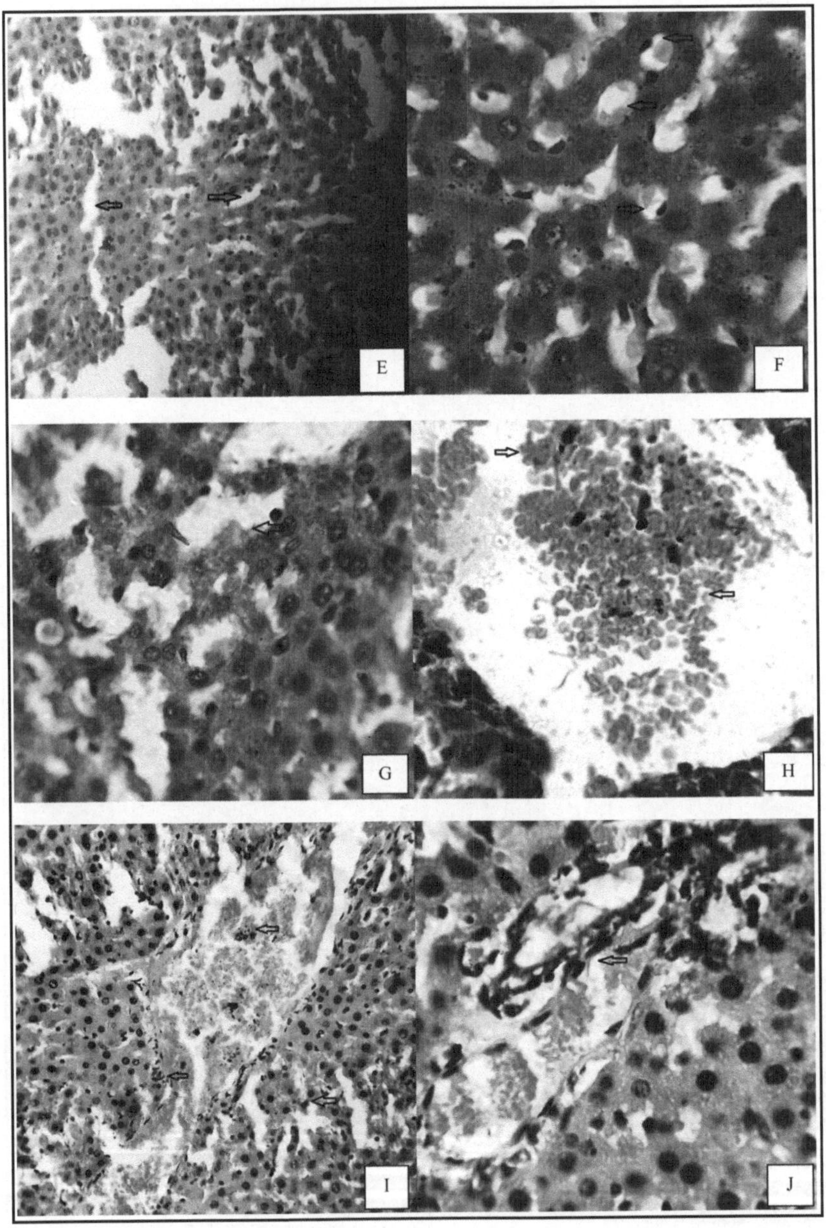

Fig. 3.4: **Cross section of liver showing microscopic view of rat cells treated with different concentration of sodium fluoridated water:**

- *Control*: Normal liver hepatocytes at 40X (A), *5 PPM*: Little disarrayed hepatocytes at 100X (B), cellular disarray and congestion at 40X (C), *10 PPM*: Central nucleic surrounded by vacuolated cytoplasm with mild fatty changes at 100X (D). *15 PPM*: Degeneration of hepatocytes at 40X (E), extensive vacuolization of cytoplasm at 100X (F), haemolysis and mild fatty changes at 100X (G). *20 PPM*: Severe haemorrhage at 100X (H), separated hepatic cells with necrosis with round cell infiltration at 40X (I), haemolysed necrotic damage at 100X (J). (Changes showed with arrow) ⟹

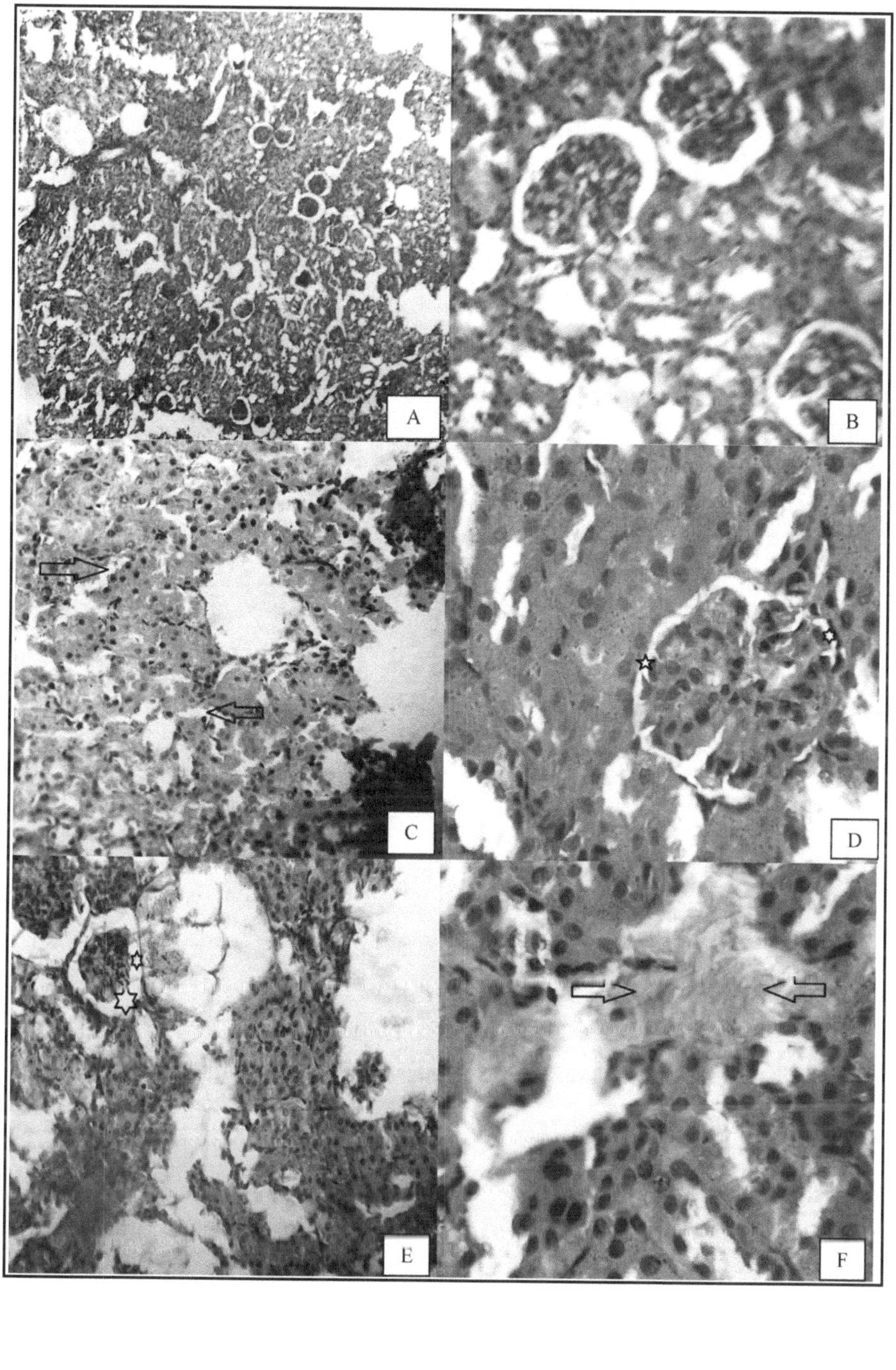
A
B
C
D
E
F

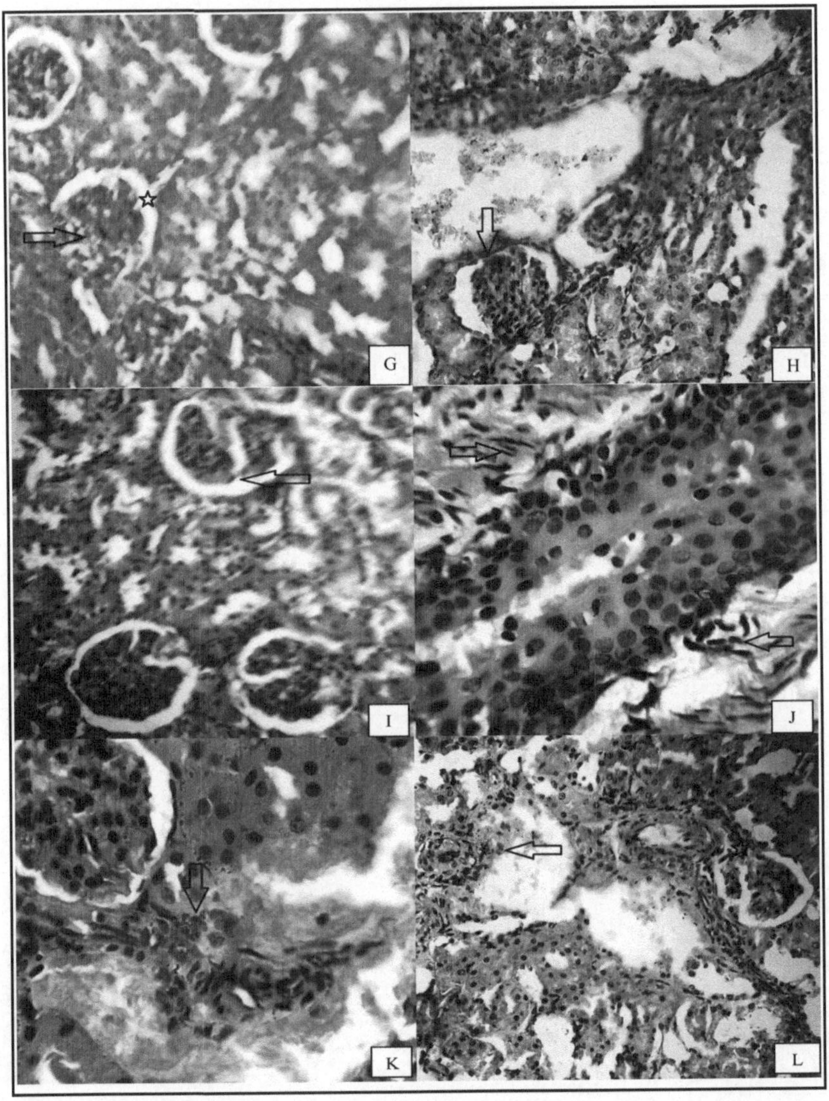

Fig. 3.5: **Cross section of kidney showing microscopic view of rat cells treated with different concentration of sodium fluoridated water:**

- *Control*: Normal histological structure of glomerulus and tubuli at 40X (A), normal kidney cell with normal glomeruli at 100X (B). *5 PPM*: Renal tubule with marked diluted lumen at 10X (C), shrunken lumen of bowman's capsule at 100X (D). *10 PPM*: Thickening of lumen of bowman's capsule at 10X (E), thickening of renal convoluted tubule at 100X (F). *15 PPM*: Damaged glomeruli and widen bowman's capsule at 100X (G), adhesion of bowman in between visceral and parietal layers at 10X (H), lobulation in glomelular tufts with haemorrhagic lesions at 100X (I). *20 PPM*: Pyknotic nucleic with interstitial haemorrhage at 100X (J), infiltrative inflammatory cells like lymphocytes and monocytesin interstitial tissue with haemorrhage at 100X (K), infiltrative inflammatory cells with necrotic change in glomeruli at 10X (L).

(Changes shown with arrows and asterix) ⟹ ☆

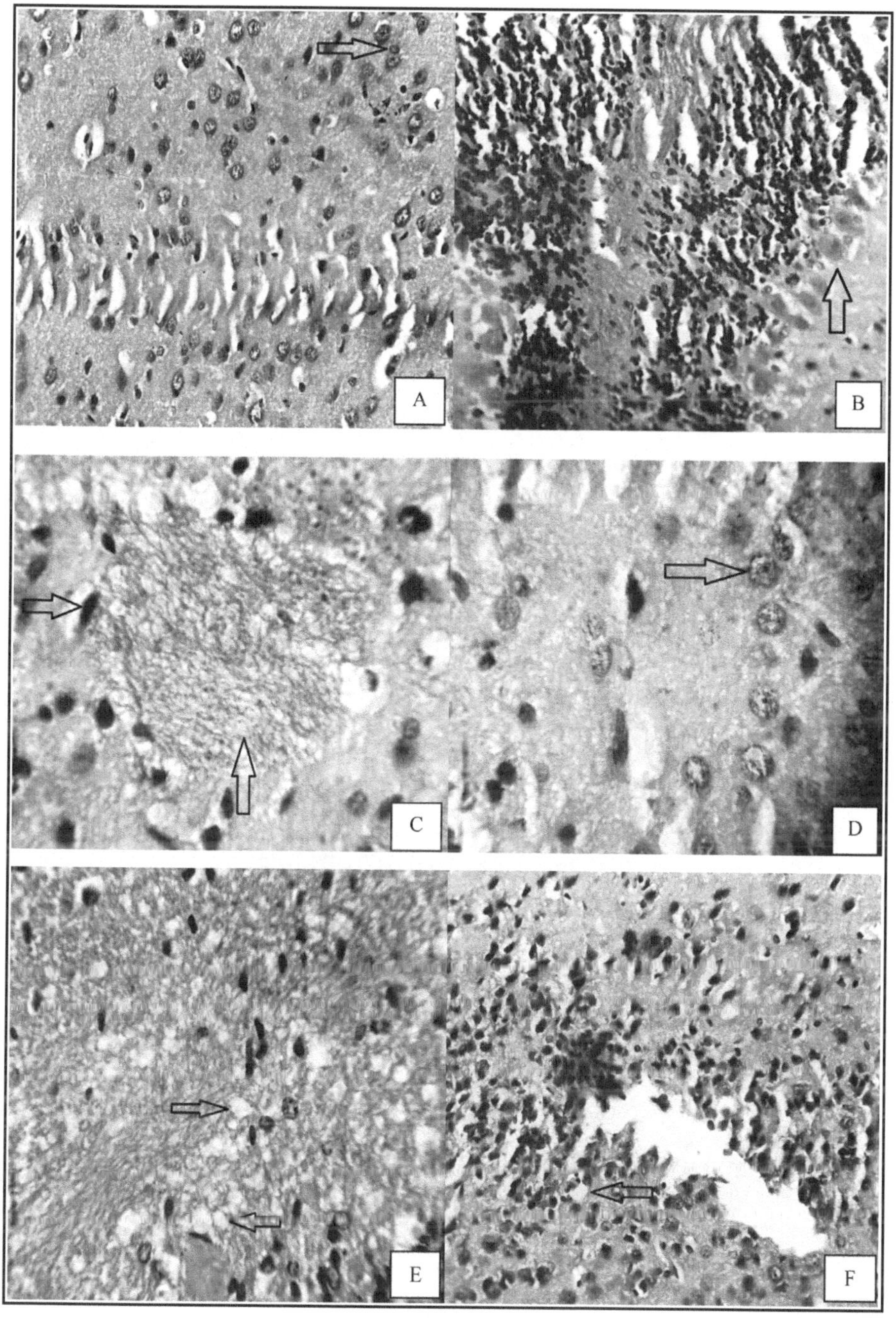
A
B
C
D
E
F

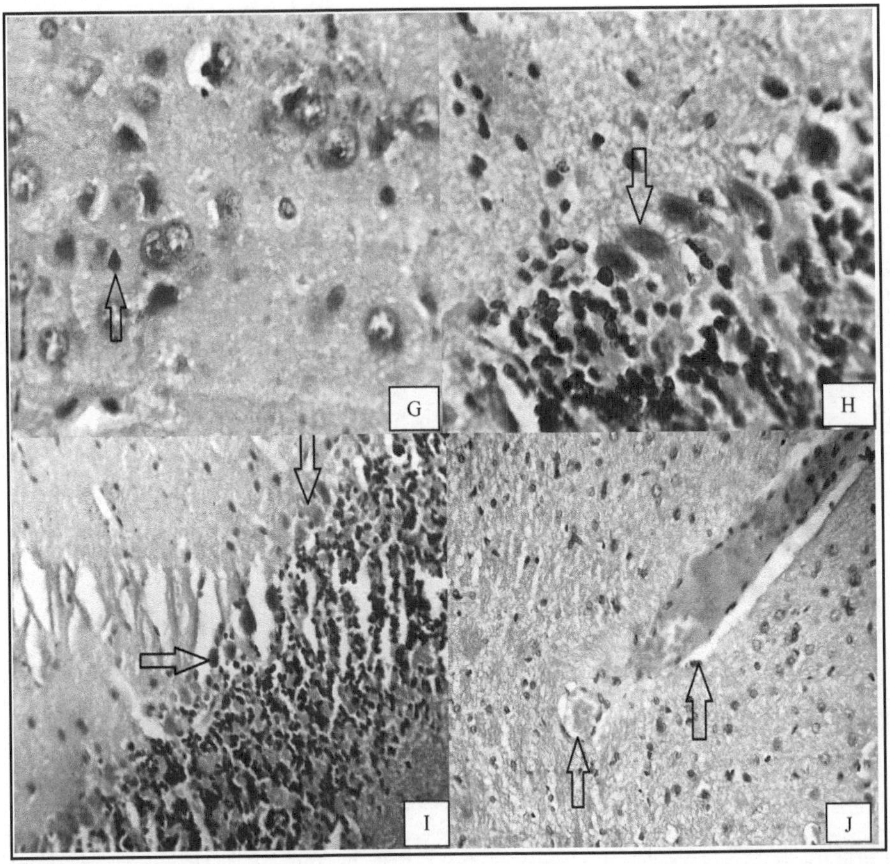

Fig. 3.6: **Cross section of brain showing microscopic view of rat cells treated with different concentration of sodium fluoridated water:**

- *Control*: Brain showing appearance of spheroid bodies in neuroglial cells or control at 100X (A), cerebelar cortex showing normal array of purkinje cells at 100X (B). *5 PPM*: Visible astrocytes with degenerated neurons at 100X (C), swollen astrocytes at 100X (D). *10 PPM*: Diffuse gliosis and pericellular oedema in the transverse section of cerebral cortex at 100X (E), astrocytes with visible oedema at 100X (F). *15 PPM*: CA1 region of hippocampal control with degenerated neuron at 100X (G), pyriformed purkinje cells at 100X (H). *20 PPM*: Cellebelar cortex showing disorganised array of Purkinje cell layer at 100X (I), transverse section through brain showing chromatolysis in Purkinje neurones and cells nucleus is in periphery and nissle substances revealed degeneration at 100X (J). (Changes showed with arrows) ⟹

Liver is the major organ of metabolism of toxic components produced during systemic processes and exogenous source. So liver is the detoxification organ. NaF causes necrosis, hyperplasia, vacuolization in liver (Shasi A *et al.* 2001). NaF induces hepatotoxicity by oxidative stress (Chattopadhyay A *et al.* 2011).

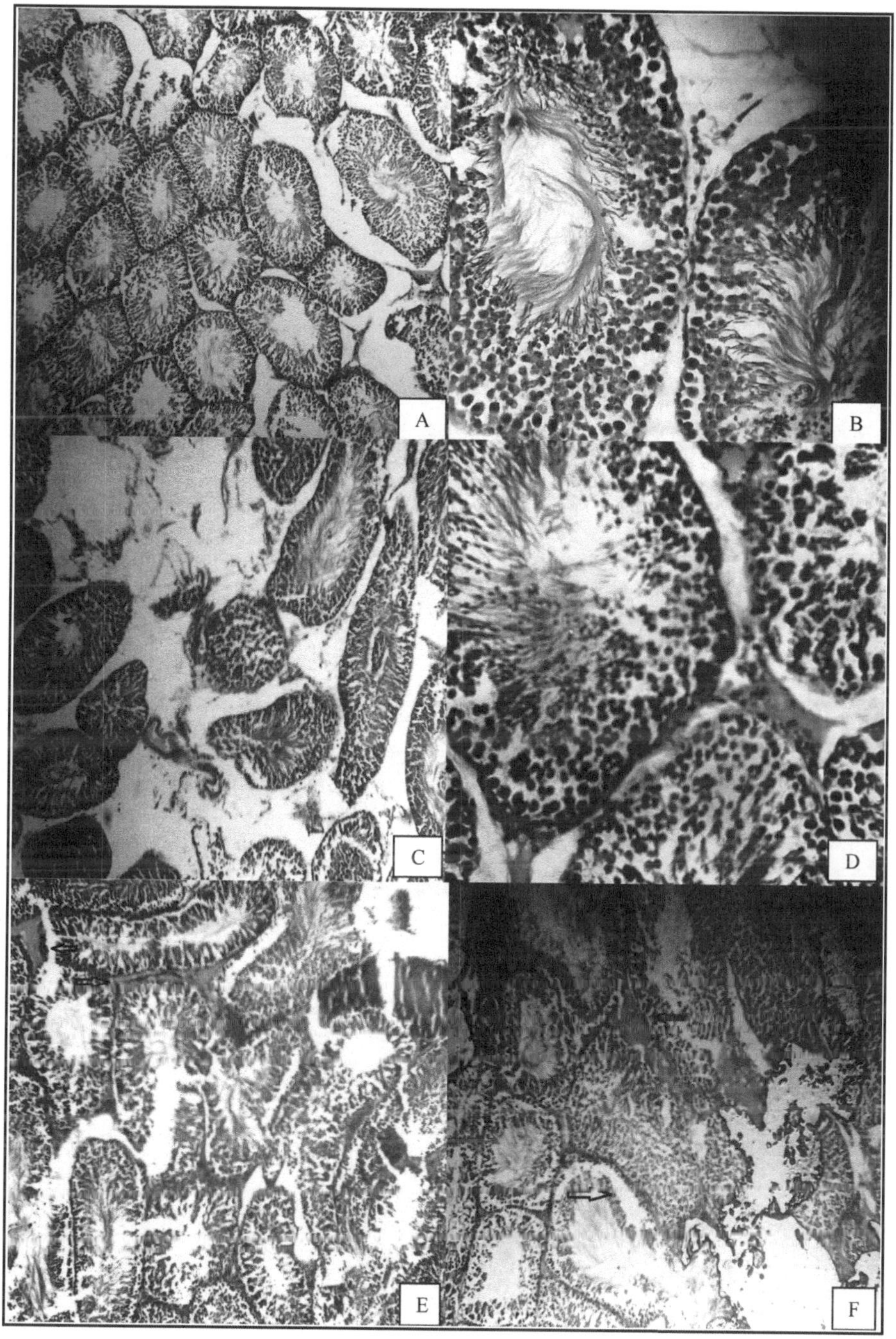
A
B
C
D
E
F

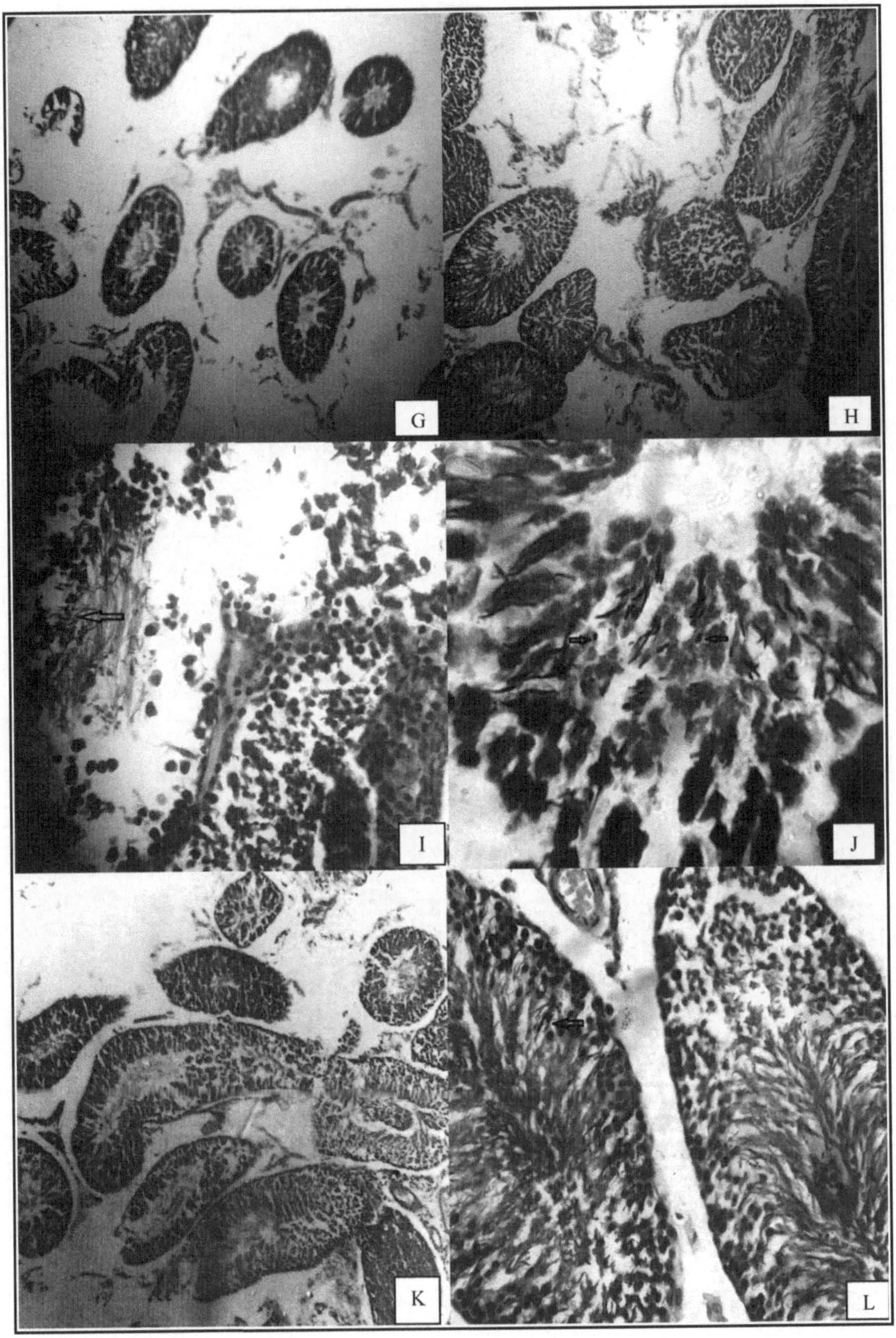
G
H
I
J
K
L

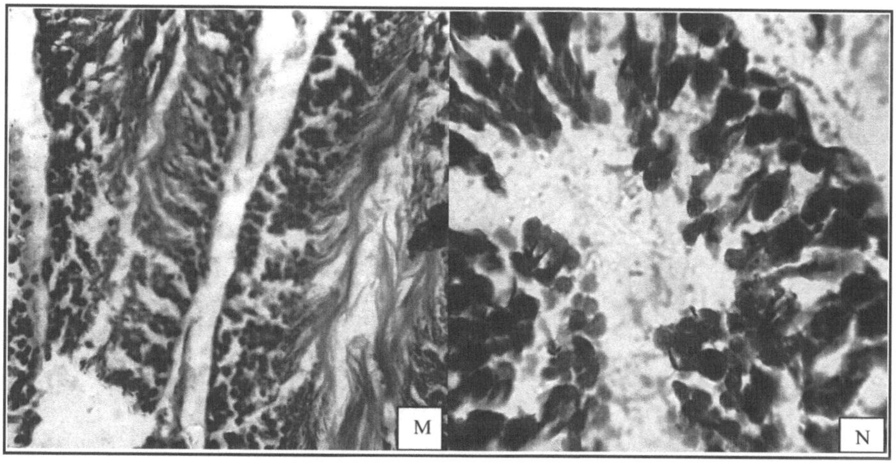

Fig. 3.7: **Cross section of testis showing microscopic view of rat cells treated with different concentration of sodium fluoridated water:**

- *Control*: Normal testicular tissue at 10X (A), health spermatids and testicular tissue at 40X (B). *5 PPM*: Diffused semineferous tubules at 10X (C), diffused testicular atropy at 40X (D), congestion of testicular vessel at 10X (E). *10PPM*: Congestion in testicular vessel and defoliation of spermatogonial cells at 10X (F), degenerative necrotic damage at 10X (G), degenerative diffused semineferous tubules with scanty spermatids at 10X (H). *15 PPM*: Aggregation of spermatids at 100X (I), blunt spermatids at 100X (J), severe degenerative necrotic damage in semineferous vessels with no spermatids visible at 10X (K). *20 PPM*: Serious exudation in semiferous tubules and aggregated spermatids at 40X (L), scanty spermatids at 40X (M), scanty crocked spermatids at 100X (N). (Chnages showed with arrows) ⟹

From the observation of fluoride treated groups under light microscopy, we find deformed glomeruli, tubal dilation and leakage (Fig. 3.3). Fluoride nephrotoxicity causes pathological glomerular changes in proximal, distal and collecting tubules of experimental animals (Bouaziz *et al*. 2007). Bowman's capsule was observed with adhesion between visceral and parietal layers (Fig. 3.3). Interstitial hemorrhage was also observed (Fig. 3.3). Other damage like degeneration of cytoplasm and infiltration by inflammatory cells was also common (Fig. 3.3).

In this work, NaF induced damage and disorganization of purkinjee cells, those are arranged in layer in control group. Vacuolated cytoplasm was observed in purkinjee cells. Multiple vacuolated areas were also observed. Ingestion of fluoride accumulated in cerebellum and stimulates neurotoxicity, cell damage and death (Trabelsi M *et al*. 2001). Histopathological changes observed like chromatolysis of nissele's granules and gliosis of rat brain and nucleus coming in periphery. Impaired and swollen astrocytes indicate impaired repair and scarring process of brain (Fig. 3.4).

We observed vacuolar dystrophy in seminal vesicles. Decreased number of spermatozoa was also observed (Fig. 3.5). Few seminal vesicles are devoid of spermatozoa, where others show tissue destruction, disorganized epithelium of seminiferous tubule.

Discussion

In this study, we observed a significant decrease of the weight of kidney, heart, liver and brain which may be a direct effect of fluoride water on vital organs. Decreased in vital organs weight after NaF water treatment was reported in mammals (Simon and Suttie, 1968; Weber and Reid, 1969).

From our work it was observed that the values obtained for serum biochemical parameters like total protein showed significant reduction whereas, cholesterol, phospholipid showed significant increase ($p \leq 0.001$) with higher fluoride contents as compared to control. SGOT and SGPT are markers of liver function. The significant ($p<0.001$) increase in enzyme activity of SGOT and SGPT following sodium fluoride treatment was observed. Therefore, increased activities of SGOT and SGPT may be due to fluoride intoxication.

The altered tissue biochemistry of liver and heart may be due to toxic effect of fluoride. A significant decrease in hepatic total lipids, triglycerides, free fatty acids, phospholipids was investigated (Kaur S and Kaur D., 1995); and cholesterol has also been reported earlier (Machoy-Mokrzynska A *et al.* 1994). It was reported that ingestion of fluoride causes decrease in the ionized calcium (Srivastava RN *et al.* 1989; and Teotia and Teotia, 1972).

It is well known that ionic calcium is one of the important ions for the initiation and maintenance of activity of vital organs and muscular skeletal system. Fluoride decreases the absorption of cholesterol and bile salts from plasma and intestine which could result in a increased conversion of bile acids in the liver, and bile acids are known to inhibit cholesterol synthesis. This may be an indicative of hepatobiliary disturbances in fluoride intoxication (Bennis *et al.* 1993).

In the present investigation we observed a significant fluoride associated decrease in R.B.C a W.B.C count and the levels of hemoglobin. Similar observation was also found previously in rats (Kahl S *et al.* 1973), rabbits (Valjavec M, 1932) and children (Balazova G, 1971). The fluoride induced anemia observed in this study may result from inhibition of globulin synthesis, depression of erythropoisis or a decrease in the level of blood folic acid (Obrig *et al.* 1971; Hoogstratten 1965).

It is known that fluoride enhances lipid peroxidation and inhibits the antioxidative enzymes in liver, kidney and heart. It is also reported that fluroacetamide inhibits GST activity in rat liver in a dose dependent manner (Dierickx PJ and DeBeer JO, 1983). Patel PD and Chinoy NJ (1998) concluded that fluoride decreased the functioning of SOD, GST and catalase enzymes in ovary of mice. Sun X *et al.* 1998 also reported a decrease in SOD activity in liver, kidney and heart of fluoridated mice. Our present results also shows (Table 3.7) that SOD, GST and catalase activities were decreased in brain in accordance with earlier reports in liver, kidney and heart (Dierickx and Beer,

1983; Patel PD and Chinoy NJ, 1998 , Sun *et al.* 1998). Thus the present investigation shows that fluoride increases free radical production and at the same time inhibits the antioxidant enzymes SOD, GST and catalase, which probably make the tissue more susceptible to biochemical injury.

From the results of our study and others, we may conclude that excess fluoride water exposure caused altered blood cell, change the serum biochemistry causes hepatotoxicity and also produce toxic effects on brain, heart and kidney.

Hepatotoxicity in rabbit exposed to NaF may cause oxidative stress along with histopathologic changes in liver impairing architecture with altered function (Wang YN *et al.* 2000). In addition, Shashi and Thapar (A. Shashi and S.P. Thapar, 2001), have reported albino rabbits exposed to sodium fluoride show hepatocellular necrosis, hepatic hyperplasia, extensive vacuolization in hepatocytes, dilation of central vein and sinusoids in liver. The dilation and congestion of sinusoids, ballooning of hepatocytes with pycnotic nuclei and focal necrosis was observed by Dikshit *et al.* 1980. In present investigation histoarchitecture of liver showed mild fatty changes (Fig. 3.4D), extensive vacuolization of cytoplasm (Fig. 3.4F), severe haemorrhage (Fig. 3.4H) and necrosis with cellular infiltration (Fig. 3.4I).

Histological results revealed that the NaF exposer lead to extensive damage on renal cortex as compared to control rats including glomerular degeneration like lobulation (Fig. 3.5I), hypertrophy or shrinkage (Fig. 3.5D) with extended bowman's capsule (Fig. 3.5E). Marked tubular lumen dilution (Fig. 3.5F), vacuolar degeneration, cell swelling, lysis may indicate cell necrosis (Fig. 3.5L). Infiltration (Fig. 3.5K) was observed with NaF exposer. These results indicate kidney filtration barrier was distorted with NaF toxicity leading to interstitial nephritis. Many reports are similar to our results (C. Xue *et al.* 2000; E. Karaoz *et al.* 2004). In rabbits, exposure to high concentration of sodium fluoride for 15 weeks caused to necrotic and degenerative changes in kidney (A. Shashi and S.P. Thapar, 2001).

The neurotoxic changes in brain of our rats indicate damage of neuron and neuroglial cells due to fluoride intoxication. Data suggest the direct relationship between fluoride exposer and brain damage, and may cause paralysis, tremors, brain dysfunction etc. In the present study, most purkinjee neurons showed chromatolysis (Fig. 3.6J) and disintegration of nuclei (Fig. 3.6H) and swollen diffuse gliosis was observed upon F intoxication (Fig. 3.6F). Cellular chromatolysis was also reported on monkey brain tissue after F exposer (4.5 mg F/day) for six months (Wadhwani TK and Ramaswamy AS, 2013). Central and peripheral nerves were damaged with fluoride exposer along with altered function of motor nerves in vertebrates (Li J and Cao S, 1994). Fluoride accumulation (Burgstahler AW and Colquhoun JC, 1996) in brain hippocampus of rats was reported. Fluoride intoxication decreases the cholesterol, free fatty acids, proteins and RNA level in rabbit brain (Shashi A *et al.* 1992).

Histological observation revealed that damaged testis with necrotic changes. Sekhar PR *et al.* 2011 found degenerative changes with increased lumen of seminiferous tubules. The histopathological study justifies that NaF act as a toxicant triggering testicular tissue degeneration and abnormalities in spermatozoa. Our study revealed conjested testicular vessels (Fig. 3.7E), presence of scanty (Fig. 3.7H) and crocked (Fig. 3.7N) sprmatids upon sodium fluoride exposer to rats, that have a overall negative effect on fertility of rats.

Conclusion

It was observed that chronic fluoride intoxication markedly enhanced lipid peroxidation in rats. Adaptive changes apparently occurred in antioxidant systems in the blood, brain, and liver of rats to counteract fluoride-induced oxidative stress on prolonged exposure. This provides further support for the theory of free radical damage as an important mechanism for F toxicity. The present study suggests that chronic F intoxication markedly affects antioxidant defense, which may result in dysfunctions of in brain, liver, kidney, heart and testicular cells. Further studies are warranted to elucidate the complex signalling pathways of all of the three major apoptosis pathways: the mitochondrial, the death receptor, and the endoplasmic reticulum pathways. Understanding the mechanisms of F-induced toxicity may provide novel approaches for attenuating fluorosis. Prevention and control of fluorosis require an integrated approach for diagnosis and patient management, contrary to prevailing practices. The results of this study suggest more purification to remove fluoridation of drinking water, milk, fruit juices, and salt by health authorities.

REFERENCES

1. Aebi H. Catalase in vitro. Methods in Enzymology. 1984 Dec 31;105:121-6.
2. Ames B.N., Cathcart R., Schwiers E., Hochstein P. Uric Acid Provides an Antioxidant Defense in Humans against Oxidant-and radical-caused aging and Cancer: A Hypothesis. Proceedings of the National Academy of Sciences. 1981 Nov. 1;78(11):6858-62.
3. Ayoob S., Gupta AK. Fluoride in drinking Water: A Review on the Status and Stress Effects. Critical Reviews in Environmental Science and Technology. 2006 Dec 1; 36(6):433-87.
4. Baez R.J., Podariu A., Marthaler T.M., Baez M.X., Floarea L. Urinary fluoride Excretion by Children and Elderly Individuals in Romania (Timisoara and Bucarest). Oral Health and Dental Management. 2007; 6:3-11.
5. Balazova G. Long-term Effect of fluoride emission upon Children. Fluoride. 1971;4(2):85-8.
6. Benagiano A., The Effect of Sodium Fluoride on Thyroid Enzymes and Basal Metabolism in the Rat. Annali Di Stomatologia 1965 14: 601-619.
7. Bennis A., Kessabi M., Hamliri A., De La Farge F., Braun J.P. Plasma Biochemistry of Adult Goats with chronic fluoride Poisoning in Morocco. *Fluoride*. 1993; 26(4):241-6.
8. Beyer W.F., Fridovich I. Assaying for Superoxide Dismutase Activity: Some large Consequences of Minor Changes in Conditions. Analytical Biochemistry. 1987 Mar 1;161(2):559-66.

9. Bouaziz H., Croute F., Boudawara T., Soleilhavoup J.P., Zeghal N. Oxidative Stress Induced by Fluoride in Adult Mice and their Suckling Pups. *Experimental and Toxicologic Pathology*. 2007 Apr 26; 58(5): 339-49.
10. Burgstahler A.W., Colquhoun J.C. Neurotoxicity of Fluoride. *Fluoride*. 1996; 29(2):57-8.
11. Chattopadhyay A., Podder S., Agarwal S., Bhattacharya S. Fluoride-induced Histopathology and Synthesis of Stress Protein in Liver and Kidney of Mice. *Archives of Toxicology*. 2011 Apr 1; 85(4):327-35.
12. Chinoy N.J., Sharma M., Michael M. Beneficial Effects of ascorbic Acid and Calcium on Reversal of Fluoride Toxicity in Male Rats. *Fluoride*. 1993; 26(1):45-56.
13. Choubisa SL. Chronic Fluoride Intoxication (fluorosis) in Tribes and their Domestic Animals. *International Journal of Environmental Studies*. 1999 Aug. 1; 56(5):703-16.
14. Chouhan S., Flora S.J. Arsenic and Fluoride: Two Major Ground Water Pollutants. *Indian Journal of Experimental Biology*. 2010 Jul 1;48(7):666.
15. Clark R.A. Neutrophil Iodination Reaction Induced by Fluoride: Implications for Degranulation and Metabolic Activation. *Blood*. 1981 May 1; 57(5):913-21.
16. Crosby WH. The Metabolism of Hemoglobin and bile Pigment in hemolytic Disease. *The American Journal of Medicine*. 1955 Jan 31;18(1):112-22.
17. Curnutte J.T., Babior B.M., Karnovsky M.L. Fluoride-mediated Activation of the Respiratory Burst in Human Neutrophils. A Reversible Process. *Journal of Clinical Investigation*. 1979 Apr; 63(4):637.
18. Dikshith T.S., Raizada R.B., Datta K.K. Interaction of phosphamidon and benzene in Female Rabbits. *Indian Journal of Experimental Biology*. 1980 Nov; 18(11):1273-7.
19. Dierickx P.J., DeBeer J.O. Interaction of fluoroacetamide with rat-liver glutathione s-transferases-evidence for a detoxication role by Defluorination. *Fluoride*. 1983 Jan 1;16(3):145-51.
20. Eren E., Özturk M, Mumcu E.F., Canatan D. Fluorosis and its hematological Effects. *Toxicology and Industrial Health*. 2005 Oct 1;21(9):255-8.
21. Ericsson Y., Forsman B. Fluoride Retained from mouthrinses and dentifrices in Pre-school Children. *Caries Research*. 1969;3(3):290-9.
22. Gupta R., Kumar A.N., Bandhu S., Gupta S. Skeletal fluorosis mimicking seronegative arthritis. *Scandinavian Journal of Rheumatology*. 2007 Jan 1;36(2):154-5.
23. Habig W.H., Pabst M.J., Jakoby W.B. Glutathione S-transferases the first Enzymatic Step in Mercapturic Acid Formation. *Journal of Biological Chemistry*. 1974 Nov 25;249(22):7130-9.
24. Hall S.K. Metal Exposure and Toxic Responses. Chemical Exposure and Toxic Responses. 1996 Oct 21;1:21.
25. Harrison PT. Fluoride in Water: A UK Perspective. *Journal of Fluorine Chemistry*. 2005 Dec 31; 126(11):1448-56.
26. Hoogstratten B., Leone NC, Shupe J.L., Greenwood D.A., Lieberman *J. Effect of Fluorides on Hematopoietic System, Liver, and thyroid gland in Cattle*. JAMA. 1965 Apr 5;192(1):26-32.
27. Kahl S., Wojcik K., Ewy Z. Effect of fluoride on some Hematological Indices and 59Fe Distribution in the Blood and Iron-storing Tissues in Rats. Bulletin. Serie des Sciences Biologiques. 1973.
28. Kapoor V., Prasad T., Bhatia KC. Effect of Dietary fluorine on Histopathological Changes in Calves. *Fluoride*. 1993;26(2):105-10.

29. Kaur S., Kaur D. Alterations in hepatic Lipid Metabolism of the Rabbits in Experimental Fluorosis. *Journal of Ecotoxicology and Environmental Monitoring*. 1995;5(2):143-6.
30. Karaoz E., Oncu M., Gulle K., Kanter M., Gultekin F., Karaoz S., Mumcu E. Effect of chronic Fluorosis on Lipid Peroxidation and Histology of Kidney Tissues in First-and Second-generation Rats. *Biological Trace Element Research*. 2004 Dec 1;102(1-3):199-208.
31. Kumar A.R., Susheela A.K. Effects of chronic fluoride Toxicity on the Morphology of ductus epididymis and the Maturation of spermatozoa of Rabbit. *International Journal of Experimental Pathology*. 1995 Feb; 76(1):1.
32. Lee CC. The Absorption, Distribution, Excretion, and Toxicity of trifluoroamine Oxide. *Toxicology and Applied Pharmacology*. 1968 Jul 31;13(1):76-88.
33. Leone N.C., Shimkin M.B., Arnold Jr F.A., Stevenson C.A., Zimmermann E.R., Geiser P.B., Lieberman J.E. Medical aspects of Excessive fluoride in a Water Supply. *Public Health Reports*. 1954 Oct; 69(10):925.
34. Li J, Cao S. Recent Studies on endemic Fluorosis in China. Fluoride. 1994; 27(3):125-8.
35. Lowry O.H., Rosebrough N.J., Farr A.L., Randall R.J. Protein Measurement with the Folin phenol Reagent. *J. Biol Chem*. 1951 Nov 1;193(1):265-75.
36. Machalinska A., Wiszniewska B., Tarasiuk J., Machalinski B. Morphological Effects of Sodium fluoride on hematopoietic Organs in mice. *Fluoride*. 2002 Nov 1;35(4):231-8.
37. Machoy-Mokrzynska A., Put A., Ceglecka M., Mysliwiec Z. Influence of Essential phospholipids (EPL) on Selected Biochemical Parameters of Lipid Metabolism in Rats Chronically Exposed to ammonium Fluoride vapours. *Fluoride*. 1994 Oct 1;27(4):201-4.
38. Maurer J.K., Cheng M.C., Boysen B.G., Anderson R.L. Two-year carcinogenicity Study of Sodium fluoride in Rats. *Journal of the National Cancer Institute*. 1990 Jul 4; 82(13):1118-26.
39. Montgomery R. Determination of glycogen. Archives of Biochemistry and Biophysics. 1957 Apr 1;67(2):378-86.
40. Mullenix P.J., Denbesten P.K., Schunior A., Kernan W.J. Neurotoxicity of Sodium Fluoride in Rats. *Neurotoxicology and Teratology*. 1995 Apr 30;17(2):169-77.
41. Obrig T., Irvin J., Culp W., Hardesty B. Inhibition of Peptide Initiation on reticulocyte Ribosomes by Edeine. *European Journal of Biochemistry*. 1971 Jul 1;21(1):31-41.
42. Pandey B., Yeragi S., Reddy A., Hagiwara A. Fluoride in Water in Parts of Raniganj Coalfield, West Bengal. Current Science. 2008 Feb. 10; 94(3):309.
43. Patel P.D., Chinoy N.J. Influence of Fluoride on Biological Free Radical Reactions in Ovary of Mice and Its Reversal. *Fluoride*. 1998; 31:S27-S27.
44. Pillai KS. Biological Magnification of Fluoride Toxicity. Proceedings, Assessment of Environmental Pollution, Academy of Environmental Biology Aurungabad (India). 1985:135-41.
45. Podder S., Chattopadhyay A., Bhattacharya S., Ray MR. Differential in vivo genotoxic Effects of Lower and Higher Concentrations of Fluoride in mouse bone Marrow Cells. *Fluoride*. 2008 Oct 1;41(4):301-7.
46. Pushpalatha T., Srinivas M., Reddy P.S. Exposure to High Fluoride Concentration in Drinking Water will Affect Spermatogenesis and Steroidogenesis in Male albino Rats. *Biometals*. 2005 Jun 1;18(3):207-12.
47. Roe J., Kuether C. Estimation of ascorbic Acid. *J Biol Chem*. 1943;147:3999.
48. Rzeuski R., Chlubek D., Machoy Z. Interactions between Fluoride and Biological Free Radical Reactions. *Fluoride*. 1998 Feb;31(1):43-5.

49. Samal A.C., Bhattacharya P., Mallick A., Ali M.M., Pyne J., Santra S.C. A Study to Investigate Fluoride Contamination and Fluoride Exposure dose Assessment in lateritic zones of West Bengal, India. *Environmental Science and Pollution Research*. 2015 Apr 1;22(8):6220-9.
50. Sarkar A., Bishayee A., Chatterjee M. Beta-carotene prevents Lipid Peroxidation and Red Blood Cell Membrane Protein Damage in Experimental hepatocarcinogenesis. Cancer Biochemistry Biophysics. 1995 Nov;15(2):111-25.
51. Sekhar P.R., Savithri Y., Kishore S., Jayasankar A., Rao K.J. Synergistic Effect of Sodium Fluoride and cypermethrin on the somatic index and Histopathology of Albino Mice Testes. *Fluoride*. 2011 Apr 1; 44(2):103-11.
52. Shashi A., Singh J.P., Thapar S.P. Toxic Effects of Fluoride on Rabbit Kidney. *Fluoride*. 2002 Feb 1;35(1):38-50.
53. Shashi A., Singh J.P., Thapar SP. Protein-degradation in skeletal-muscle of Rabbit during Experimental Fluorosis. *Fluoride*. 1992 Jan 1;25(3):155-8.
54. Shashi A., Thapar SP. Histopathology of fluoride-induced hepatotoxicity in Rabbits. *Fluoride*. 2001 Feb 1;34(1):34-42.
55. Shivarajashankara Y.M., Shivashankara A.R., Bhat P.G., Rao SH. Brain lipid Peroxidation and Antioxidant Systems of young Rats in chronic Fluoride Intoxication. *Fluoride*. 2002 Aug 1;35(3):197-203.
56. Shulman J.D., Wells L.M.. Acute Fluoride Toxicity from Ingesting Home use Dental Products in Children, Birth to 6 Years of Age. *Journal of Public Health Dentistry*. 1997 Sep 1;57(3):150-8.
57. Simon G., Suttie J.W. Effect of Dietary Fluoride on Food Intake and Plasma Fluoride Concentration in the Rat. *Journal of Nutrition*. 1968;96:152-6.
58. Srivastava R.N., Gill D.S., Moudgil A., Menon R.K., Thomas M., Dandona P. Normal ionized calcium, Parathyroid Hypersecretion, and Elevated osteocalcin in a Family with Fluorosis. Metabolism. 1989 Feb 28;38(2):120-4.
59. Sun X., Lee H.S., Lee S., Yang X.Q., McBreen J. A Novel lithium battery electrolyte based on lithium fluoride and a tris (pentafluorophenyl) borane anion receptor in DME. Electrochemical and solid-state letters. 1998 Dec 1;1(6):239-40.
60. Susheela A.K., Jha M. Effect of Fluoride ingestion on Cortical and Cancellous bone-composition. IRCS Medical Science-Biochemistry. 1981 Jan 1;9(11):1021-2.
61. Takamori T. The Heart Changes of Growing albino Rats fed on Varied Contents of Fluorine In: Gordonoff T, editor. *The Toxicology of Fluorine Symposium* 1962. 1962;1517.
62. Teotia M., Rodgers A., Teotia S.P., Wandt A.E., Nath M. Fluoride metabolism and fluoride content of stones from children with endemic vesical stones. *British Journal of Urology*. 1991 Oct 1;68(4):425-9.
63. Teotia S.P., Teotia M. Hyperactivity of Parathyroid Glands in Endemic Osteofluorosis. *Fluoride Official Quarterly Journal of International Society for Fluoride Research*. 1972 Jan 1;5(3):115.
64. Trabelsi M., Guermazi F., Zeghal N. Effect of Fluoride on thyroid Function and cerebellar Development in Mice. *Fluoride*. 2001 Aug 1;34(3):165-73.
65. Valjavec M. The Blood Picture in Rabbits Poisoned Experimentally with Sodium fluoride. *Z Ges Exp Med*. 1932;85:382-6.
66. Vani M.L., Reddy K.P. Effects of Fluoride Accumulation on some Enzymes of Brain and Gastrocnemius Muscle of Mice. *Fluoride*. 2000 Feb 1;33(1):17-26.

67. Wadhwani T.K., Ramaswamy AS. Pathological changes in the Tissues of Rats (albino) and monkeys (Macaca radiata) in Fluorine Toxicosis. *Journal of the Indian Institute of Science*. 2013 Nov 28;35(3):223.

68. Waldbott GL. Incipient Fluorine Intoxication from Drinking Water. Acta Medica Scandinavica. 1956 Jan 12;156(3):157-68.

69. Waldbott GL. Chronic Fluorine Intoxication from Drinking Water. *International Archives of Allergy and Immunology*. 1955 Jul 1;7(2):70-4.

70. Wang Y.N., Xiao K.Q., Liu J.L., Dallner G., Guan ZZ. Effect of Long-term Fluoride Exposure on Lipid Composition in Rat Liver. *Toxicology*. 2000 May 5;146(2):161-9.

71. Weber C.W., Reid B.L. Effect of Dietary cadmium on mice. *Toxicology and Applied Pharmacology*. 1969 May 1;14(3):420-5.

72. Whitford GM. Fluoride. Biochemical and Physiological Aspects of Human Nutrition. (Stipanuk, MH, ed.). WB Saunders Company, Philadelphia, PA. 2000:810-24.

73. Wilson J.D., Lindsey Jr CA. Studies on the influence of Dietary cholesterol on Cholesterol Metabolism in the isotopic Steady state in Man. *Journal of Clinical Investigation*. 1965 Nov; 44(11):1805.

74. Wintrobe MM. The erythrocyte in man. Medicine. 1930 May 1;9(2):195.

75. World Health Organization. Fluorine and Fluorides, Environmental Health Criteria 36, WHO, Geneva. 1984; 1-136.

76. Xiang Q., Liang Y., Chen L., Wang C., Chen B., Chen X., Zhou M., Shanghai PR. Effect of Fluoride in Drinking Water on Children's Intelligence. *Fluoride*. 2003 May 1;36(2):84-94.

77. Xu H., Jin X.Q., Jing L., Li GS. Effect of Sodium fluoride on the Expression of bcl-2 Family and osteopontin in Rat Renal tubular Cells. *Biological Trace Element Research*. 2006 Jan 1;109(1):55-60.

78. Xue C., Chen X., Yang K. [Study on antagonistic effects of selenium and zinc on the renal impairments induced by fluoride in rats]. Wei sheng yan jiu= *Journal of hygiene research*. 2000 Jan; 29(1):21-3.

79. Zak B., Boyle A.J., Zlatkis A. A Method for the Determination of Cholesterol. *Journal of Clinical Medicine*. 1953;41:486-92.

80. Zilversmits D.B., Davis A.K. Estimation of phospholipids. *Journal of Laboratory and Clinical Medicine*. 1950;35:100-10.

Page 64-78

MICROBIAL ENVIRONMENT AND BIOREMEDIATION

Edited by : Dr. Alka Chauhan; Dr. Ashok K. Rathoure & Dr. Raaz K Maheshwari

Edition : 2017

ISBN : 978-93-5056-856-9

Published by : Discovery Publishing House Pvt. Ltd., New Delhi (India)

4

Identification of Polymorphism by Rapd Markers in Indian *Solanum* Species

G. Tanmaya

D.S. Nishchitha

S. Rajashekara*

ABSTRACT

Genetic diversity refers to the variation of genes within species i.e., genetic variation between distinct population of the same species. Study was carried out on genetic diversity of Solanum spp., – S. melongena, S. scarbrum and S. gilo using six different decamer oligonucleotide random primers. Four primers out of six showed the positive amplification. Random Amplified Polymorphic DNA (RAPD) patterns obtained for only two varieties were clear and distinct. A low degree of polymorphism was detected with most of the primers especially Arbit 2, Arbit 3, CPDK and PPDK. Solanum melongena and S. scarbrum showed amplified bands with the primer CPDK indicating that these two varieties are closely related ones. During plant breeding and characterization it is necessary to study and to analyse polymorphism in specific plants. The potential use of RAPD analysis was evaluated as a source of development of alternative genetic marker for studying genetic variation, genetic relationship and genetic diversification of Solanum species.

INTRODUCTION

Solanum melongena L. (2n=24) is known as brinjal or eggplant, aubergine or guinea squash, is an important vegetable crop of tropical and temperate parts of the world. It is a rather small plant growing up to 1.5m high. Brinjal is classified as herb because of its non-woody stem. The simple leaves are oblong to oval, slightly lobed, and have an undersurface that is a paler green than the

* Centre for Applied Genetics, Department of Studies in Zoology, Bangalore University, Jnana Bharathi Campus, Bengaluru, India 560 056.

upper surface. Both leaves and stem are covered with fine hairs. The flowers sprout singly or in small clusters from the leaf axils. Individual flowers are star-shaped, light purple in colour and have short stalks. There are five stamens attached to the corolla tube and a single superior ovary. Its root system is fibrous. The fruits are berries with many seeds. The fruits are either long or round and vary in colour according to the variety: white, orange, green, purple or black. Based on fruit shape, brinjal has been divided into three main types namely: egg-shaped (*S. melongena* var. *esculentum*); long slender shaped (*S. melongena* var. *serpentium*) and dwarf type (*S. melongena* var. *depressum*). It is a perennial with fruits growing all year round.

Solanum torvum is a wild brinjal plant found in Malaysia and India. Certain indigenous varieties of the plants seem to be unique to certain parts of the world. The question of centre of origin of brinjal has been debated but is generally believed to have originated in India. The plant was first domesticated in India. The Persians then introduced brinjal to Africa from India while the Arabs introduced it to Spain. It presumably spread from Spain to the rest of Europe (Polunin 1987). Today, many varieties of brinjal plants are found growing throughout the warmer parts of the world. In Southeast Asia, countries where it is commercially grown include Malaysia, Thailand and Indonesia.

Brinjal has been cultivated for the last 4,000 years in India. Among the Solanaceous vegetables, brinjal is the most common vegetable crop grown in many geographical parts in India. Brinjal has become an intrinsic part of Indian folklore and tradition. The area under brinjal cultivation is estimated at 0.55 million hectares with a total production of 8.2 million tons (www.faostat.fao.org). About 1.4 million small, marginal and resource-poor farmers grow brinjal. It is an important cash crop for poor farmers producing two or three crops, each of 150 to 180 days duration.

It is a warm season crop and is very susceptible to frost. Late round varieties are more tolerant of frost than the early long varieties. Cool nights and short summers are unfavorable to its satisfactory yields. It requires a long growing season with the high average day and night temperatures. Its seed germinates well at 77°F temperature. A daily mean temperature of 13-21°C is most favorable for successful production (Polunin 1987).

Though it can be grown on different types of soils, yet it is grown with considerable success in fine and rich loam soils that are deep and well-drained. The soil pH should not be higher than pH 5.5 to 6.0 for its better growth and development. As the crop remains in the field for a number of months therefore, the soils should be well prepared by being ploughed 4-5 times before transplanting the seedlings. When the field is well prepared and leveled, the beds of suitable size are made in the field before transplanting.

Brinjal is a good source of vitamins and minerals especially iron. Hence, it is considered as a common vegetable in our diet since ancient time. Its composition per 100g of edible portion is 24g of calories, 92.7 per cent of moisture content, 4 per cent of carbohydrates, 1.4g of proteins, 0.3g of fat, 3mg of sodium, 0.17mg of copper, 2mg of potassium, 44mg of sulphur, 52mg of chlorine, 1.3g of fibre, 18mg of oxalic acid, 18mg of calcium, 16mg of magnesium, 47mg of phosphorous, 0.9mg of iron, 124 IU of vitamin A, 12 IU of vitamin C, 0.04 IU of thiamine, 0.11 IU of riboflavin, 0.74 IU of β-carotene (Darbie and Granberry 1990).

Solanum spp., is a main vegetable of the plains available more or less throughout the year. It is used primarily as cooked vegetable. Brinjal is popular for the preparation of various dishes in different regions of the country. It is rich in Vitamin A and B (Wee 1992). Besides being used as an important vegetable, eggplant has been exploited extensively in traditional medicine as it contains certain medicinal properties, it is used in ayurvedic medicines.

All parts of the plant can be used to stop intestinal bleeding. The fruit of the plant is used as an antidote in cases of mushroom poisoning. The parts of the plant are used as a purgative. The ashes of the fruit are used in dry, hot poultices to treat haemorrhoids. To treat ulcers, the root is pounded and applied inside the nostrils. The Amboinese take the juice of the root from a wild variety of the plant to ease a difficult labour (Wee 1992).

The diseases of the *Solanum* spp., are *(i)* Damping Off is a serious disease of brinjal seedlings and mainly occurs in nursery bed. The disease infected seedlings rot at ground level and then the plants fall over ground. The seedlings die in patches (Daunay *et al.* 1991). *(ii)* Phomopsis Blight and/or Fruit Rotis a serious disease of brinjal. The fungus attacks all parts of the plants above ground. Dark brown lessions appear on the stem and round to oval spots are formed on the leaves (Kashyap *et al.* 2003). *(iii)* Little Leaf of Brinjal is the affected plant produces numerous tiny yellow leaves and does not bear fruits. The disease is transmitted by leaf hopper (Daunay *et al.* 1991).

Several workers have contributed to the characterization of the largest genus of *Solanaceae* family (Correll 1962; Seithe and Anderson 1982; Whalen 1984; Bohs 1999; Furini and Wunder 2004). Great degree of taxonomic confusion exists as regard to genus *Solanum* (Daunay and Lester 1988). *Solanum* L. is a complex and large genus of the family *Solanaceae* has an unresolved proper delineation of the species. The genus consists of approximately 2000 species (Bohs 2001). They are morphologically varied, numerically diversified and vastly eco-geographicaly distributed. Several species of vegetable *Solanum* is important for human diet and are referred as eggplant (Daunay *et al.* 2001). The taxonomy of the eggplant *Solanum* has remained challenging due to species' large size, overlapping eco-geographical distribution (Levin *et al.* 2005), morphological plasticity, similar genomes (Okoli 1988) and existence of swamps of natural hybrids (Obute *et al.* 2006; Oyelana and Ugborogho 2008).

DNA-based markers provide powerful tools for discerning within crop germplasm and for studying evolutionary relationships (Gepts 1993). Among the various molecular markers, Random Amplified Polymorphic DNAs (RAPDs) have been extensively used to characterization of organisms in genetic research owing to their speed and simplicity (Williams *et al.* 1990; Welsh and McClelland 1990). Most variability/taxonomic affinity studies in eggplant have focused mainly on morphology (Deb 1989; Karihaloo *et al.* 1995), crossability (Hasan and Lester 1990a), anatomy (Hasan and Lester 1990b), isozyme (Deb 1989; Lester and Hasan 1991; Isshiki *et al.* 1994) and chloroplast DNA diversity (Sakata *et al.* 1991; Sakata and Lester 1994; Sakata and Lester 1997). In another study Amplified Fragmented Length Polymorphism (AFLP) was found to be an excellent tool for the determination of genetic relationship among the species of *Solanum* (Mace *et al.* 1999).

Information regarding genetic diversity and genetic relationships among different genotypes is very valuable in crop improvement (Daunay *et al.* 1991; Weising *et al.* 1995; Doganlar *et al.* 2002). No comprehensive work related to the RAPD-PCR analysis of the varieties of *Solanum* species done. Hence we made an attempt to investigate the genetic relationship between the varieties of *Solanum* species using RAPD markers for the present study.

Materials and Methods

Study was carried out on genetic diversity of *Solanum* spp., during the experiment initially the seeds were sowed to cultivate the plants which were selected for the present study. The details of methodologies and techniques adopted in the above studies are explained hereunder.

Selection of the Plant Sources

The plants of different varieties were selected for the conduction of the present study belonging to the following classification:

- *Kingdom*: Plantae.
- *Division*: Magnoliophyta.
- *Class*: Magnoliopsida.
- *Subclass*: Asteridae.
- *Order*: Solanales.
- *Family*: Solanaceae.
- *Group:* Solanum L.
- *Species: Solanum spp.*

The plants of different varieties of *Solanum* spp., selected for the conduction of the present experiments is given below (Figure 4.1-4.3).

Fig. 4.1: *Solanum melongena*

Fig. 4.2: *Solanum scarbrum*

Fig. 4.3: *Solanum gilo*

Sample Collection

The leaves of *Solanum* spp., (brinjal) from three different varieties (such as: long purple, oblong purple and round white) were used as material for DNA extraction. The seeds were collected from the Lalbagh Botanical Garden and sowed, and then allowed it to germinate in Bhat's Laboratory, Bengaluru 560 070.

DNA Extraction

Total Genomic DNA

Total genomic DNA was isolated from three week old leaves according to the method followed by the Doyle and Doyle (1987) with minor modifications. The leaves were weighed about 0.5g and ground into a fine paste using mortar and pestle. The ground paste was transferred to 2ml vials and 700µl of Cetyl Trimethyl Ammonium Bromide (CTAB) buffer was added, and incubated at 50°C for 15 min in hot water bath for CTAB activity to take place (Murray and Thompson 1980). An equal volume of Chloroform: Isoamylalcohol (24:1) was added and kept in shaker for about 30 min at room temperature. The vials were centrifuged at 10,000 rpm for 12 min at room temperature. The supernatant was collected and transferred to new 2ml vials. To this 0.5 volume of 5M NaCl was added and mixed well. The DNA was precipitated by adding isopropanol and the vials were stored at -20°C overnight. The vials were centrifuged at 10,000 rpm for 12 min at 4°C. The pellet was dissolved in 700µl of TE buffer and 6-8µl of RNase was added to remove RNA and incubated at 37°C in hot water bath for 30 min. An equal volume of Phenol: Chloroform: Isoamylacohol was added and mixed by gentle inversion and centrifuged at 10,000 rpm for 12 min at room temperature. The supernatant was collected and transferred to 2ml vials and an equal volume of Chloroform: Isoamylalcohol (24:1) was added and centrifuged at 12,000 rpm for 12 min at room temperature. The upper layer was collected and 0.1 volume of 3M sodium acetate and full volume of absolute alcohol (ethanol) was added and stored at -20°C overnight. The DNA was recovered by centrifuging at 12,000 rpm for 12 min at 4°C. The pellet was dissolved with 70 per cent ethanol and centrifuged at 12,000 rpm for 12 min at 4°C. The pellet was dissolved in 30µl of TE buffer. 10µl of DNA isolated along with gel loading dye was run on 20ml of 0.8 per cent agarose gel to get good photographs.

Agarose Gel Electrophoresis

The edges of a clean gel-casting tray was sealed which was transparent to UV to form a mould. The mould was set on the horizontal section of the bench. The sufficient electrophoresis buffer [1x Tris-acetate-EDTA buffer (TAE buffer)] was prepared to fill the electrophoresis tank and to cast the gel tray. The mixture of TAE buffer and agarose was heated on a hot plate until the agarose dissolved. When the molten gel has cooled (to 50-60°C), Ethidium Bromide (stock concentration-5mg/ml) was added. The solution was mixed by gentle swirling. While the agarose solution is cooling, the appropriate comb for forming the slots in the gel was chosen and the agarose solution was poured into the mould. The gel was allowed to set completely, and tape and comb were carefully removed and gel was mounting in the electrophoresis tank. The electrophoresis buffer was poured to cover the gel to a depth of 1mm. The sample mixture is slowly loaded into the slots of the submerged gel using a disposable micropipette tip and the gel was electrophoresed at 50-100 V. The lid of gel tank was closed and the electrical leads were attached so that the DNA will migrate towards the positive electrode. If the leads have been attached carefully, bubbles should be generated at the anode and cathode (due to electrolysis), and within a few minutes, the Bromophenol blue should migrate from the wells into the body of the gel. When the sample or dye is migrated a sufficient distance through the gel, turn off the electric current and remove the leads and lid from the gel tank. Examination of the gel done by the illumination of Ultraviolet sources and photograph was taken.

Polymerase Chain Reaction (PCR)

PCR was invented by Kary Mullis in 1983. Mullis's idea was to develop DNA which could be artificially multiplied through repeated cycles of duplication driven by an enzyme called DNA Polymerase. The DNA samples of about 10µl each from 3 varieties of *Solanum* spp., were subjected to PCR along with 2.5µl assay buffer, 2.5µl dNTPs, 1µl Taq polymerase, 0.5µl of different forward and 0.5µl of different reverse primers for each variety is added and the volume is made upto 25µl with sterile water. All these are mixed and prepared for the total number of reactions including a 3µl positive control with a primer and template and Taq polymerase. The contents of the tubes are mixed with a brief spin and transferred to PTC 200 thermal cycler. The initial denaturation at 94°C for 3 min is done. The annealing of primers is done at 94°C for 30 sec, 55°C for 30 sec and 72°C for 1 min. The final extension is done at 72°C for 5 min. PCR amplification with each of the primer was done twice before checking the presence or absence of bands. The agarose gel electrophoresis was done to detect the different banding patterns.

Amplification of DNA Using RAPD-PCR

The following reaction is set up in the same order-10µl template DNA, 2.5µl dNTPs, 2.5µl assay buffer, 1µl primers, 1µl Taq DNA polymerase and the volume is made upto 25µl with sterile water. Prepare the master mix for one template DNA of one variety with one primer along with the blank. As there are three varieties used and with one blank, total tubes come up to 4 tubes. All those mentioned ingredients are mixed and prepared for the total number of reactions including a blank with a particular primer excluding template. The calculated volume of masters mix is then transferred to labeled PCR tubes with template source and primer. The contents of the tube are mixed with a brief spin and transferred to PTC 200 thermal cycler and the programme with 30 cycles at 94°C for 1 min, 35°C for 1 min, 72°C for 1 min is selected for amplification. The agarose gel electrophoresis was done to detect the amplified bands of DNA.

Template DNA

Optimal concentration of templates DNA per reaction may vary substantially from typical conditions (25ng per reaction) depending on the primer template combination used (Carlson *et al.* 1991). Crude DNA preparation is adequate. Slightly degraded or sheared DNA may amplify more readily because it denatures more easily, allowing better primer access. Only very small amount of DNA should be used. The less DNA used the fewer unintended amplification products will be present. Amplification of single copy of genes is readily accomplished in 30 cycles from less than 0.5g of plant DNA.

Williams *et al.* (1990) suggested that the minimum useful primer length is an Oligonucleotide of nine bases and GC content should be 40 per cent or greater to generate detectable levels of amplification products. The number of amplified products may be related to the GC content of primer and template DNA sequence rather than to the primer length (Caetano-Anollés *et al.* 1991). If two of the primers anneal to the template on opposite strand, in the appropriate orientation and within amplifiable distance, the discrete fragment will be amplified. The differences among random primers in the estimation of intra and inter population relationships may be due to minor changes in the PCR reaction conditions (Hedrick 1992; Bardakci and Skibinski 1994). The primer design is usually constrained by three factors, GC per cent (50-70%), no palindromes greater than six bases and no complementarily at the 3′ end (Williams *et al.* 1990).

Deoxynucleoside Triphosphate (dNTPs)

High purity dNTPs are supplied by several manufactures either as four individual stock solutions or as a mixture of all four dNTPs. PCR is normally performed with dNTP concentration around 100µl, although at lower dNTP concentration (10-100µl), Taq DNA polymerase has a high fidelity (Innis *et al.* 1988). The four dNTPs should be used at equivalent concentration to minimize disincorporation errors (Innis and Gelfand, 1990). The optimal concentration of dNTPs depends on several factors including $MgCl_2$ concentration, reaction stringency, primer concentration, length of the amplified product and number of cycles of PCR (Eckert and Kunkel, 1990).

Thermus Aquaticus (TAQ) DNA Polymerase

The recommended concentration of Taq DNA polymerase varies between 1-2.5 units per 100µl reaction mixture when other parameters are optimum to high enzyme concentration resulted in the accumulation of the non-specific background products. While at too low concentration of enzyme, the yield will be insufficient (Lawyer *et al.* 1989). Meunier and Grimont (1993) reported that variability in commercial preparation of Taq polymerase was a major source of variation in PCR reaction. Jayasanker and Dharnalingam (1997) reported that the same DNA template amplified with two different commercial preparation of Taq polymerase generated different bands.

A set of six available primers such as: Arbit 1, Arbit 2, Arbit 3, CPDK, FP1 and PPDK available was used to assess the genetic variability for *Solanum* spp. These markers were synthesized from GeNei™. The sequence information of the primer used is presented in the Table 4.1.

Table 4.1: Primer set for assessing genome of *Solanum* spp., populations

Primer name	Sequence
CPDK	5′ACAGAACCACCAAAGGAG3′
PPDK	5′CGTAAGATTGCTGTGGA3′
FP1	5′TCTCAGTGGGCGTTCTTATG3′
Arbit 1	5′GACTGCGTACGAATTAAT3′
Arbit 2	5′GACTGCGTACGAATTTGC3′
Arbit 3	5′GACTGCGTACGAATTGAC3′

Results

Genomic DNA Isolation

The genomic DNA was isolated from *Solanum melongena, S. scarbrum* and *S. gilo* respectively by using CTAB extraction method. A good concentration and pure quality of bands were obtained on the gel photograph.

Rapd-PCR

After confirming the presence of genomic DNA in the samples, the quality of genomic DNA was checked by quality PCR. The positive control along with primer specific to it was loaded into 0.8 per cent agarose gel. All the genomic DNA samples along with positive control showed amplified fragments in agarose gel indicating that all genomic DNA sample quality was good.

Screening of Rapd–Primers

The RAPD analysis of isolated plant genomic DNA was carried out with six different decamer oligonucleotide random primers. Out of six random primers tested for *Solanum* spp., only four primers showed amplification with the samples. Hence only four selected primers were used to study polymorphism in three *Solanum* varieties. The agarose gel electrophoresis was carried out along with gel loading dyes was carried out on 80ml gel of 1.6 per cent agarose gel.

The RAPD-PCR technique provides sufficient polymorphisms for characterization of different types of *Solanum* spp. The genomic DNA isolated from the three varieties – *S. melongena, S. scarbrum* and *S. gilo* using CTAB buffer were subjected to RAPD screening to detect polymorphism with six random oligonucleotide primers. A low degree of polymorphism was detected with most of the primers especially Arbit 2, Arbit 3, CPDK and PPDK. *Solanum melongena* and *S. scarbrum* showed amplified bands with the primer CPDK indicating that these two varieties are closely related ones whereas *S. gilo* did not show any amplified bands with any of these primers (Table 4.2). This revealed that *S. gilo* is distantly related to *S. melongena* and *S. scarbrum*. Therefore from the present study, we can conclude that only two selected varieties – *S. melongena* and *S. scarbrum* was closely related as they showed low polymorphism and *S. gilo* is distantly related.

Table 4.2: Presence or absence of polymorphic bands in different primer sets

Primer	*Solanum melongena*	*Solanum scarbrum*	*Solanum gilo*
Arbit 1	-	-	-
Arbit 2	-	+	-
Arbit 3	-	+	-
CPDK	+	+	-
FP1	-	-	-
PPDK	-	+	-

+indicates presence; -indicates absence

Discussion

Among the six random primers tested, only four primers showed amplification with the samples for *Solanum* spp., by using the RAPD analysis of isolated plant genomic DNA. The RAPD-PCR technique provides sufficient polymorphisms for characterization of three varieties – *S. melongena*, *S. scarbrum* and *S. gilo*. This revealed that low degree of polymorphism was detected with Arbit 2, Arbit 3, CPDK and PPDK-primers. *Solanum melongena* and *S. scarbrum* showed amplified bands with the primer CPDK indicating that these two varieties are closely related ones whereas *S. gilo* did not show any amplified bands with any of these primers. This showed that *S. gilo* was distantly related to *S. melongena* and *S. scarbrum*. Therefore from the present study, we can conclude that only two selected varieties – *S. melongena* and *S. scarbrum* were closely related as they showed low polymorphism and *S. gilo* was distantly related. Similarly, the molecular techniques are used for analyzing genetic diversity in *Solanum* spp. by the earlier workers (Prohens *et al.* 2003; Munoz-Falcon *et al.* 2008; Mishra *et al.* 2014). Such studies are however imperative for the information they supply for the germplasm management and breeding efforts using collected genetic material. RAPD screening showed a high degree of polymorphism with most of the primers indicating a wide range of diversity at DNA level and also among germplasm accessions.

The genetic diversity among diverse genotypes of *Solanum* spp., can be analyzed using RAPD technique. Twenty RAPD primers were used to amplify genomic DNA from 24 brinjal genotypes. Out of 20 primers, only 5 primers showed 6.5 per cent polymorphism and the other 15 showed polymorphism. The DNA fragments of various sixes were amplified in various *Solanum* spp. genotypes. Cluster analysis showed that genotypes were clustered in two groups based on distinct and significant genotypes. Thus the genotypes included in diverse clusters could be used as a parent for hybridization in order to obtain a heterotic response and better segregates in eggplant. Therefore, an identification of genetically distinct varieties using a RAPD marker could be a potential tool for eggplant improvement (Mishra *et al.* 2014).

Singh *et al.* (2006) showed all accessions produced a large number of distinct fragments for each primer using the same RAPD analysis. Twenty eight samples of eggplants were collected from different parts of India. Eighty selected arbitrary primers generated a total of 44 scorable bands of which 14 were polymorphic. Furthermore, RAPD profile for the 28 accessions yielded by two primers produced the maximum number of bands. With combination of suitable primers, all accessions could be identified by having accession-specific band, or by lacking a band that was present in all other accessions. The value of Jaccard's coefficient ranged from 0.05 to 0.82. The similarity result indicated the presence of high level of genetic diversity in eggplants and dendrogram was constructed by Unweighted Pair Group Method with Arithmetic Average (UPGMA) method and showed that *S. incanum* is closest to *S. melongena* followed by *S. nigrum*. Only one accession of *S. nigrum* and *S. surattense* showed grouping with each other (Singh *et al.* 2006). The explanation for the observed high degree of variation could be due to the fact that the analysis of DNA variability is based on RAPD markers. Thus, this technique was used for the assessment of the relationships between the 28 accessions of eggplant representing five species.

Caguiat and Hautea (2014) showed that a sum total of 41 SSR primers for polymorphism in seven representative genotypes consisted of two commercial cultivars (*S. melongena* cv. and F1 hybrid (Morena)), three landraces (*S. melongena* accessions 8257) and two wild related species (*S. americanum* and *S. torvum*). Among the 41 SSR primer pairs, 33 (88.48%) generated the expected PCR products with 28 mapped and 5 unmapped SSR markers loci. Twenty-eight of the 33 SSR primer pairs amplified a polymorphic locus. Twelve out of the 28 polymorphic SSR markers were detected in both cultivated eggplant and wild species used. Nine out of 12 primers genomic SSRs (75%) while only three out of the 12 (25%) were EST-SSRs. Seven SSR markers were detected only among *S. melongena* genotypes. Two SSR markers were monomorphic among the *S. melongena* genotypes. More alleles were detected in the cultivated eggplant (37-40) than in the wild related species. The calculated polymorphism information content values among the 7 accessions varied between 0.0263 and 0.6785. This study provided significant information for the need to increase the present eggplant collection and to widen the genetic diversity of currently cultivated eggplant varieties in the Philippines (Caguiat and Hautea 2014).

Further, the genetic relationships between ten genotypes of *Solanum* spp., were studied using Inter-Simple Sequence Repeats (ISSR) molecular markers. Seven out of 20 ISSR primers were used to assay the levels of polymorphism among the Egytpian cultivars of *Solanum* spp. Some variations in banding patterns were observed among these ten genotypes where 24 monomorphic and 47 polymorphic distinct fragments (61% of polymorphism) which appeared as a high level of polymorphism between them. The results obtained from ISSR markers demonstrated the relationship that refers to the best six cultivars which have broad genetic background and must be introduced in genetic breeding to produce hybrid seeds of *Solanum* spp., On the whole it could declare that these molecular markers are useful tools for the breeder to decrease the time of breeding programme (Mahmoud and El-Mansy 2012).

Four highly polymorphic RAPD primers were used to describe both the genetic relatedness and variability of 25 accessions of eggplant from South-western Nigeria. At a truncated line of 65 per cent, five clusters and two ungrouped samples were distinguishable from the dendrogram revealed that *S. dasyphyllum* is more closely related to *S. melongena*, a probability of being progenitors from a common ancestral lineage was also shown. Occurrence of *S. scarbrum* and *S. nigrum* in the same clusters different from *S. melongena* was an indication of distant relatedness to *S. melongena* and close relatedness between them. High level of polymorphism was observed by the co-efficient of variation that exhibited a good separation from a conserved region of the genome and revealed that a wide and diverse genetic base in Nigerian *Solanum* spp. (Sifau *et al.* 2014).

Conclusion

Thus, polymorphism between genotypes is due to either a nucleotide base change that alters the ability of the primer to anneal to the DNA template or an insertion/deletion within the amplified fragment. Therefore the polymorphism is generally seen as presence or absence of particular RAPD product. The level of polymorphism detected by RAPDs appears to be similar to the amount detected by RFLPs and RAPD loci are distributed as randomly throughout the genome. These RAPD markers can help in the identification of varieties at a faster and more accurate rate than the conventional technique as it can avoid the manual mistakes which are subjected to happen during manual scoring of the fruit characters.

Thus, genetic diversity provides the means for species to adapt to a changing environmental condition in the future. This diversity also provides the means for species that might suffer or even die out due to rapid changes in climate (Pan *et al.* 2004). The extent and distribution of genetic variation in a species determines the chance of its long-term survival (Levin *et al.* 2005). In conclusion, the genetic diversity of *Solanum* spp., will be a great boon to the resource poor vegetable farmers of India. This will go a long way in reducing pesticide usage in agriculture thus protecting human health, biodiversity and environment.

REFERENCES

Bardakci, F. and Skibinski, D.O.F (1994). Application of the Random Amplified Polymorphic DNA Technique in tilapia Fish Species and Subspecies Identification hereditary. *Nature,* 37: 117-123.

Bohs, I. (1999). *Cyphomandra (Solanaceae) Flora Neotropica. Monograph,* Botanical Garden, New York, 63.

Bohs, L. (2001). Revision of *Solanum* Section *Cyphomandropsis (Solanaceae) Systematic Botany Monographs,* 61:1-85.

Caetano-Anollés, Bassam, J.B.and Gresshoff, M.P. (2001). DNA amplification Finger Printing: A Strategy for Genome Analysis. *Plant Molecular Biology Reporter,* 9(4): 294-307.

Caguiat, X.G.I. and Hautea, D.M. (2014). Genetic Diversity Analysis of Eggplant (*Solanum melongena* L.) and Related wild Species in the Phillipines using morphological and SSR Markers. *Sabrao Journal of Breeding and Genetics* 46(2): 183-201.

Cantello-Anolle, G. (1998). DAF Optimization using Taguchi Methods and the Effect of Thermal Cycling Parameter on DNA Amplification. *Biotechniques,* 25: 472-480.

Carlson, J.E., Tulsieram, L.K., Glaubitz, J.C., Luk, W.W.K., Kauffedt, C.and Rutledge, R. (1991). Segregation of Random Amplified DNA Markers in F1 Progeny of Conifers. *Theoretical and Applied Genetics,* 83: 194-200.

Correll, D.S. (1962). The Potato and Its Wild Relatives *Botanical Studies,* S4: 1-606.

Daunay, M.C. and Lester, R.N. (1988). The Usefulness of Taxonomy for *Solanaceae* breeders with Special Reference to the genus *Solanum* and to *Solanum melongena* L. (eggplant). *Capsicum Newsletter,* 7: 70-79.

Daunay M.C., Lester, R.N., Gerbhardt, C., Hennart, J.W., Jahn, M., Frary, A. and Dognalar, S. (2001). Genetic Resources of Eggplant (*Solanum melongena* L.) and Allied Species: A New Challenge for Molecular Geneticists and Eggplant Breeders. In: van den Berg RG, Barendse GWM, van der Weerden GM and Mariani (eds), *Solanaceae VAdvances in Taxonomy and Utilization* 354.

Daunay, M.C., Lester, R.N. and Laterroot, H. (1991). *Solanaceae III: Taxonomy-Chem-Evolution.* In: Hawakes, J.G., Lester, R.N., Nee, M. and Estrada, N. (eds), *The Royal Botanical Gardens,* Kew, London, 3: 389-412.

Deb, D.B. (1989). *Solanum Melongena* vs. *Solanum incanum* (*Solanaceae*). *Taxon,* 38: 138-139.

Doganlar, S., Frary, A., Duanay, M.C., Lester, R.N. and Tanksley, S.D. (2002). A Comparative Genetic linkage Map of Eggplant (*Solanum melongena*) and its Implications for Genome Evolution in the *Solanaceae. Genetics,* 161: 1697-1711.

Doyle, J.J. and Doyle, J.L. (1987). A Rapid DNA Isolation Procedure for Small Quantities of Fresh Leaf Tissue. *Phytochemistry Bulletin,* 19: 11-15.

Eckert, F.C. and Kunkel, T.A. (1990). High Fidelity DNA Synthesis by the Thermus Aquaticus DNA Polymerase. *Nucleic Acids Research,* 18(13): 3739-3744.

Furini, A. and Wunder, J. (2004). Analysis of Eggplant (*Solanum melongena*) Related Germplasm: Morphological and AFLP Data Contribute to phylogenetic Interpretations and Germplasm Utilization. *Theoretical Application Genetics,* 108: 197-208.

Gepts, P. (1993). The use of Molecular and Biochemical Markers in crop Evolution Studies. *Evolutionary Biology,* 27: 51-94.

Hasan, S.M.Z. and Lester, R.N. (1990a). Comparitive Micomorphology of the Seed Surface of *Solanum melongena* L. (Eggplant) and Allied Species. *Pertanika,* 13: 1-8.

Hasan, S.M.Z. and Lester, R.N. (1990b). Crossability Relationship and *in vitro* Germination of F1 hybrids between *Solanum melongena* L.X *Solanum punduriforma* F. Meyer (*Solanum incanum* L. Sensu ampl). *Sabrao Journal of Breeding and Genetics,* 22: 65-72.

Heath, J., Douglas, C.W.I., Hampton, K.K. and Preston, F.E. (1993). Identity of Viridians Streptococci Isolated from Cases of Infective Endocarditis. *Journal of Medical Microbiology,* 39: 179-182.

Hedrick, P. (1992). Shooting the Random Amplified Polymorphic DNA. *Nature,* 355: 668-679.

Innis, M.A. and Gelfand, D.H. (1990). Thermostable DNA Polymerase. In: Innis, M.A., Gelfand, D.H., Snisky, J.J. and White, T.J. (eds) PCR Protocols – A Guide to Methods and Applications. *Academic Press,* San Diego, 3-13.

Innis, M.A., Myambo, K.B., Gelfand, D.H. and Brow, M.A. (1988). DNA Sequencing with Thermus Aquaticus DNA Polymerase and Direct Sequencing of Polymeras chain Reaction-amplified DNA. *Current Issue,* 85(24): 9436-9440.

Isshiki, S., Okubo, H. and Fuzaida, K. (1994). Phylogeny of Eggplant and Related *Solanum* Species Constructed by Allozyme Variation. *Scientia Horticulturae* 59: 171-176.

Jayasankar, P. and Dharmalingam, K. (1997). Potential Application of RAPD and RAHM Markers in Genome Analysis of scromboid Fishes. *Current Science* 72: 383-390.

Karihaloo, J.L. and Gottileb, L.D. (1995). Random Amplified Polymorphic Variation in the Eggplant, *Solanum melongena* L. (*Solanaceae*). *Theoretical Application of Genetics*, 90: 767-770.

Kashyap, V., Kumar, S.V., Collonnier, C., Fusari, F., Haicour, R., Rotino, G.L., Sihachakr, D. and Rajam (2003). Biotechnology of Eggplant, *Scientia Horticulturae*, 97: 1-25.

Lawyer, F.C., Stoffel, S., Saiki, R.K. and Myambo, K. (1989). Isolation, Characterization and Expression in *Escherichia coli* of the DNA Polymerase gene from Thermus Aquaticus. *The Journal of Biological Chemistry*, 264: 6427-6437.

Lester, R.N. and Hasan, S.M.Z. (1991). Origin and Domestication of the Brinjal Eggplant *Solanum melongena* from *S. incanum* in Africa and Asia. In: *Solanaceae III: Taxonomy-Chem-Evolution*, Hawakes, J.G., Lester, R.N., Nee, M. and Estrada, N. (eds), *The Royal Botanical Gardens*, Kew, London, 369-388.

Levin, R.A., Watson, K. and Bohs, L. (2005). A Four-gene Study of Evolutionary Relationships in *Solanum* Section Acanthophora. *American Journal of Botany*, 92(4): 603-612.

Mace, E.S., Lester, R.N. and Gebhardt, C.G. (1999). AFLP Analysis of Genetic Relationship among the Cultivated Eggplant *Solanum melongena* and its wild Relatives *Solanaceae. Theoretical Application Genetics*, 99: 626-633.

Mahmoud, M.I. and El-Mansy, A.B. (2012). Molecular Identification of Eggplant Cultivars (*Solanum melongena* L.) using ISSR Markers. *Journal of Applied Sciences Research*, 8(1): 69-77.

Meunier, J.R. and Grimont, P.A.D. (1993). Factors Affecting Reproducibility of Random Amplified Polymorphic DNA Finger Printing. *Research in Microbiology*, 144(5): 373-379.

Mishra, S., Singh, M. and Sharma, R.S. (2014). Assessment of Genetic Diversity in Diverse Genotypes of Eggplant (*Solanum melongena* L.) using RAPD Markers. *The Bioscan*, 9(4): 1739-1742.

Muñoz-Falcón, J.E., Prohen, J., Vilanova, S. and Nuez, F. (2008). Characterization, Diversity and Relationships of the Spanish Striped (Listada) Eggplants: A Model for the Enhancement and Protection of Local Heirlooms. *Euphytica*, 164: 405-419.

Murray, M.G. and Thompson, W.F. (1980). Rapid Isolation of High Molecular Weight DNA; DNA. *Nucleic Acids Research*, 8: 4321-4325.

Obute, G.C., Benjamin, C.N. and Okoli, B.E. (2006). Cytogenetic Studies on some Nigerian Species of *Solanum* L. (*Solanaceae*). *American Journal of Botany*, 5(9): 689-692.

Okoli, B.E. (1988). Cytotaxonomic Studies of five West African Species of *Solanum* L. (*Solanaceae*). *Feddes Repert*, 99(5-6): 183-187.

Oyelana, O.A. and Ugborogho, R.E. (2008). Phenotypic Variation of F1 and F2 Populations from three Species of *Solanum* L. (*Solanaceae*). *American Journal of Botany*, 7(14): 2359-2367.

Pan, Y., Burner, D.M., Legendro, B.L., Grisham, M.P. and White, W.H. (2004). An Assessment of the Genetic Diversity within a Collection of *Saccharum spontaneum* with RAPD-PCR *Genetic Resources and Crop Evolution*, 51: 895-903.

Polunin, I. (1987). Plants and Flowers of Singapore. *Singapore: Times Editions* 148.

Prohens, J., Valca´rcel, J.V., Fernandezde, C.P. and Nuez, F. (2003). Characterization and Typification of Spanish Eggplant Landraces. *Capsicum Eggplants Newsletter*, 22: 135-138.

Sakata, Y. and Lester, R.N. (1994). Chloroplast DNA Diversity in Eggplant (*Solanum melongena*) and its Related Species *S. incanum* and *S. marginatum*. *Euphytica,* 80: 1-4.

Sakata, Y. and Lester, R.N. (1997). Chloroplast DNA Diversity in Eggplant (*Solanum melongena*) and Related Species. *Euphytica,* 97: 295-301.

Sakata, Y. Nishio, T. and Mathews, P.J. (1991). Chloroplast DNA Analysis of Eggplant (*Solanum melongena*) and Related Species for their Taxonomic Affinity. *Euphytica,* 55: 21-26.

Seithe, A. and Anderson, G.J. (1982). Hair Morphology and the Relationships of Species in *Solanum* Section Basarthun. *Plant Systematics and Evolution,* 139: 229-256.

Sifau, Oyekunle, M., Ogunkanmi, Adebayo, L., Adekayo., Olajide, K., Oboh, Olufunmilayo, B., Ogundipe and Temitayo, O. (2014). Partitioning and Distribution of Random Amplified Polymorphic DNA (RAPD) variation among Eggplant *Solanum* L. in Southwest Nigeria. *International Journal of Genetics and Molecular Biology,* 6(1): 1-7.

Singh, A.K., Singh, M., Singh, R., Kumar, S. and Kalloo, G. (2006). Genetic Diversity within the Genus *Solanum* (Solanaceae) as Revealed by RAPD Markers. *Current Science,* 90: 711-715.

Wee, Y.C. (1992). A Guide to Medicinal Plants. *Singapore: Singapore Science,* Centre 140.

Weising, K., Nybom, H., Wolff, K. and Meyer, W. (1995). DNA Finger Printing in Plants and Fungi, CRC Press, Boca Raton K.

Welsh, J. and McClelland, M. (1990). Finger Printing Genomes using PCR with Arbitrary Primers. *Nucleic Acids Research,* 18: 7213-7218.

Whalen, M.D. (1984). Conspectus of the Species Group in *Solanum* sub genus *Leptostemonum Genetics Herbarium,* 12: 179-282.

Williams, J.G.K.A.R., Kubelik, K.J., Livak, J.A., Rafalski and Tingey, S.V. (1990). DNA Polymorphisms Amplified by Arbitrary Primers are useful as Genetic Markers. *Nucleic Acids Research,* 18: 6531-6535.

www.faostat.fao.org

Page 79-94

MICROBIAL ENVIRONMENT AND BIOREMEDIATION
Edited by : Dr. Alka Chauhan; Dr. Ashok K. Rathoure & Dr. Raaz K Maheshwari
Edition : 2017
ISBN : 978-93-5056-856-9
Published by : Discovery Publishing House Pvt. Ltd., New Delhi (India)

5 Role of Plasmid in Aquatic Microbiology

Husne Banu[1]
Pramod Kumar Pandey[2]

ABSTRACT

Plasmids are not integral part of bacteria as their absence makes no harm. But the extraordinary properties carried by plasmids make them attractive to study their usefulness for microbes in a hostile environment and it has tremendous contribution for molecular biotechnology. There are many classification of plasmids based on property, compatibility or replication pattern but still many unidentified useful plasmids are remaining. Probably there are many researches on antibiotic resistance group of bacteria which transfer their determinants through R-Plasmids. The transfer of these plasmids is quite harmful for aquatic animals as well as for human being as it increases dose resistance to therapeutics. Microbes are ultimate stage of food chain where everything on earth has to be recycled. Researchers have identified a process called Bioremediation where a group of useful plasmids diversify bacteria to tolerate high concentration of pollutants and to degrade it. With the increase in human population pollution is a big challenge in front. So study of plasmids having crucial role in bioremediation will definitely have vast scope in future.

INTRODUCTION

Importance of Bacterial Genomic Diversity

The dynamics of bacterial genome has aroused from a long series of evolutionary events. These evolutionary events are responsible for unique

1. ICAR-Central Institute of Fisheries Education, Panch Marg, off Yari Road, Versova, Andheri (W), Mumbai - 400 061, Maharasta, India.
2. College of Fisheries Central Agricultural University Lembucherra, Agartala - 799 210, Tripura, India.

set of biological function in large number of bacteria. Bacteria have two separate genetic systems such as: chromosomal DNA and extra-chromosomal DNA. Both genetic systems can undergo gene transfer by various means which accelerates process of evolution in bacterial community. Genetic diversity led by evolution is main cause of bacterial adoptability to vast range of conditions. Bacteria are present everywhere even at extreme conditions such as: high salinity, extremely high and low temperature where no higher animal will survive. They have different phenotypic characters along with diverse metabolic activity. There are many processes involved in bacterial genomic diversity such as: mutation, recombination and Horizontal gene transfer. Mutations are natural alteration during DNA replication or it may occur due to a mutagen. Recombination most commonly takes place between closely related bacterial strains and its frequency decreases with decreasing sequence similarity between the donor and recipient. While mutation brings variation in existing genome, recombination serves alteration within a species. But both of them has little contribution for microbial evolution in comparison to the horizontal gene transfer which alters the genes across the species boundaries (Syavnen, 1994; Syvanenand Kado, 1998; Tendencia and de la Pena, 2001). There are three process of horizontal gene transfer mechanism such as: conjugation, transformation and transduction. The frequency at which gene transfer occur in aquatic ecosystem is not known. Each one has different probabilities to occur in various conditions like availability of external DNA and presence of favorable environmental conditions (nutrient composition, cell density, temperature and salinity) but they have a common means of gene transfer that is through Plasmid.

Role of Plasmid in Gene Transfer

Extra-chromosomal DNA is highly folded circular self-replicating independent body found in most bacteria. Necessary genetic information are stored in chromosomal DNA whereas other additional characteristic such as: UVC resistance, catabolism of unusual carbon sources, resistance to antibiotics, heavy metals and pesticides, degradation of complex organic matter are coded in plasmids (David, 2005). This is why plasmids are regarded as accessory genetic element to bacterial chromosome. Genetic diversity in bacteria is due to the active transport of genes which are incorporated with accessory elements like plasmids. These plasmids survive in host by vertical transmission and adapt to new conditions by horizontal gene transfer. Horizontal gene transfer through plasmids has received much attention due to the incidence of antibiotic resistance of certain pathogenic bacteria. The plasmids carrying resistance gene are supposed to transfer those genes to other bacteria and helps in spreading the resistance. This kind of plasmid transformation in aquatic ecosystem has potential impact on human health. There are applications of bacterial transformation which carry and spread plasmid having xenobiotic degradation genes. These can be used for bioremediation of heavy metals and toxic chemicals.

This paper is a review on activity of plasmid in aquatic microbes. It will cover the description regarding their types, distribution in aquatic environment, transportation mechanism and various properties.

Types of Plasmid and their Function

Plasmids are commonly found in variable amounts in bacteria isolated from various aquatic environments, with frequencies of plasmid incidence reported at 23 to 46 per cent (Hada and Sizemore, 1981; Trevors *et al.* 1987; Schutt, 1988). Plasmids are classified depending on their different function in a host. Depending on their replication property broadly we can classify them as compatibility and incompatibility groups. When two different plasmids can coexist stably in a cell then they are called compatibility plasmid. In opposite when two plasmids with similar replicon or replication elements are unable to coexist, then it is known as incompatibility of plasmids. It was first described for the F plasmid in the early 1960s. Classification based on this property of plasmid was developed in the early 1970s (Chabbert *et al.* 1972; Richards and Datta, 1979; Sagai *et al.* 1976; Sasakawa *et al.* 1980). At present, about 30 incompatibility groups are recognized among plasmids of enteric bacteria and 7 are recognized among staphylococcal plasmids (Couturier *et al.* 1988). It is most common method of plasmid classification but it has a limitation that it does not consider plasmids with high homology and different replication control genes. Depending on their property plasmids are classified as F plasmids, colicinogenic (Col) plasmids and R plasmids (Wang *et al.* 2009).

- *F plasmid:* F (fertility) factor of *Escherchia coli* K-12 was the first plasmid to be described. Lederberg *et al.* (1952) and Hayes (1953) reported the occurrence of a peculiar infective inheritance mediated by an agent called F which controls system of sex compatibility in *E. coli* K-12 strain (Lederberg *et al.* 1952; Hayes, 1953). Original K-12 strain and most of its descendants show no mating limitations, but a few derivative strains have more recently been found which are not crossing with one another. These cross-incompatible strains are called F-, while strains showing the normal, apparently homothallic condition have been termed as F +.
- *Col plasmid:* These are group of small multicopy colicinogenic plasmids which encode the genes to synthesize colicins (bacteriocines). These plasmids need DNA polymerase I for replication and are amplified by chloramphenicol with the exception of ColE2. The Col plasmid groups such as: CoL4, ColD, ColK, and ColEl share a number of replication characteristics (Zverev *et al.* 1984). Has reported that ColA, ColD, and ColK each contain DNA sequences homologous to the region of ColEl which is involved in autonomous replication. These plasmids are widely

used in gene cloning process. They are also used as a good model for gene replication, transcription and translation.

- *R plasmid:* During 1980s most of the *Shigellaflexneri* bacterium found in Korea were resistant to many drugs and it was of high human health concern. Some of the strains were showing multiple resistant to the six drugs like: chloramphenicol (Cm), tetracycline (Tc), streptomycin (Sm), sulfisomidine (Su), ampicillin (Ap) and trimethoprim (Tp). This resistant property was co-transferred to *E. coli* by conjugation, indicating that the resistance was R plasmid-mediated. Most of them belong to incompatibility group of plasmids (*Inc*FIl & *Inc* B) (Chun *et al.* 1984).
- *Suicide plasmids*: These are plasmids which get transfer to another bacterial cell but do not replicate further and also known as mobilizable plasmids. These plasmids are mostly used for transposon and gene replacement experiment. Most of the suicidal/mobilizable plasmids are based on broad host range plasmids R388 plasmid (IncW) and RP4 plasmid (IncPα) (Demarre *et al.* 2005) but there is more advantage if it is based on small narrow host range plasmids.
- *Virulence plasmids*: Presence of these plasmids increases pathogenicity of microbes. There is an excellent review on virulent plasmids of *E. coli* by Johnson *et al.* (2005). Some of them are highly stable where others are unstable. Most of them has originated from a single strain and diversified by accumulating traits which is necessary for respective virulence. There are different types of *E. coli* virulence plasmids exist, including those essential for the virulence of enterotoxigenic *E. coli*, enteroinvasive *E. coli*, enteropathogenic *E. coli*, enterohemorrhagic *E. coli*, enteroaggregative *E. coli*, and extraintestinal pathogenic *E. coli*.

Mode of Plasmid Transfer

The genetic information encoded in an self-replicating extrachromosomal DNA (plasmid) of bacteria are transferred across a broad range of microorganism through conjugation, transformation and transduction. In case of conjugation the donor cell must have a conjugative plasmid and establish a strong physical contact with the recipient cell. In contrast later two methods do not require any physical contact with in donor and recipient.

- *Conjugation:* This requires cell to cell contact of donor and recipient cells and DNA metabolism of donor cell. It is postulated that conjugation is a two step process. In first step, the DNA that is covalently linked to recipient is initially transported in a passive manner, trailing on the relaxase where pilus helps in transporting DNA across several membrane barriers in recipient cell and second step is active pumping of the DNA to the recipient, using the already available T4SS transport conduit (LIosa *et al.* 2002). There are reports of inter-kingdom genetic exchange by conjugation. Heinemann and Sprague has reported that transfer function encoded by two plasmids such as: R751 and F (fertility factor) and two mob/oriT system are able to transfer DNA from bacteria to yeast by conjugation process (Heinemann and Sprague, 1989). Even there are reports of conjugative transfer between Escherichia coli, the RK2 plasmid system and Chinese hamster ovary CHO K1 cells (Waters, 2001). Conjugative plasmid, such as: RP4 has extremely broad host range and these plasmids contribute a lot to genetic diversity. There is much information regarding gene transfer by conjugative mechanism in aquatic ecosystem. Sengelov and Sørensen have selected donor and recipient bacteria in lake water microcosm that received plasmid RP4 by conjugation on filters (Sengeløv and Sørensen, 1998). Research in marine ecosystem with adetection system for gene transfer based on the green fluorescent protein (GFP) has shown that conjugative plasmid pBF1 from *Pseudomonas putida* to indigenous bacteria in seawater (Dahlberg *et al.* 1998).

- *Transduction:* It represents plasmid mediated gene transfer in bacterial community through the bacteriophages which are viruses infecting bacteria. It can be generalized transduction (ability of transducing any gene into bacterial chromosome) or specialized transduction (it can transduce a particulargenes). Jiang and Paul has done a transduction related experiment using marine water bacterial isolates, group of bacterial community as recipient of Plasmid pQSR50 and marine phase host isolates (Jiang, and Paul, 1998). The results revealed that transduction frequency were $1.33\ 3 \times 10^{27}$ to $5.13\ 3 \times 10^{29}$ in bacterial isolates group and $1.58\ 3 \times 10^{28}$ to $3.7\ 3 \times 10^{28}$ in bacterial community. It has been concluded that $1.3\ 3 \times 10^{14}$ transduction events per year could occur in the Tampa Bay Estuary. Transduction in freshwater ecosystem is reported in *P. aeruginosa* streptomycin resistance by a generalized transducing phage, F116, in an experiment conducted with a flow-through environmental test chamber for 10 days period. Mean transduction frequencies ranged from 1.4×10^{-5} to 8.3×10^{-2} transductions per recipient (Morrison *et al.* 1978). A pseudo-lysogenic, generalized transducing bacteriophage, UT1, isolated from a natural freshwater habitat, is capable of mediating the transfer of both chromosomal and plasmid DNA between strains of *P. aeruginosa* (Ripp *et al.* 1994).
- *Transformation:* It is the most common method of bacterial gene transfer in nature. The process requires competent cells which is ready to accept extracellular plasmid and further stable replication inside recipient cells. Artificial transformation by preparing competent *E. coli bacterial* cells in lab is a common and widely used method in gene cloning. But there are many naturally occurring competent bacteria which participate in natural transformation like: *Streptococcus pneumoniae* and *Neisseria gonorrhoeae* (Lorenz and Wackernagel, 1994; Lunsford, 1998).

Plasmids Distribution in Aquatic Environment

Even though DNases are ubiquitous in the environment, because there may be > 90 per cent DNase producing bacteria in aquatic and soil environment (Greaves and Wilson 1970; Maeda and Taga, 1974) extracellular plasmidis found everywhere. Gene transfer via plasmids may occur through extracellular environmental DNA. Natural plasmid transformation is a means of plasmid acquisition by aquatic bacterial population. Plasmids are released to environment through both abiotic (*e.g.*, ionic strength, pH, temperature (Paul and David, 1989) and biotic factors. Bacteriophage infection and predation by protozoa are probably the main biotic factors of the presence of extracellular DNA in the aquatic environment (Børsheim, 1993; Turk *et al.* 1992). The persistency of free plasmid in soil has been evaluated by Romanowski *et al.* (Romanowski *et al.* 1993) in an experiment period of 60 days with plasmid pUC8-ISP DNA introduced into 10-g samples of various soils and kept at 23°C. The data concludes that half-life period of plasmid varies in different type of soils from 9.1 to 28.2 and persist for a long period enough to be available for uptake by natural competent cells. Later studies by him through PCR and electroporation conformed that transforming activity was found up to 60 days after inoculation of the soils (Romanowski *et al.* 1992). Plasmid transformation mostly in marine environment has extensively studied by many authors (Bruns *et al.* 1992; Frischer *et al.* 1990, 1993; Lorenz and Wackernagel, 1990; Stewart and Sinigalliano, 1989). Stewartand Sinigalliano (1989) has demonstrated the first marine model for natural transformation in *P. stutzeri* ZoBell. The transformation was detected by ajauni plate method and frequency detected by filter transformation process. He concluded that transformation by cell contact is 10-fold lesser that purified DNA. But first proof of plasmid transformation in natural water body was given by Paul *et al.* (1991). He has reported that in water column, transformation frequencies ranged from 1.7×10^{-6} to 2.7×10^{-10} transformants per recipient, with highest frequencies occurring when low levels of nutrients (peptone and yeast extract) were added. The result of transformation frequency in sediments is comparatively less to marine water. It is experimentally proved that 45 per cent of Vibrio genera contained 1–3 plasmids (Zhang *et al.* 2012). The high-frequency-of-transformation (HFT) estuarine Vibrio strains (D1-9) were transformable with the broad host range plasmids with frequencies ranging from 1.1×10^{-8} to 1.3×10^{-4} transformants per recipient with plasmid DNA (Dahlberg *et al.* 1998). Transformants can be easily verified by colony hybridization with probes for the transforming DNA. The evidence of gene transformation in natural fresh water body has come late and most of the natural transformation related work is done with marine water bacteria. *E coli* found in natural ecosystem under goes natural competency development which is a method of plasmid transformation (Baur *et al.* 1996). The natural transformation in freshwater is influenced by temperature fluctuation but do not depends on high temperature. It may also occur at low concentration of Calcium ion (1-2mM).

Properties of Plasmid

Heavy Metal Tolerance

Microbial method for heavy metal detoxification is widely used due to its high specificity for target heavy metal where as other alternatives are not so specific in action. Plasmid mediated heavy metal tolerance is well studied as this phenomena is older than antibiotic resistance of bacteria. General mechanisms involved in such kind of tolerance are enzymatic alteration of the toxic compound, enzymatic modification of the target site, development of alternate metabolic pathways, and extrusion of the toxic compound from the cell (Foster, 1983). Studies related to toxic metal ion tolerant bacteria increased rapidly after the discovery of mercury-resistant bacteria which can volatilize mercury (Summers, A.O., and Silver, 1972). Apart from mercury there are other highly specific metal tolerance systems such as: arsenic, copper, cadmium, zinc, cobalt, nickel, tellurite, silver and other toxic metal ions (Silver, 1996). Each bacteria has different mode of detoxification. But most of them involve a group of genes that is known as operon system. An example of such kind of well-studied operon is *mer* operon for mercury resistant bacteria. This operon is well studied both in Gram + and Gram – bacteria. It consists of series of genes such as: *mer*R, *mer*A, *mer*B and *mer*D whose product are engaged in breaking of mercury-carbon bond, intracellular detoxification and transport of toxic chemical across the cell membrane. This system slightly varies in gram+ and Gram-bacteria due to the expression pattern of *mer*R which encodes regulator protein that controls polymerase activity. Second most studied heavy metal tolerance is Arsenic operon system. There are five different types of operon and among them plasmid R773 is extensively studied which consists of genes such as: ArsA, ArsB, ArsC, ArsD and ArsR. ArsC gene is involved in Arsenate reduction where as ArsA, ArsB are involved in ATP dependent membrane transport of toxic arsenite and ArsR is a regulatory gene. In 1983 T.J. Tetaz and R.K.J. Luke reported a copper tolerant *E. coli* strain found in effluent of a piggery where the pig was fed with copper sulfate supplemented feed (Tetaz and Luke, 1983). The resistance was due to a 78-megadalton plasmid designated as pRJ1004. Latter it was experimentally proved that there is an operon of genes named as pcoABCD which is followed by two regulatory genes, pcoR and pcoS. The pcoA, pcoC are two periplasmic proteins and pcoB, pcoD are outer and inner membrane proteins respectively. All together helps in reducing intracellular copper concentration and efflux of toxic copper outside the cell. There are other similar copper resistance mechanism found in *Pseudomonas* (Cooksey, 1994) *Xanthomonas* (Lee *et al.* 1994). There are reports of other metal resistant bacteria controlled by plasmids such as: Cadmium and Chromate and tellurite etc.

Nitrogen Fixation

Nitrogen fixing prokaryotic organism are unique for having N_2 fixing ability as well as most of them (Blue green algae) are autotrophs. Nitrogen fixing genes are conserved in chromosomal DNA and plasmids. Molecular study of Cyanobacteria strains shows that it contains several plasmids (Van *et al.* 1979). There are many reports regarding presence of *nif* genes in prokaryotes like: *Klebsiella pneumoniae, P.stutzeri* and group of cyanobacteria. The DNA hybridization of Klebsiella with other bacteria demonstrates that there is a high homology of nif genes between interspecies bacteria (Ruvkunand Ausubel. 1980). Most of the *nif* genes are encoded by chromosomal DNA but hybridization of plasmids isolated from *Rhizobiwn Zegwninosarum* with cloned *nif*gene of Klebsiella reveals that at least few *nif* genes are located in plasmids (Krol *et al.* 1980). The interspecific transfer of nitrogen-fixing ability (Nif) from strains of *R. trifolii* containing P1 group R plasmids to other bacterium explains about plasmid mediated transfer of this gene. Bishop *et al.* 1977 has reported an intergeneric transformation between *Nif* mutant of *Azotobactervinelandii* and *R. trifolii which* may be due to the whole plasmid transformation (Bishop *et al.* 1977). Other plasmid related experiments shows that certain hybrid *nif plasmids* drastically inhibit the expression of the chromosomal *nif genes* of *K. pneumoniae* (Riedel *et al.* 1983). The inhibition is due to polypeptides made by plasmid which interferes with Nif expression or it is due to the inhibitory plasmid DNA which interacts directly with a macromolecule in the cell and inhibits *nif*gene expression. Masterson *et al.* (1982) has reported about the presence of structural nif gene on large plasmids of all fast-growing *R. japonicum* but slow growing strains do not have nif gene on their plasmid (Masterson *et al.* 1982).

Sulfur Utilization

There are a group of bacteria known as sulfur utilizing bacteria which metabolize sulfur and this activity is useful for sulfur cycling in nature. Most of sulfur compounds are oxidized by Archaea and Bacteria. These compounds are used as electron donors for anaerobic phototrophic and aerobic chemotrophic growth, and are mostly oxidized to sulfate. The common energy sources for such bacteria are hydrogen sulfide (H_2S), sulfur and thiosulfate ($S_2O_3^{2-}$). Monticellc *et al.* (1985) has reported that oxidiation of dibenzothiophene (DBT) which includes many sulfur containing polyaromatic hydrocarbons, is mediated by plasmid-borne functions in *Pseudomonas* isolates. Two Pseudomonas species which oxidized DBT to water-soluble, sulfur-containing products harbored the 55-megadalton plasmid in contrast none of the 50 Dbt⁻ colonies which are grown in medium supplemented with novobiocin (30ug/ml) harbored a plasmid. Zillig *et al.* (1984) has reported that *Sulfolobus ambivalens* is able to live in an anaerobic mode of chemolithoautotrophy by using Co_2 as carbon source and reduces sulfate to

H_2S as aenergy source. They have correlated this mode of growth with amplification of a plasmid, pSL10. From athermoacidophilic archaea *S.islandicus*, multicopy plasmids were isolated and a 5.3 kb plasmid. pRNl, is completely sequenced which may be useful as cloning vectors in Sulfolobales (Keeling *et al.* 1996). A 14 kb plasmid isolated from green sulfur bacteria *Chlorobiumlimicola* f. sp. *thiosulfatophilum* is experimentally proved for carrying genes necessary for thiosulfate utilization or regulating such gene expression (Mendez *et al.* 1994).

Hydrocarbon Degradation

Biodegradation of hydrocarbon are of major concerned with environmental pollution and its harmful impact. Such harmful impact of hydrocarbon pollution are oil spillage, poly aromatic hydrocarbon pollution which are adsorbed to sediment and accumulated in aquatic animals like: fish and shellfish followed by transfer to human through seafood consumption (Meador *et al.* 1995). Microbial degradation of hydrocarbon is a useful technique of bioremediation without any adverse impact on environment. This property of microbes has evolved from a series of adaptation process in which they acquired few genes which are necessary to survive and propagate in a hydrocarbon reach environment. They require appropriate catabolic genes to be a good hydrocarbon degrader. Such special genes are often carried on plasmids of bacteria (Johnsen *et al.* 2005). Plasmids which carry structural genes for organic matter or xenobiotic degradation are known as degradative or catabolic plasmids. It is experimentally proved that plasmids encode the enzymes required for metabolism of naphthalene, salicylate, camphor, octane, xylene, and toluene (Chakrabarty, 1976). Hada and Sizemore (1981) had isolated 440 Vibrio from an operational oil field and control site located in the northwestern Gulf of Mexico. They were screened for the presence of plasmids and 31 per cent showed distinct plasmid bands on agarose gels with estimated molecular masses of 10×10^6 or less. The oil field area had noticeably more plasmid containing strains in comparison to control fields (35 vs. 23%) and number of plasmids per cell was more in bacteria isolated from polluted area (2.5 plasmids, versus 1.5 in the control site). This finding indirectly proves that plasmids are providing additional adaptability to microbes for organic compound degradation. Plasmids have a great role in PAH degradation and spreading this capacity among all other microbial community. For example naphthalene degradation capacity has experimentally marked to be transferred at low frequency by conjugation from strain NCIB 9816 into a plasmid-free strain of *P. putida*, PaW340 and the transconjugant, PaW701, containing the naphthalene plasmid pWW60-1, metabolize Naphthalene and salicylate by ortho pathway. Pseudomonads genes encode the upper and lower pathways of naphthalene degradation in the NAH plasmids which encodes for the enzymes that can metabolize a broad range of nutrition (Foght and Westlake, 1996). Yen and Serdar (1988) has explained how naphthalene is catabolized by *Pseudomonas* in a series of reactions to salicylic acid, which is further degraded to Krebs cycle intermediates. The naphthalene catabolic genes have been located on self-transmissible plasmids and among them NAH7 is best studied. It consists of two operons involved in host utilization of naphthalene and salicylate as a carbon and energy source. Among all genes nahR codes for regulatory protein which is required to turn on the operon in presence of Salicylate as an inducer. These genes are highly unstable as it can undergo structural alteration by involving insertion or deletion during conjugation or altered nutritional condition. Li *et al.* (2004) for the first time reported complete naphthalene catabolic plasmid sequence of Pseudomonas sp., which consists of 101,858 bp nucleotide according to the whole-genome-shotgun approach [36]. pND6-1encodes 102 putative coding sequences (CDSs). Among them, 23 CDSs were predicted to be involved in naphthalene catabolism and rest of the CDSs indirectly helps in plasmid functioning. These all catabolic plasmids (pDTG1, NAH7 and pND6-1) have high sequence homology but they are highly versatile in their activity (Obayori and Salam 2010). Other high molecular weight PAH degraders such as: *Mycobacterium* sp., are reported to degrade pyrene and they carry large plasmids but hybridization results shows that extrachromosomal DNA are not involved in degradation. Most of the pyrene degradative proteins are encoded by chromosomes. But in contrast Lin and Cai (2008) reported the isolation of plasmid from two strains, *Bacillus cereus* Py5 and *Bacillus megaterium* Py6 are involved in Pyrene degradation and after these plasmids transformed to *E. coli,* it was shown to degrade pyrene. Plasmid pNL1 which is isolated from *S. aromaticivorans* F199 strain is suggested to be a broader host range plasmid, because it was transferred without any obvious structural changes to *S. yanoikuyae* B1, *Sphingomonas* sp. SS3, and *S. herbicidovorans (Basta et al.* 2004). So it concludes that these broad host range plasmids are likely to spread PAH degradation capacity. Most of these degradative plasmids are evolved in a short time period by acquiring genes from bacterial chromosomes or self alteration due to the external influence.

Drug Resistance

Multiple drug resistance of bacteria is a major issue since early 1960s when there were many reports for antibiotic resistance of Shigellae in south east countries like: Japan and Korea. This drug resistance has marked to be transferred to other Enterobacteriaceae by conjugation (Anderson, 1965). Resistance to antibiotics is acquired from the factors called R-factors which are plasmids carrying resistant determinants (R-determinants) and resistance transfer factors (RTF). Anderson *et al.* (1965) has reported that these two components of R-plasmid are effective when present in a single cell. R-determinants are not transferable without RTF and alone RTF cannot develop drug resistant criteria. The transfer of drug resistance is dependent on temperature and other physicochemical parameters of water. For example drug resistance of *Salmonella typhi* isolated in Korea from 1968 to 1975 was more efficiently transferred to *E. coli at* 25°C than at 37°C (Chun *et al*. 1977). Most of the drug resistance studies are aimed towards antibiotic resistance of human pathogenic bacteria for example Salmonella and shigellae. But it is also concerned with veterinary medicines which are indirectly transferred to human. The antibiotics which are resistant to bacteria are ampicillin (A), chloramphenicol (C), neomycin (N), kanamycin (K), streptomycin (S), sulphonamides (Su), and tetracycline (T). Most of the R-factor elicits multiple drug resistance patterns for example *S. typhimurium* have common resistance patterns such as: ST Su; A S T Su; and S T N K Su (Anderson, 1965). These resistant pattern changes due to incorporation of more drugs resistance. Disease occurrence in fish and shrimp culture system is increased due to the intensification of culture practice and in proportion to that antibiotic application has also increased. Due to improper and frequent application of antibiotic, tolerance level of pathogenic bacteria increases and the effective dose has to be increased or replaced with other drugs. In developed countries like: the EU, the USA, Canada and Norway, there is strong regulation over use of certain antibiotics in aquaculture but in developing countries such regulation is still not implemented. Akinbowale *et al*. (2006) has reported about the antimicrobial resistance in Australian aquaculture system and briefly explained about drug resistance in aquaculture. There are many reports of bacterial drug resistance in finfish culture farms as well as in shellfish hatcheries and ponds Tjahjadi *et al*. 1994; Tendencia and de, 2001; Ho *et al*. 2000; Hossain *et al*. 2012; Manjusha and Sarita, 2013). Antibiotic resistance is also observed in natural condition. It has been reported that frequency of pigmented bacteria and occurrence of bacterial antibiotic resistance were higher at the air-water interface than in the bulk water (Hermansson *et al*. 1987). Sandaa and Enger (1994) has reported that in case of fish-pathogenic bacterium *Aeromonas salmonicida* plasmid, pRAS1 encodes for tetracycline resistance is transferred at a high frequency in marine sediments even in the absence of a selective factor. The presence of oxytetracycline increases transfer frequency to 3.4×10^{-1}transconjugant per recipient and 3.6 transconjugants per donor cell.

Conclusion

Every animal has adaptation mechanism by which they survive on earth for a long period. For bacteria like: prokaryote, Plasmid is essential for adaptation by means of genetic diversity. Plasmids carry properties of xenobiotic degradation and heavy metal tolerance which makes them useful in bioremediation of toxic chemicals in eco-friendly manner. Whereas properties like: antibiotic resistance is the consequence of indiscriminate use of drugs in culture system by farmers. The practice of genetic engineering of microbes and development of superior varieties is useful in comparison to chemical method of toxic remediation. A superior catalyst is made through combination of catabolic segments from different organisms within one recipient strain and such segments are frequently found in plasmids. Today we are using many plasmid vectors in gene cloning experiments but incorporation of antimicrobial resistance mediated selection method is harmful for ecosystem. It is important to investigate more regarding plasmids and their properties so that we will come to understand more about bacteria and their means of survival.

REFERENCES

1. Akinbowale, O.L., Peng, H., and Barton, M.D. (2006). Antimicrobial Resistance in Bacteria Isolated from Aquaculture Sources in Australia. *Journal of Applied Microbiology*, 100(5), 1103-1113.
2. Anderson, E.S. (1965). Origin of Transferable Drug-resistance Factors in the Enterobacteriaceae. *Br Med J.*, 2(5473), 1289-1291.
3. Basta, T., Keck, A., Klein, J., and Stolz, A. (2004). Detection and Characterization of Conjugative Degradative Plasmids in xenobiotic-degrading Sphingomonas Strains. *Journal of Bacteriology*, 186(12), 3862-3872.
4. Baur, B., Hanselmann, K., Schlimme, W., and Jenni, B. (1996). Genetic Transformation in Freshwater: Escherichia Coli is Able to Develop Natural Competence. *Applied and Environmental Microbiology*, 62(10), 3673-3678.
5. Bishop, P.E., Dazzo, F.B., Appelbaum, E.R., Maier, R.J., and Brill, W.J. (1977). Intergeneric Transfer of Genes Involved in the Rhizobium-legume Symbiosis. *Science*, 198(4320), 938-940.
6. Børsheim, K.Y. (1993). Native Marine Bacteriophages. *FEMS Microbiology Letters*, 102(3), 141-159.
7. Bruns, S., Reipschläger, K., Lorenz, M.G., and Wackernagel, W. (1992). Characterization of Natural Transformation of the Soil Bacteria Pseudomonas stutzeri and Acinetobacter calcoaceticus by Chromosomal and Plasmid DNA. In *Gene Transfers and Environment* (pp. 115-126). Springer Berlin Heidelberg.
8. Chabbert, Y.A., Scavizzi, M.R., Witchitz, J.L., Gerbaud, G.R., and Bouanchaud, D.H. (1972). Incompatibility Groups and the Classification of fi" Resistance Factors. *Journal of Bacteriology*, 112(2), 666-675.
9. Chakrabarty, A.M. (1976) Plasmids in pseudomonas. *Annual Review of Genetics*, 10(1), 7-30.
10. Chun, D., Cho, D.T., Seol, S.Y., Suh, M.H. and Lee, Y.C., (1984). R plasmids Conferring Multiple Drug Resistance from shigella isolated in Korea. *Journal of Hygiene*, 92(02), pp. 153-160.
11. Chun, D., Seol, S.Y., Cho, D.T., and Tak, R. (1977). Drug Resistance and R plasmids in Salmonella Typhi Isolated in Korea. *Antimicrobial Agents and Chemotherapy*, 11(2), 209-213.
12. Cooksey, D.A. (1994). Molecular Mechanisms of Copper Resistance and Accumulation in Bacteria. *FEMS Microbiology Reviews*, 14(4), 381-386.

13. Couturier, M.A.R.T.I.N.E., Bex, F., Bergquist, P.L., and Maas, W.K. (1988). Identification and Classification of Bacterial Plasmids. *Microbiological Reviews*, 52(3), 375.
14. Dahlberg, C., Bergström, M., and Hermansson, M. (1998). In situ Detection of High Levels of Horizontal Plasmid Transfer in Marine Bacterial Communities. *Applied and Environmental Microbiology*, 64(7), 2670-2675.
15. David C. Sigee. (2005). Freshwater Microbiology. In Genetic Interactions. pp. 294-300. John Wiley and Sons, Ltd., Chichester, UK.
16. Demarre, G., Guérout, A.M., Matsumoto-Mashimo, C., Rowe-Magnus, D.A., Marlière, P., and Mazel, D. (2005). A New Family of Mobilizable Suicide Plasmids based on Broad Host Range R388 Plasmid (IncW) and RP4 Plasmid (IncPα) Conjugative Machineries and their cognate Escherichia coli Host Strains. *Research in Microbiology*, 156(2), 245-255.
17. Foght, J.M., and Westlake, D.W. (1996). Transposon and Spontaneous Deletion Mutants of Plasmid-borne Genes Encoding polycyclic Aromatic Hydrocarbon Degradation by a Strain of Pseudomonas fluorescens. *Biodegradation*, 7(4), 353-366.
18. Foster, T.J. (1983). Plasmid-determined Resistance to Antimicrobial Drugs and Toxic Metal Ions in Bacteria. *Microbiological Reviews*, 47(3), 361.
19. Frischer, M. E., Thurmond, J. M., and Paul, J.H. (1990). Natural Plasmid Transformation in a High-frequency-of-transformation Marine Vibrio Strain. *Applied and Environmental Microbiology*, 56(11), 3439-3444.
20. Frischer, M.E., Thurmond, J.M., and Paul, J.H. (1993). Factors Affecting Competence in a High Frequency of Transformation Marine Vibrio. *Microbiology*, 139(4), 753-761.
21. Greaves, M.P., and Wilson, M.J. (1970). The Degradation of Nucleic Acids and Montmorillonite-nucleic-acid Complexes by Soil Microorganisms. *Soil Biology and Biochemistry*, 2(4), 257-268.
22. Hada, H.S., and Sizemore, R.K. (1981). Incidence of Plasmids in Marine Vibrio spp., Isolated from an Oil field in the Northwestern Gulf of Mexico. *Applied and Environmental Microbiology*, 41(1), 199-202.
23. Hayes, W. (1953). Observations on a Transmissible Agent Determining Sexual Differentiation in Bacterium Coli. *J. Gen. Microbiol*. 8: 72.
24. Heinemann, J.A., and Sprague Jr, G.F. (1989). Bacterial Conjugative Plasmids Mobilize DNA Transfer between Bacteria and Yeast. *Nature*, 340(6230), 205-209.
25. Hermansson, M., Jones, G. W., and Kjelleberg, S. (1987). Frequency of Antibiotic and Heavy Metal Resistance, Pigmentation, and Plasmids in Bacteria of the Marine Air-Water Interface. *Applied and Environmental Microbiology*, 53(10), 2338-2342.
26. Ho, S.P., Hsu, T.Y., Chen, M.H., and WANG, W.S. (2000). Antibacterial Effect of Chloramphenicol, thiamphenicol and florfenicol against Aquatic Animal Bacteria. *Journal of Veterinary Medical Science*, 62(5), 479-485.
27. Van den Hondel, C.A.M.J. J., Keegstra, W., Borrias, W.E., and Van Arkel, G.A. (1979). Homology of Plasmids in Strains of unicellular cyanobacteria. *Plasmid*, 2(3), 323-333.
28. Hossain, M.S., Aktaruzzaman, M., Fakhruddin, A.N.M., Uddin, M.J., Rahman, S.H., Chowdhury, M.A.Z., and Alam, M.K. (2012). Prevalence of Multiple Drug Resistant Pathogenic Bacteria in Cultured Black Tiger Shrimp (Penaeus monodon fabricius). *Global J. Environ Res*, 6(3), 118-124.
29. Jiang, S.C., and Paul, J.H. (1998). Gene Transfer by Transduction in the Marine Environment. *Applied and Environmental Microbiology*, 64(8), 2780-2787.

30. Johnsen, A.R., Wick, L.Y., and Harms, H. (2005). Principles of Microbial PAH-degradation in Soil. *Environmental Pollution*, 133(1), 71-84.
31. Keeling, P.J., Klenk, H.P., Singh, R.K., Feeley, O., Schleper, C., Zillig, W., and Sensen, C.W. (1996). Complete Nucleotide Sequence of the Sulfolobus islandicus Multicopy Plasmid pRN1. *Plasmid*, 35(2), 141-144.
32. Krol, A.J.M., Hontelez, J.G.J., Van den Bos, R.C., and Van Kammen, A. (1980). Expression of Large Plasmids in the endosymbiotic form of Rhizobium leguminosarum. *Nucleic Acids Research*, 8(19), 4337-4348.
33. Lederberg, J., Cavallli, L. and Lederberge, M. (1952). Sex Compatibility in Escherichia coli. Genetics, 37: 720.
34. Lee, Y.A., Hendson, M., Panopoulos, N.J., and Schroth, M.N. (1994). Molecular Cloning, Chromosomal Mapping, and Sequence Analysis of Copper Resistance genes from Xanthomonas campestris pv. juglandis: Homology with Small blue Copper Proteins and Multicopper Oxidase. *Journal of Bacteriology*, 176(1), 173-188.
35. Li, S., Zhao, H., Li, Y., Niu, S., and Cai, B. (2012). Complete Genome Sequence of the Naphthalene-degrading Pseudomonas putida strain ND6. *Journal of Bacteriology*, 194(18), 5154-5155.
36. Li, W., Shi, J., Wang, X., Han, Y., Tong, W., Ma, L., ... and Cai, B. (2004). Complete Nucleotide Sequence and Organization of the Naphthalene Catabolic plasmid pND6-1 from Pseudomonas sp., Strain ND6. *Gene*, 336(2), 231-240.
37. Lin, Y., and Cai, L.X. (2008). PAH-degrading Microbial Consortium and Its Pyrene-degrading Plasmids from Mangrove Sediment Samples in Huian, China. *Marine Pollution Bulletin*, 57(6), 703-706.
38. Llosa, M., Gomis Rüth, F.X., Coll, M., and Cruz, F.D.L. (2002). Bacterial Conjugation: A Two Step Mechanism for DNA Transport. *Molecular Microbiology*, 45(1), 1-8.
39. Lorenz, M.G., and Wackernagel, W. (1990). Natural Genetic Transformation of Pseudomonas Stutzeri by Sand-adsorbed DNA. *Archives of Microbiology*, 154(4), 380-385.
40. Lorenz, M.G., and Wackernagel, W. (1994). Bacterial gene Transfer by Natural Genetic Transformation in the Environment. *Microbiological Reviews*, 58(3), 563-602.
41. Lunsford, R.D. (1998). Streptococcal Transformation: Essential Features and Applications of A Natural Gene Exchange System. *Plasmid*, 39(1), 10-20.
42. Maeda, M., and Taga, N. (1974). Occurrence and Distribution of Deoxyribonucleic Acid-hydrolyzing Bacteria in Sea Water. *Journal of Experimental Marine Biology and Ecology*, 14(2), 157-169.
43. Manjusha, S., and Sarita, G.B. (2013). Characterization of Plasmids from Multiple Antibiotic Resistant Vibrios Isolated from Molluscan and Crustacean of Kerala. *International Food Research Journal*, 20(1).
44. Masterson, R.V., Russell, P.R., and Atherly, A.G. (1982). Nitrogen Fixation (nif) Genes and Large Plasmids of Rhizobium Japonicum. *Journal of Bacteriology*, 152(2), 928-931.
45. Meador, J.P., Stein, J.E., Reichert, W.L., and Varanasi, U. (1995). Bioaccumulation of Polycyclic aromatic Hydrocarbons by Marine Organisms. In *Reviews of Environmental Contamination and Toxicology* (pp. 79-165). Springer New York.
46. Mendez-Alvarez, S., Pavón, V., Esteve, I., Guerrero, R., and Gaju, N. (1994). Transformation of Chlorobiumlimicola by a Plasmid that Confers the Ability to Utilize Thiosulfate. *Journal of Bacteriology*, 176(23), 7395-7397.

47. Monticello, D.J., Bakker, D., and Finnerty, W.R. (1985). Plasmid-mediated Degradation of dibenzothiophene by Pseudomonas Species. *Applied and Environmental Microbiology*, 49(4), 756-760.
48. Morrison, W.D., Miller, R.V., and Sayler, G.S. (1978). Frequency of F116-mediated Transduction of Pseudomonas aeruginosa in a Freshwater Environment. *Applied and Environmental Microbiology*, 36(5), 724-730.
49. Obayori, O.S., and Salam, L.B. (2010). Degradation of Polycyclic Aromatic Hydrocarbons: Role of Plasmids. *Sci. Res. Essays*, 5(25), 4093-4106.
50. Paul, J.H., Frischer, M.E., and Thurmond, J.M. (1991). Gene Transfer in Marine Water Column and Sediment Microcosms by Natural Plasmid Transformation. *Applied and Environmental Microbiology*, 57(5), 1509-1515.
51. Paul, J.H., and David, A.W. (1989). Production of Extracellular Nucleic Acids by Genetically Altered Bacteria in Aquatic-Environment Microcosms. *Applied and Environmental Microbiology*, 55(8), 1865-1869.
52. Richards, H., Datta, N., (1979). Reclassification of Incompatibility Group L (IncL) Plasmids. Plasmid 2: 293-295.
53. Riedel, G.E., Brown, S.E., and Ausubel, F.M. (1983). Nitrogen Fixation by Klebsiella pneumoniae is inhibited by Certain Multicopy hybrid nif plasmids. *Journal of Bacteriology*, 153(1), 45-56.
54. Ripp, S., Ogunseitan, O.A., and Miller, R.V. (1994). Transduction of a Freshwater Microbial Community by a New Pseudomonas aeruginosa Generalized Transducing Phage, UT1. *Mol. Ecol.* 3: 121-126.
55. Romanowski, G., Lorenz, M.G., and Wackernagel, W. (1993). Use of Polymerase Chain Reaction and Electroporation of Escherichia coli to Monitor the Persistence of Extracellular Plasmid DNA Introduced into Natural Soils. *Applied and Environmental Microbiology*, 59(10), 3438-3446.
56. Romanowski, G., Lorenz, M.G., Sayler, G., and Wackernagel, W. (1992). Persistence of Free Plasmid DNA in Soil Monitored by Various Methods, Including a Transformation Assay. *Applied and Environmental Microbiology*, 58(9), 3012-3019.
57. Ruvkun, G.B., and Ausubel, F.M. (1980). Interspecies Homology of Nitrogenase Genes. *Proceedings of the National Academy of Sciences*, 77(1), 191-195.
58. Sagai, H., Hasuda, K., Iyobe, S., Bryan, L.E., Holloway, B.W., Mitsuhashi, S., (1976). Classification of R Plasmids by Incompatibility in Pseudomonas aeruginosa. Antimicrob. Agents Chemother. 10: 573-578.
59. Sandaa R.A. and Enger O. (1994). Transfer in Marine Sediments of the Naturally Occurring Plasmid pRASi Encoding Multiple Antibiotic Resistance. *Appl. Environ. Microbiol.* 60:4234-4238.
60. Sasakawa, C., Takamatsu, N., Danbara, H., Yoshikawa, M., (1980). A Method of Plasmid Classification by Integrative Incompatibility. *Plasmid* 3: 116-127.
61. Schutt, C. (1988). Plasmid-DNA in Natural Bacterial Populations of Four Brownwater Lakes (South Sweden). *Arch. Hydrobiol. Beih.* 31:133-139.
62. Sengeløv, G., and Sørensen, S.J. (1998). Methods for Detection of Conjugative Plasmid Transfer in Aquatic Environments. *Current Microbiology*, 37(4), 274-280.
63. Silver, S. (1996). Bacterial Resistances to Toxic Metal Ions – A Review. *Gene*, 179(1), 9-19.

64. Stewart, G.J., and C.D. Sinigalliano. (1989). Detection and Characterization of Natural Transformation in the Marine Bacterium Pseudomonas stutzeri Strain ZoBell. *Arch. Microbiol.* 152: 520-526.

65. Summers, A.O., and Silver, S. (1972). Mercury Resistance in a Plasmid-bearing Strain of Escherichia coli. *Journal of Bacteriology*, 112(3), 1228-1236.

66. Syvanen, M. (1990). Migrant DNA in Bacterial World. *Cell* 60: 7-8.

67. Syavnen, M. (1994). Horizontal Gene Flow: Evidence and Possible Consequences. *Annu. Rev. Genet.* 28: 237-261.

68. Syvanen M. and Kado, C.I. (1998). Horizontal Gene Transfer, chapman and Hall, London.

69. Tendencia, E.A. and de la Pena, L.D. (2001). Antibiotic Resistant Bacteria from shrimp Ponds. *Aquaculture* 195: 193-204.

70. Tetaz, T.J., and Luke, R.K. (1983). Plasmid-controlled Resistance to Copper in Escherichia coli. *Journal of Bacteriology*, 154(3), 1263-1268.

71. Timothy J. Johnson and Lisa K. Nolan. (2009). Pathogenomics of the Virulence Plasmids of Escherichia coli. *Micro and Mol Bio Rev.*, 73:750-774.

72. Tjahjadi, M.R., Angka, S.L. and Suwanto, A. (1994). Isolation and Evaluation of Marine Bacteria for Biocontrol of luminous Bacterial Disease in Tiger Shrimp Larvae (Penaeus monodon, Fab.). *Asia Pac J. Mol Biol Biotechnol* 2: 347-352.

73. Trevors, J.T., Barkey, T. and Bourquin, A.W. (1987). Gene Transfer among Bacteria in Soil and Aquatic Environments: A Review. *Can. J. Microbiol.* 33:191-198.

74. Turk, V., Rehnstam, A.S., Lundberg, E., and Hagström, Å. (1992). Release of Bacterial DNA by Marine Nanoflagellates, An Intermediate Step in phosphorus Regeneration. *Applied and Environmental Microbiology*, 58(11), 3744-3750.

75. Wang, Z., Jin, L., Yuan, Z., Wegrzyn, G., Wegrzyn A. (2009). Classification of Plasmid Vectors using Replication Origin, Selection Marker and Promoter as Criteria. *Plasmid* 61: 47-51.

76. Waters, V.L. (2001). Conjugation between Bacterial and Mammalian Cells. *Nature Genetics*, 29(4), 375-376.

77. Yen, K.M and Serdar, C.M. (1988). Genetics of Naphthalene catabolism in Pseudomonas. *Crit. Rev. Microbiol.* 15: 247-267.

78. Zhang, R., Pan, L., Zhao, Z., and Gu, J. D. (2012). High Incidence of Plasmids in Marine Vibrio Species Isolated from Mai Po Nature Reserve of Hong Kong. *Ecotoxicology*, 21(6), 1661-1668.

79. Zillig, W., Yeats, S., Holz, I., Böck, A., Gropp, F., Rettenberger, M., and Lutz, S. (1984). Plasmid-Related anaerobic Autotrophy of the Novel archaebacterium *Sulfolobus ambivalens*. *Nature*, 313(6005), 789-791.

80. Zverev, V.V., Kuzmin, N.P., Zuyeva, L.A., Burova, E.I., Alexandrov, A.A., and Khmel, I.A. (1984). Regions of Homology in Small colicinogenic plasmids. *Plasmid*, 12(3), 203-205.

MICROBIAL ENVIRONMENT AND BIOREMEDIATION
Edited by : Dr. Alka Chauhan; Dr. Ashok K. Rathoure & Dr. Raaz K Maheshwari
Edition : 2017
ISBN : 978-93-5056-856-9
Published by : Discovery Publishing House Pvt. Ltd., New Delhi (India)

6 Vermicompost
A Potential Bio-fertilizer

BL Jat[1]
Priyanka Bishnoi[2]
Raaz K Maheshwari[2]

ABSTRACT

For sustainable development in agriculture, it is essential to improve the soil organic carbon status that has deteriorated under intensive chemical farming. Among the several bio-fertilizers, farmers may use vermicompost on account of its simple preparation technology, favourable climatic support and easy availability of raw materials. Farmers can use vermicompost by mixing with chemical fertilizers almost in every agro production for increasing the effectiveness of the chemical fertilizers. It performs better in floriculture, horticulture, house plants, potting soil, fruit and vegetable productions. However, for any application, better result can be obtained if farmers apply the estimated amount after knowing its per cent of organic carbon and nitrogen (C : N) ratio.

Keywords: Chemicals; Farming; Fauna; Agro-ecosystem; Eisenia foetida; Eudrilus Eugenia; NPK; Organic materials.

INTRODUCTION

It is true that we have alleviated hunger from the world by introducing the components of 'Green Revolution' technologies *viz;* high yielding varieties (HYV) seeds, fertilizers, pesticides and farm machineries. India's food production has also improved significantly due to successful implementation of this technology since mid 1960's. in spite of this remarkable achievement, recently, farmers are facing problems in harvesting crops for stagnant

1. Department of Botany, Dayanand College, MDSU, Ajmer, Rajasthan.
2. Department of Chemistry, SBRM Government PG College, Nagaur, Rajasthan.

productivity and associated hazards of the technology as it requires a huge amount of chemical fertilizer, pesticide, insecticide and even water, chemicals accumulate gradually into the soil that causes the deterioration of soil fertility and environmental quality. A review of over 300 published reports showed that most of the environmental indicators which have decreasing trends are floral diversity, faunal diversity, habital diversity, landscape, soil organic matter, soil biological activity, soil structure, soil erosion, nitrate leaching, pesticide residue, CO_2, N_2O, CH_4, NH_3, nutrient use, water use and energy use. However, organic farming system performed significantly better in all the above factors and performed worse in none (Stolze, *et al.* 2000). For eradicating these ill effects of modern agriculture, peasants are considering growing food without chemical fertilizers and pesticides throughout the world. Meanwhile, the global organic-food market has already crossed 31 billion US $ by 2005. Though the production cost in the organic farming is slightly higher, yet it will be sustainable alternative on account of its biological, ecological and environmental supportive natural approaches. Government of India has already constituted a 'Task Force' to popularise the organic farming. According to the opinion of the task force, the application of the organic manure is the only option to improve the soil organic carbon for sustenance of soil quality and future agricultural productivity (Prasad, 2005).

Vermicompost as A Bio-fertilizer

Efforts are required to grow crops and vegetables by using organic manure, which may come from microbial fertilizer, bio-fertilizer and also vermicompost. Among these, use of vermincompost as an organic manure is important, because of its ability to release nutrients slowly and the technology for its preparation being very simple. In rural Bengal, traditional concept of using bio-fertilizer in agriculture has become completely absent in modern approach of farming on account of inputs of machineries and rejection to consider animal husbandry as a component of farm management. Nevertheless, as a tropical zone, the climate is suitable for composing huge green manure, bio-solids, crop residues and even food processing wastes. Our attitude of frequent and injudicious use of chemical fertilizers, pesticides and herbicide in farm practices has destroyed the soil micro, meso and macro fauna (Ali, *et al.* 2006). Even earthworms that decompose the agricultural wastes naturally and supply organic manure in the form of cast, have also left from our fields now. Hence, the percentage of organic carbon in the harvested soil gradually decreases to such a minimum level that hampers the exchange of plant macronutrients. At this juncture we can reintroduce the earthworms into our field by preparing and using vermicompost as a source of bio-fertilizer. It is biologically active mound containing thousands of bacteria, enzymes, remnants of plant material formed during the breakdown of organic matter. It also provides many binding sites for plant nutrients *e.g.*, calcium, iron, potassium, sulphur and phosphorus. It dissolves slowly rather than allowing immediate nutrient leaching. It has excellent soil structure, porosity, aeration and water retention capabilities, which can insulate plant roots from extreme temperatures, reduce erosion and control weeds (Appelhof, 1982).

Local Efforts

Earthworms play a variety of important roles in agro-ecosystem. Their feeding and burrowing activities ingest organic matter into the soil. They can easily decompose agricultural wastes, several domestic wastes, even any green plant material. So they can also be used to manage the agricultural waste, municipal solid waste, livestock manure and wastewater for its higher consumption and decomposition abilities. There are 2,200 earthworms species found all over the world. Therefore, the selection of earthworm species is important in terms of their breeding rate and cast formation ability. Out of these species two important species namely: *Eisenia foetida* and *Eudrilus eugenia* are generally considered for vermicomposting, because of their breeding and cast formation rate (Annexure-IA). The technology for preparing vermicompost is so simple that it can be imparted to the farmers knowledge for their own purposes (Lee, 1985). Now-a-days several standard projects for preparing vermicompost are available in CAPART (Council of Advancement of Peoples Action and Rural Technology), New Delhi and elsewhere. In west Bengal, this technical know-how is currently available from following centres: *(i)* Farmers Training Institute, Kalayani, *(ii)* Matar-Benay Trust, Hatsimul, Burdwan, *(iii)* Nimpith, Narendrapur, South 24-Paragana and *(iv)* Vishva-Bharti, Santiniketan. In spite of this readily available managing technology, the use of vermicompost as a bio-fertilizer in agriculture is not so familiar to our farmers community. Therefore, farmers need a motivation for using vermicompost as a bio-fertilizer to increase the soil organic matter (SOM) and also to provide binding sites for the inorganic plant nutrients. A small group of activists is engaged in the preparation of vermicompost and motivation work for the last five years under Paschim Banga Vigyan Mancha at Matar-Benay Trust campus, Burdwan, West Bengal.

Chemical Quality and Precautions

Casting contain 5× the available nitrogen, 7× the available potash and 5.5× more calcium than that found in 15 cm of good top soil. Moreover, vermicomposting adds valuable attributes *viz;* water retention, texture, nutrient availability and an ability to fight soil-borne plant diseases like root rotten (Edwards, 1995). In spite of these advantages, the use of vermicompost either in pure or mixed with chemical fertilizer as a farm manure, is still rare because the technology has not gone into farmers' concept. Aforesaid activists group in 'Matar-Benay Trust' campus has been experimenting the use of vermicompost in different crop production for the last eight years. Out of

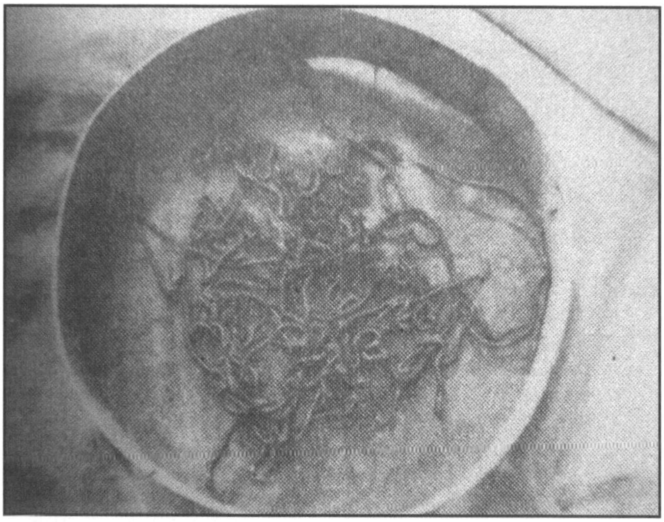

curiosity, eight different vermicopmost samples were collected from different farmers, farmers' co-operative and NGOs and estimated its percentage of carbon content and NPK values in *'Shibaprasad Bandyopadhayay Maati Parikshagar'* (soil laboratory) at Matar-Benay trust campus, Hatsimul, Burdwan, West Bengal. The results obtained are shown in the Table 6.1 below.

Table 6.1: Percentage of different macronutrients in eight Vermicompost samples

Sample	pH	% of Organic Carbon	% of Nitrogen	% of P_2O_5	% of K_2O
1.	6.60	3.83	0.40	0.074	0.301
2.	6.56	3.25	0.33	0.220	0.220
3.	6.54	2.66	0.27	0.160	0.280
4.	-	13.06	1.41	1.502	0.258
5.	7.22	15.30	1.60	0.405	0.960
6.	8.75	6.85	0.68	0.040	1.400
7.	8.53	3.64	0.36	0.100	0.570
8.	6.98	2.78	0.30	0.095	0.210

Table 6.1 reflects the estimated results of eight different vermicompost samples which show a very high variation of carbon content (2.66 to 15.3%) and also the percentage of nitrogen content in the vermicompost sample, which is obvious. But the problem is whether farmers know the percentage of carbon content and C : N ratio of the used vermicompost sample or not. Therefore, the nutrient content, particularly the C : N ratio of each vermicompost sample should be measured before applying it into the field even if the vermicompost is indigenously prepared by the farmers themselves.

Values of C : N ratio can be improved by using different animal manure as a feeding material to the earthworms, instead of using cow-dung only. In order to project this idea, some relevant data (Tisdale, *et al.* 1995) regarding the animal manure are shown in the Table 6.2.

Table 6.2: Approximate dry matter and fertilizer nutrient composition of various types of animal manure

Type of Livestock	% of Dry Matter	Nutrient (kg/tonne in Raw Waste)			
		NH_4-N	Total-N	P_2O_5	K_2O
Swine	18	2.72	4.54	4.08	3.63
Beef cattle	15	1.81	4.99	3.18	4.54
Dairy cattle	18	1.81	4.08	1.81	4.54
Poultry	35	11.79	14.87	21.77	15.42

Table 6.2 indicates that certainly the per cent carbon content, C : N ratio and NPK values of the vermicast will be higher by using the poultry litter as feeding material. This trend of higher NPK values is also reflected in the vermicast NPK values (Table 6.1) intensive care is required for protecting the vermicompost pit from ant, birds, rat and direct sunlight. Shortly a large number of vermicompost products are coming into market packed within beautiful containers without mentioning the percentage of organic matter and C : N ratio. Whereas farmers are now being advised to use vermicast as an organic manure to increase the effectiveness of the chemical fertilizer also, hence for the optimum benefit from the organic manure, information regarding bio-fertilizer should be authenticated or verified thoroughly.

Vermicompost Application

It has been established that the earthworms are ore one of the most useful and active agents in introducing suitable chemical, physical and microbiological changes in the soil, thereby directly increasing the fertility of the soil (Joshi and Kelkar, 1951). Vermicompost should be used, after checking the nutrient content and mixing with the chemical fertilizers in suitable proportions. Institute of National Organic Agriculture (INORA) has applied the vermicompost in different proportions with chemical fertilizer in sugarcane production at different places of Maharastra, Gujarat, and Karnataka. It has been established that 1 : ! vermicompost and chemical fertilizer is most effective in sugarcane production. In a certain region of New Zealand, grass production became doubled after introducing some European earthworm species. Researchers of Mississippi State University have shown that the mixture casting with peat moss at the ratio of 1 : 1, 2 : 1 and 3 : 1 performed better in all growth parameters of Marigold production. They have also shown that earthworm casting increases the germination rate in seeding development of cucumber nicely (Annexure-IB).

In Bangalore, earthworms successfully decomposed residual from sugar factory and turned them into a soil nutrient which enabled 50 per cent reduction in the use of chemical fertilizer. Earthworm castings are the best imaginable potting soil for houseplant as well as gardening and farming. It can also be used as a planting soil for trees, vegetables, shrubs and flowers (Gaddie and Douglas, 1975). It was also observed at the 'Matar-Benay' Trust campus that vermicompost performed better in flowers, vegetables, fruits and nursery productions. It can also be used, by mixing with chemical fertilizers, in any agro-production for raising the effectiveness of the chemical fertilizer.

Anexure-IA

These worms can consume any organic waste to an amount of even 2-5× their body weight. After using only 5-10 per cent of the ingested materials for their growth, they excrete the rest amount in mucous coated form as worm cast. Vermicomposting, is therefore, the technology of composting wide ranges of organic wastes with the help of epigeic group of earthworms which generally resdes in the soil surface and feeds upon various organic materials (Gaur and Singh, 1995).

Anexure-IB

While studying occurrence of beneficial microorganisms on cowdung under conventionally decomposed and vermicomposed condition, it was observed that vermicompost contain considerably higher concentration of phosphate stabilizing bacteria as well as nitrogen fixing bacteria. Since existing microbial population generally fails to remain active in tropical soils due to lack of energy required for their activity, regular application of these vermicompost wastes is likely to improve the biological properties in addition to its positive effects on physic-chemical condition of the soil to their hgher productivity level (Bhattacharya and Chattopadhyay, 2002).

REFERENCES

Ali, S.A., Khan, I. and Ali, A.S. (2006). *Science Reporter,* 43, No. 1, pp. 28-30.

Applehof, M. (1982). *Worms Eat My Garbage,* pp. 68.

Bhattacharya, S.S. and Chattopadhyay, G.N. (2002). *J. Env. Quality,* 31, pp. 2116-2119.

Edwards, C.A. (1995). *Bio Cycle,* 36, pp. 56-58.

Gaddie, R.E. and Douglas, D.E. (1975). *Scientific Earthworm Farming,* 1, pp. 175.

Gaur, A.C. and singh, G. (1995). *In Tandon, HLS (ed) Recycling of Waste in Agriculture,* F.D.C.O. pp. 31-47.

Joshi, N.V. And Kelkar. B. (1951). *Ind. J. Agrl. Sci.,* 22, pp. 189-196.

Lee, K.E. (1985). *Earthworms, Their Ecology and Relationship with Soils and Land Use,* New York : Academic Press.

Prasad, R. (2005). *Current Sci.,*89, pp. 252-254.

Samanta, T. (2008). *Everyman's Science,* Vol. XLIII, No. 3, pp. '73-177.

Stolze, M., Piorr, A., Haring, A. and Dabbert, S. (2000). *Organic Farming In Europe : Economics and Policy,* University of Hohenheim, Hohenheim ,Germany.

Tisdale, S.L., Nelson, W.L. Beaton, J.D. and Havlin, J.L. (1995). *Soil Fertility and Fertilizers,* 5th Editon, pp. 598, Prentice Hall of India Pvt. Ltd., New Delhi.

Page 102-114

MICROBIAL ENVIRONMENT AND BIOREMEDIATION
Edited by : Dr. Alka Chauhan; Dr. Ashok K. Rathoure & Dr. Raaz K Maheshwari
Edition : 2017
ISBN : 978-93-5056-856-9
Published by : Discovery Publishing House Pvt. Ltd., New Delhi (India)

7

Food Antioxidants
Sources Mechanism and its Impact on Health

Priyadarshini[1]
Ravindra Singh[2]
Priyanka Shukla[3]

ABSTRACT

An antioxidant is a molecule stable enough to donate an electron to a rampaging free radical and neutralize it, thus reducing its capacity to damage. Free radicals are generated by our body by various endogenous systems, exposure to different physiochemical conditions or pathological states. Free radicals thus adversely alter lipids, proteins, and DNA and trigger a number of human diseases. Hence application of external source of antioxidants can assist in coping this oxidative stress. The plant sources are rich of antioxidants, phyto-constituents are capable to terminate free radical reactions and prevent our body from oxidative damage. Vegetables and fruits are also important sources of antioxidant substances. Different phyto-constituents and herbal product which are safer then synthetic medicine and beneficial in the treatment of diseases caused by free radicals, it also protect the body by prevent the free radicals to cause tissue injury. Synthetic antioxidants such as: butylated hydroxyl toluene and butylated hydroxyl anisole have recently been reported to be dangerous for human health. Thus, the search for effective, nontoxic natural compounds with anti oxidative activity has been intensified in recent years.

1. Department of Food and Agriculture Engg., Faculty of Engg. and Technology M.G.C.G.V Chitrakoot, Satna (M.P.) India - 485 780.
2. (H.O.D) Department of Biological Sciences, Faculty of Science and Environment M.G.C.G.V Chitrakoot, Satna (M.P.) India - 485 780.
3. Department of Food and Agriculture Engg., Faculty of Engg. and Technology M.G.C.G.V Chitrakoot, Satna (M.P.) India - 485 780.

INTRODUCTION

Antioxidants are substances that help prevent certain types of cell damage, especially those caused by oxidation. An 'antioxidant' is actually not a substance; it's a behaviour. Any compound that can donate electrons and counteract free radicals has antioxidant properties. When certain types of oxygen molecules are allowed to travel freely in the body they cause what is known as oxidative damage which is the formation of free radicals. Free radicals are very dangerous to the body's tissues and have been connected to cancer and premature aging. The body uses antioxidants to prevent itself from the damage caused by oxygen. Oxidative damage plays a major role in disease today and has been linked to health conditions like: heart disease, cancer and dementia.

Antioxidants are any substance that delay or inhibits oxidative damage to a target molecule. At a time one antioxidant molecule can react with single free radicals and are capable to neutralize free radicals by donating one of their own electrons, ending the carbon-stealing reaction. Antioxidants prevent cell and tissue damage as they act as scavenger. Cell produce defense against excessive free radicals by their preventative mechanisms, repair mechanisms, physical defenses and antioxidant defenses (Jacob R.A. 1995).

To mitigate the harmful effect of free radicals, aerobic cells have developed antioxidant defense mechanisms. A biological antioxidant may be defined as a substance that significantly delay oxidation of a substrate. Antioxidants may be considered as the scavenger of free radicals.

Classification of Antioxidants

A variety of components act against free radicals to neutralize them from both endogenous and exogenous in origin. These include:

- Endogenous enzymatic antioxidants.
- Non-enzymatic, metabolic and nutrient antioxidants.
- Metal binding proteins like: ferritin, lactoferrin, albumin and ceruloplasmin.
- Phyto-constituents and phytonutrients.

The body produces different antioxidants (endogenous antioxidants) to neutralize free radicals and protect the body from different disease leads by the tissue injury. Exogenous antioxidants are externally supply to the body through food also plays important role to protect the body.

There are different way of classifying the antioxidants

(A) Antioxidants in Relation to Lipid per Oxidation

1. *Preventive antioxidants*: Are those that will block the initial production of free radicals and protect the cell *e.g.*, catalase, glutathione peroxidase.
2. *Chain breaking antioxidants*: Are those that inhibit the propagative phase of lipid per oxidation *e.g.*, superoxide dismutase, vitamin E and uric acid.

(B) Antioxidant According to their Location

1. *Plasma antioxidants*: Are those generally present in plasma of cell *e.g.*, β carotene, ascorbic acid, bilirubin, uric acid, ceruloplasmin and transferin.
2. *Cell membrane antioxidants*: Are those generally present in cell membrane *e.g.*, α tocopherol.
3. *Intracellular antioxidants*: Are those generally present in intracellular space in cell *e.g.*, superoxide dismutase, catalase, glutathione peroxidase.

(C) Antioxidant According to their Nature and Action

The body's internal free radical fighters, known as endogenous scavengers, are enzymes that gobble up free radicals, converting them into harmless molecules. Food and plants donate a police force of micro-nutrients called exogenous scavengers. The body has developed several endogenous antioxidant defense systems classified into two groups such as:

1. *Enzymatic antioxidants*: The body's internal free radical fighters, known as endogenous scavengers, are enzymes that gobble up free radicals, converting them into harmless molecules. The enzymatic defense system includes different endogenous enzymes like: superoxide dismutase, catalase, glutathione peroxidase, glutathione reductase.

(*a*) Superoxide dismutase is an important endogenous antioxidant enzyme act as the first line defense system to protect cells from the injurious effect of superoxide. It converts superoxide (O_2^-) to hydrogen peroxide and O_2.

$$O_2 + O_2 + 2H^+ \xrightarrow{\text{superoxide dismutase}} H_2O_2 + O_2$$

(*b*) Catalase metabolized the hydrogen peroxide produced by superoxide dismutase.

$$2\,H_2O_2 \xrightarrow{\text{catalase}} 2H_2O + O_2$$

(*c*) *Glutathione peroxidase:* It detoxifies the H_2O_2 to H_2O, while reduced glutathione (G-SH) is converted to oxidized glutathione (GS-SG). The reduced glutathione is regenerated by the enzyme glutathione reeducate utilizing NADPH. The hexose monophosphate shunt is the major source of NADPH.

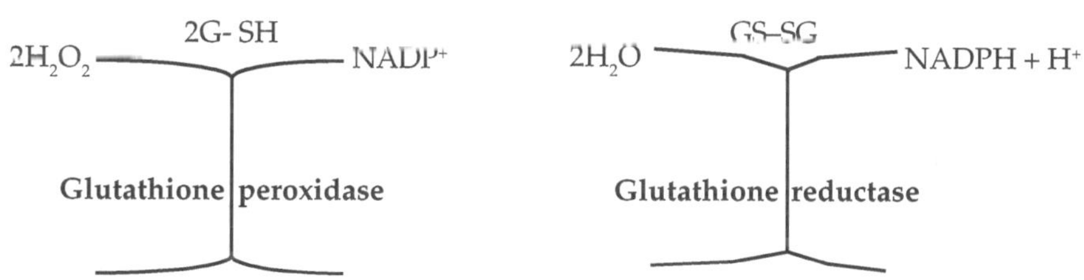

2. *Non-enzymatic:* Vitamins C and E are non-enzymatic endogenous antioxidant also exists within normal cells and react with free radicals to form radicals themselves which are less reactive than the radicals. They break radical chain reactions by trapping peroxyl and other reactive radicals 16,20,25. This included vitamin E, vitamin C and reduced glutathione (GSH) Non-enzymatic antioxidants also can be divided into metabolic antioxidants and nutrient antioxidants.

(A) *Nutrient antioxidants:* These are belonging to exogenous antioxidants, which cannot be produced in the body but provided through diet or supplements *viz;* trace metals (selenium, manganese, zinc), flavonoids, omega-3 and omega-6 fatty acids etc. Vitamin E and C are the non enzymatic antioxidants exist within normal cells as well as they can be supplied through diet. The human body naturally produces antioxidants but the process is not 100 per cent effective in case of overwhelming production of free radicals and that effectiveness also declines with age (Sies H., 1991 and Goldfarb A.H. 1993).

These following are the food source (nutrient antioxidants) of antioxidants:

(a) *Vitamin C:* It is a water-soluble vitamin found in all body fluids, so it may be one of our first lines of defense. This powerful antioxidant cannot be stored by the body, so it's important to get some regularly-not a difficult task if you eat fruits and vegetables. Important sources include: citrus fruits, green peppers, broccoli, green leafy vegetables, strawberries, raw cabbage, and potatoes.

(b) *Vitamin E:* A fat-soluble vitamin that can be stored with fat in the liver and other tissues, vitamin E (tocopherols, tocotrienols) is promoted for a range of purposes-from delaying aging to healing sunburn. While it's not a miracle worker, it's another powerful antioxidant. Important sources include: wheat germ, nuts, seeds, whole grains, green leafy vegetables, vegetable oil, and fish-liver oil.

(c) *Beta-carotene:* Beta-carotene (lycopene, carotenes) protects dark green, yellow and orange vegetables and fruits from solar radiation damage. It is thought that it plays a similar role in the body. Carrots, squash, broccoli, sweet potatoes, tomatoes, kale, collards, cantaloupe, peaches, and apricots are particularly rich sources of beta-carotene.

(d) *Selenium:* Selenium probably interacts with every nutrient that affects the antioxidant balance of the cell. This mineral is thought to help fight cell damage by oxygen-derived compounds and thus may help protect against cancer. It is best to get selenium through foods, as large doses of the supplement form can be toxic. Good food sources include: fish, shellfish, red meat, grains, eggs, chicken, and garlic. Vegetables can also be a good source if grown in selenium-rich soils.

(e) *Polyphenol antioxidants:* These are characterized by the presence of several phenol functional groups. In human health these compounds, are thought to be instrumental in combating oxidative stress. The main source of poly phenol antioxidants is nutritional, since they are found in a wide array of phyto nutrient-bearing foods. For example, most legumes; fruits such as: apples, blackberries, cantaloupe, cherries, cranberries, grapes, pears, plums, raspberries, and strawberries; and vegetables such as: broccoli, cabbage, celery, onion, and parsley are rich in poly phenol antioxidants. Red wine, chocolate, green tea, olive oil, bee pollen, and many grains are alternative sources.

(f) *Glutathione:* These protects cells from toxins such as: free radicals. The human body produces glutathione from the synthesis of three key amino acids–cysteine, glycine, and glutamic acid. Food sources with the highest amounts of naturally occurring glutathione include: asparagus, avocado, grapefruit, squash, potato, cantaloupe, peach, zucchini, spinach, broccoli, watermelon, and strawberries. Fish, meat, and foods which yield sulfur containing amino acids (*e.g.*, eggs) are the preferred sources for maintaining and increasing bodily glutathione levels. Supplemental glutathione is only available in one active form, GSH.

(g) *Peroxidase:* An enzyme occurring especially in plants, milk, and leukocytes and consisting of a protein complex with hematin groups that catalyzes the oxidation of various substances. Food sources of peroxidase include horseradishm root, soybean, mango fruit, and turnip.

(h) *Cysteine:* Cysteine is an important free radical antioxidant in cellular systems. It blocks oxidants of the free radical type that may be engaged in certain forms of cellular pathology, including: aging, carcinogenesis, diabetes mellitus, and the development of heart disease. Cysteine is incorporated in the cellular glutathione, which works along with vitamin E to protect cells against free radical oxidant damage.

(i) *Flavonoids:* Flavonoids promote antioxidant activity, cellular health and normal tisse growth and renewal throughout the body. They also work with vitamin C to reduce oxidative stress for the water based portion of the cell and may slow down some of the effects of aging. There are more than 4,000 unique flavonoids and they are most effective when several types are consumed together. Food sources include: cranberries, kale, beets, berries, red and black grapes, oranges, lemons, grapefruits, and green tea.

Table 7.1: Nutrient antioxidants and their dietary sources

Antioxidants	Dietary Sources
Vitamin E (tocopherol)	Unprocessed vegetable oils (cotton seed oil, peanut oil, sunflower oil,) whole grains, leafy vegetables, legumes.
Vitamin C Ascorbic acid	Citrus fruits (orange, lemon, grapes), goose berry (amla), guava, green vegetables (cabbage, spinach), cacliflower, melons.
β carotene (provitamin A)	Carrot, green fruits and vegetables , turnip, spinach and apricots.
Lycopene	Tomato and their products (tomato sauce), papaya, pink guava, water melon.
Leutein and zeaxanthin	Egg yolk, fruit, green vegetables (cabbage, spinach), corn, green peas.
Selenium	Sea foods, meat, organ meats, whole grain.
α-Lipoic acid	Red meat, liver, yeast.
Co enzyme Q_{10}	Organ meats (best heart), beef, chicken.
N-Acetylecystein	Available as supplement or drug.
Proanthocyanidins	Grape seeds.
Catechins	Green tea.
Curcuminoids	Turmeric.
Quercetin	Onions, red wine, green tea.

(*B*) *Metabolic antioxidants:* Are the endogenous antioxidants, which produced by metabolism in the body like: lipoid acid, glutathione, L-ariginine, coenzyme Q_{10}, melatonin, uric acid, bilirubin, metal-chelating proteins, transferring etc. (Droge W, 2006).

(*a*) *Glutathione:* The reduced glutathione (GSH) play a key role in the biological antioxidants enzyme system. The reduced glutathione (GSH) gets regenerated from the oxidized glutathione (GS-SG) through the participation of glutathione reductase and NADPH. It is suggested that the ability to synthesize GSH decrease as age advances and this has been implicated in certain disease *e.g.*, cataract.

(*b*) *Uric acid:* It is a strong scavenger of singlet oxygen ($^1O_2$) and OH^- radicals.

(*c*) *Ceruloplasmin:* Inhibit the iron and copper dependent lipid peroxidation.

(*d*) *Transferrin:* It binds to iron and prevents iron catalyzed free radical formation.

(e) *Albumin:* Can scavange the 'free radicals' formed on its surface.

(f) *Bilirubin:* This protects the albumin bound free fatty acid from peroxidation.

(g) *Haptoglobin:* Binds to free hemoglobin and prevents the acceleration of lipid peroxidation.

Food Sources of Antioxidants

Some of the better food sources of antioxidants are as following:

- *Berries*: Blueberries, blackberries, raspberries, strawberries and cranberries.
- *Beans*: Small red beans and kidney, pinto and black beans.
- *Fruits*: Many apple varieties (with peels), avocados, cherries, green and red pears, fresh or dried plums, pineapple, oranges, and kiwi.
- *Vegetables*: Artichokes, spinach, red cabbage, red and white potatoes (with peels), sweet potatoes and broccoli.
- *Beverages*: Green tea, coffee, red wine and many fruit juices.
- *Nuts*: Walnuts, pistachios, pecans, hazelnuts and almonds.
- *Herbs*: Ground cloves, cinnamon or ginger, dried oregano leaf and turmeric powder.
- *Grains*: Oat-based products.
- *Dessert*: Dark chocolate.

Following are the phytochemicals found in food

- Alkaloids - Flavanones.
- Coumarins - Stilbenes.
- Lignans - Lignin.
- Phenolic Acids - Triterpenoid.
- Phytosterols - Tannins.
- Carotenes and xanthophylls - Isoflavones.
- Volatile and essential oil Anthocyanins.
- Flavan-3-ols - Flavones.
- Flavonols.

Antioxidants may exert their activity by several mechanisms, like by suppressing the production of active species by reducing hydro peroxides and H2O2, by sequestering metal ions, termination of chain reaction by scavenging active free radicals and also caused repairing and/or clearing damage of cell. Biosynthesis of other antioxidants or defense enzymes also induced by some antioxidants. Therefore antioxidant synthesized in body or supplied from outside like phyto constituents plays important role to protect the body from free radical induced injury.

Mechanism of Free Radicals

Free radicals are atoms or groups of atoms with an odd (unpaired) number of electrons in its outermost atomic or molecular orbital, are capable of independent existence and can be *formed* when oxygen interacts with certain molecules. Once *formed* these highly reactive *radicals* can start a chain reaction. These are dangerous substances produced in the body along with toxins and wastes which are formed during the normal metabolic process of the body. Overproduction of the free radicals can responsible for tissue injury (Halliwell B. *et al.* 1999). Many radicals are unstable and highly reactive. They can either donate an electron to or accept an electron from other molecules, therefore behaving as oxidants or reductants. The most important oxygen-containing free radicals in many disease states are hydroxyl radical, superoxide anion radical, hydrogen peroxide, oxygen singlet, hypochlorite, nitric oxide radical, and per oxynitrite radical. These are highly reactive species, capable in the nucleus, and in the membranes of cells of damaging biologically relevant molecules such as: DNA, proteins, carbohydrates, and lipids. Free radicals attack important macromolecules leading to cell damage and homeostatic disruption. Targets of free radicals include all kinds of molecules in the body. Among them, lipids, nucleic acids, and proteins are the major targets.

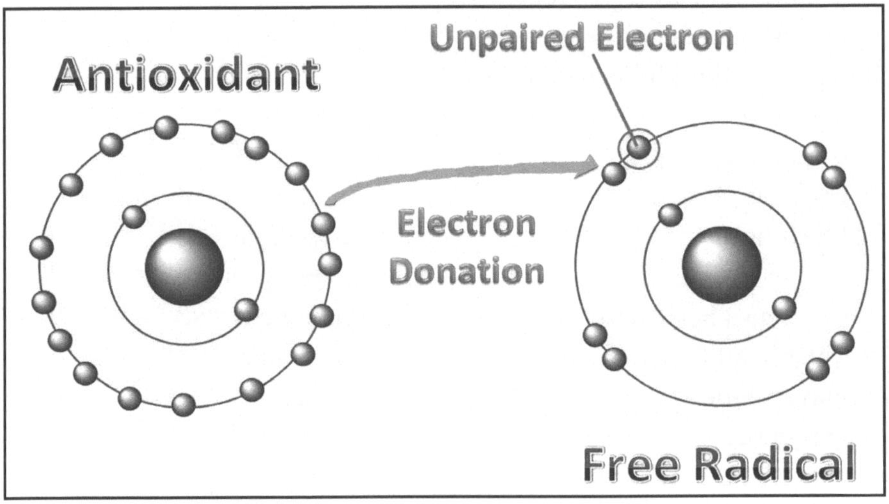

Source : www.googleimage.com

Many cell component like cell membrane (made of unsaturated fatty acid) RNA, DNA and protein enzymes are susceptible to oxidative damage. *Free radicals* can *cause damage* to parts of *cells* such as: proteins, DNA, and *cell* membranes by stealing their electrons through a process called oxidation. This is why *free radical damage* is also called 'oxidative *damage*.' Environmental agents also initiate free radical generation leads different complication in body.

The toxicity of lead, pesticides, cadmium, ionizing radiation, alcohol, cigarette smoke, UV light and pollution may all be due to their free radical initiating capability (Langseth L, 1996 and Davies KJA, 1991). Anti-oxidants are substances capable to mop up free radicals and prevent them from causing cell damage. Free radicals are responsible for causing a number of health problems which include cancer, aging, heart diseases and gastric problems etc. Antioxidants cause protective effect by neutralizing free radicals, which are toxic byproducts of natural cell metabolism. The human body naturally produces antioxidants but the process is not 100 per cent effective in case of overwhelming production of free radicals and that effectiveness also declines with age.

Sources of Free Radicals

Free radicals can be formed from both endogenous and exogenous substances. They are continuously forming in cell and environment. Different sources of free radicals are as follows: Some internally generated sources of free radicals are:

- Mitochondria.
- Xanthine oxidase.
- Peroxisomes.
- Inflammation.
- Phagocytosis.
- Arachidonate pathways.
- Exercise.
- Ischemia/reperfusion injury.

Some externally generated sources of free radicals are:

- Cigarette smoke.
- Environmental pollutants.
- Radiation.
- Certain drugs, pesticides.
- Industrial solvents.
- Ozone.

Free Radical Reactions

Free radicals generally involved in chain reactions, a series of reactions leads to regenerates a radical that can begin a new cycle of reactions. Free radical reactions take three distinct identifiable steps.

- *Initiation step: (formation of radicals)*: In this phase hydrogen atoms (H) are removed from polyunsaturated fatty acid (RH) by hydroxyl radical.

$$RH + OH^{-} \longrightarrow R^{-} + H_2O$$

- *Propagation step:* In this step required free radical is regenerated repeatedly as a result of chain reaction, which would take the reaction to completion. In this the fatty acid radicals ($R^·$) takes up oxygen form peroxy radical ($ROO^·$). This peroxy radical ($ROO^·$) in turn can remove H- atom from another PUFA (RH) to form lipid hydro peroxide (ROOH).

$$R^· + O_2 \longrightarrow ROO^·$$

$$ROO^· + RH \longrightarrow ROOH + R^·$$

The hydro peroxide are capable of further stimulating lipid peroxidation as they can form alkoxy ($RO^·$) and peroxyl ($ROO^·$) radicals.

$$2\,ROOH \xrightarrow{Fe, Cu} RO^· + ROO^· + \text{aldehyde s}$$

- *Termination step: (destruction of radicals):* Lipid peroxidation proceeds as a chain reaction until the available PUFA gets oxidized.

Free Radicals and Bio-molecules

Free radicals are highly reactive and are capable of damaging all type of bio molecules lipid, protein, carbohydrates and nucleic acids.

1. *Protein*: Free radicals cause oxidation of sulfhydryl groups, and modification of certain amino acids (*e.g.*, tryptophan, cysteine, histidine, tyrosine). They may damage the protein by fragmentation, cross linking and aggregation. So result in the loss of biological activity of protein.
2. *Lipids:* Polyunsaturated fatty acids (PUFA) are highly susceptible to damage by free radicals.
3. *Carbohydrates:* The oxidation of monosaccharides (*e.g.*, glucose) can produce H_2O_2 and oxoaldehydes at certain pH (physiological pH). The linkage of carbohydrates to protein increases the susceptibility of protein to the attack by free radicals.
4. *Nucleic acid:* Free radical may cause DNA strands breaks, fragmentation of base and deoxyribose. Such damage may be associated with cytotoxicity and mutation.

Mechanism of Action for Antioxidants

Free radicals occur continuously in all cells as part of normal function. Oxygen free radicals are detrimental to the integrity of biological tissue and mediate their injury. The mechanism of damage involves lipid per oxidation, which destroys cell structures, lipids, proteins and nucleic acids. They causes damage to cell membranes with the release of intracellular components, leading to further tissue damage (Poli G. *et al.* 2004 and Halliwell B, 1997).

Two principle mechanisms of action have been proposed for antioxidants.

1. The first is a chain-breaking mechanism by which the primary antioxidant donates an electron to the free radical present in the systems.

2. The second mechanism involves removal of reactive nitrogen species initiators (secondary antioxidants) by quenching chain-initiating catalyst. Antioxidants may exert their effect on biological systems by different mechanisms including: electron donation, metal ion chelation, co-antioxidants, or by gene expression regulation.

Diseases Occurs due to Production of Free Radicals in Body

When free radicals overrun the body and cause extensive damage-dramatically accelerates the aging process. It's also directly responsible for a host of health problems, some of which are listed below.

- AIDS.
- Alzheimer's disease.
- Arrhythmia (abnormal heartbeat).
- Atherosclerosis (hardening and clogging of the arteries).
- Autoimmune disease (destruction of healthy tissues by immune cells).
- Cancer.
- Cataracts.
- Degenerative retinal damage.
- Diabetes.
- Emphysema.
- Heart attack.
- Lupus.
- Macular degeneration (cell breakdown in the retina that leads to vision loss).
- Multiple sclerosis.
- Pancreatitis (inflammation of the pancreas).
- Respiratory disease.
- Male infertility.
- Parkinson's disease.
- Rheumatoid arthritis.
- Cardiovascular diseases (CHD).
- Other diesease.

Benefits

Some benefits of consuming antioxidant rich foods include:

- Slower aging.
- *Healthy glowing skin*: When skin is exposed to high levels of ultraviolet light, photo-oxidative damage is induced by the formation of different types of reactive species of oxygen, including singlet oxygen, superoxide radicals, and peroxide radicals. These forms of reactive oxygen damage cellular lipids, proteins, and DNA, and they are considered to be the primary contributors to erythema (sunburn), premature aging of the skin, photodermatoses, and skin cancers.

- Reduced cancer risk.
- Detoxification support.
- Longer life span.

Recommonded daily Allowances

There is no RDA or Daily Value set for antioxidants. The levels of antioxidants is evaluated by ORAC Score (oxygen radical absorption capacity) and tests the power of a plant to absorb and eliminate free radicals. These measurements were developed by the National Institute of Aging and are based on 100 grams of each food or herb.

Conclusion

Free radicals damage contributes to many chronic health problems such as: cardiovascular and inflammatory disease, cataract, and cancer. Antioxidants prevent free radical induced tissue damage by preventing the formation of radicals, scavenging them, or by promoting their decomposition. Antioxidants are thought to have a role in preventing the disease. Therefore from a public health perspective it is premature to make recommendations regarding antioxidant supplements and disease prevention.

REFERENCES

Ali A.T.M.M., Al-Swayeh O.A., Al-Rashed R.S., Al - Mofleh I.A., Al-Dohayan AD, and Al-Tuwaijri A.S. (1996). Role of Oxygen-derived Free Radicals on Gastric mucosal injury Induced by ischemia-reperfusion, *The Saudi Journal of Gastroenterology*, 2, pp. 19-28.

Bagchi K. and Puri S. (1998). Free Radicals and Antioxidants in Health and Disease, *Eastern Mediterranean Health Journal*, 4, pp. 350-360.

Cadenas E. (1989). Biochemistry of Oxygen Toxicity, *Annual Review of Biochemistry*, 58, pp. 79-110.

Cheeseman K.H. and Slater T.F. (1993). An Introduction to Free Radicals Chemistry. *Br Med Bull.*, 49, pp. 481-93.

Davies K.J.A. (1991). Oxidative Damage and Repair: Chemical, Biological and Medical Aspects, Pergamon, Oxford.

Droge, W. (2002). Free Radicals in the Physiological Control of Cell Function, *Physiological Reviews*, 82, 47-95.

Goldfarb A.H. (1993). Antioxidants: Role of Supplementation to Prevent Exercise-Induced Oxidative Stress, Medicine and Science in Sports and Exercise, 25, 232- 236.

Halliwell B,. (1997). Antioxidants and Human Diseases: A General Introduction, Nutrition Reviews, 55, pp. 44-52.

Jacob, R.A. (1995). The Integrated Antioxidant System, Nutrition Research, 15, pp. 755-766.

Krinsky N.I. (1992). Mechanism of Action of Biological Antioxidants. *Proc Soc Exp Biol Med.*, 200: 248-54.

Nagendrappa C.G. (2005). An Appreciation of Free Radical Chemistry - 3, Free Radicals in Diseases and Health, Resonance, 10, 65-73.

Pham-Huy L.A. He H. and Pham-Huy C. (2008). Free Radicals, Antioxidants in Disease and Health, *International Journal of Biomedical Science*, 4, pp. 89-96.

Poli G., Leonarduzzi G., Biasi F. and Chiarpotto E. (2004). Oxidative Stress and cell Signaling, Current Medicinal Chemistry, 11, pp. 1163-1182.

Rice-Evans C.A. and Diplock A.T. (1993). Current Status of Antioxidant Therapy. *Free Radic Biol Med.*, 15, pp. 77-96.

Sies H. (1991). Oxidative Stress: Oxidants and Antioxidants, Academic Press, London, 1991.

Tiwari, A.K. (2001). Imbalance in Antioxidant Defense and Human Disease: Multiple Approach of Natural Antioxidants Therapy, Current Science, 81, pp. 1179-1187.

Young I.S. and Woodside J.V. (2001). Antioxidants in Health and Disease. *J. Clin Pathol.* 54, pp. 176-86.

Page 115-137

MICROBIAL ENVIRONMENT AND BIOREMEDIATION
Edited by : **Dr. Alka Chauhan; Dr. Ashok K. Rathoure & Dr. Raaz K Maheshwari**
Edition : **2017**
ISBN : 978-93-5056-856-9
Published by : **Discovery Publishing House Pvt. Ltd., New Delhi (India)**

8 Bioremediation of Polluted Environment

Yadvesh[1]
Pooja Solanki[2]
Sudha Sambyal Malik[2]

INTRODUCTION

Our planet 'Earth' is enriched with wealth of natural resources such as: forests, wildlife, land, soil, air, water, wind, plants and animals. The race begins when humans started living a stable life rather than a nomadic life. Since the advent of civilization the use and overuse, and now the misuse has led to depletion of various natural resources to an extent that today half of our natural wealth are either depleted or at the edge of depletion (Gosavi *et al.* 2004). Earlier it was believed that our land and its resources are in abundance and will remain available for decades. However, today the existing state of our resources shows carelessness and negligence in using them. There are various examples which indicate the exploitation of natural resources by the use of chemical fertilizers in agriculture, release of industrial waste, anthropogenic activities and burning of fossil fuels etc.

Contaminated lands generally result from past industrial activities when awareness of the health and environmental effects connected with the production use, and disposal of hazardous substances were less well recognized than today. The use of chemical fertilizers, pesticides and herbicides in agriculture has improved the crop yield and productivity but led to the addition of detrimental amount of nitrogen and phosphorus in soil and terrestrial ecosystem. Similarly, the release of toxic contaminants from various man made sources resulted in contamination of natural resources

1. Institute of Environment Science, Kurukshetra University, Kurukshetra, Haryana, India.
2. Department of Environmental Science, M.D. University, Rohtak, Haryana, India.

leading to scarcity of clean water and loss of soil fertility (Kumari *et al.* 2013). The problem is worldwide, and the estimated number of contaminated sites is significant (Adriaens *et al.* 1993). It is now widely recognized that contaminated land is a potential threat to human health, and its continual discovery over recent years has led to international efforts to remedy many of these sites, either as a response to the risk of adverse health or environmental effects caused by contamination or to enable the site to be redeveloped for use.

Bioremediation is the process by which living organisms degrade or transforms hazardous organic contaminants to inorganic compounds such as: CO_2, H_2O and NO_3 (Nandal *et al.* 2015). The process of bioremediation involves the use of various microorganisms or plants to treat environment contaminated with organic molecules which can be living or non-living, natural or genetically engineered. These toxic heavy metals molecules are otherwise very difficult to break or mitigate by transforming them into innocuous products (Li and Li, 2011).

Types of Bioremediation

Bioremediation explores the genetic diversity and metabolic versatility of microbes for the transformation of contaminants into less harmful end products which are then integrated into natural bio-geochemical cycles (Liu and Suflita, 1993). The diversity of bioremediation system depends on the constituent of contaminants and it involves a multidisciplinary approach requiring knowledge from individuals having expertise in chemistry, microbiology, geology, environmental engineering, chemical engineering, soil science etc. Bioremediation techniques are of different types (Nandal *et al.* 2015):

1. *Bioaugmentation*: Addition of bacterial cultures to a contaminated medium, frequently used in bioreactors and *ex-situ* system. It is used when the proportion of degradative microbial flora to contaminant needs to be increased.
2. *Biomineralization/Biocrystallization:* The process whereby microbially generated ligands or microbially mediated changes in the cellular microbial environment cause precipitation of heavy metals as biomass-bound crystalline deposits.
3. *Biostimulation:* The process including: the introduction of adequate amounts of water, nutrients, and oxygen into the soil, in order to enhance the activity of indigenous microbial degraders. It can be applied when the addition of nutrients is necessary.
4. *Bioattenuation:* A method of monitoring the natural programme of degradation to ensure that contaminant concentration decreases with time at relevant sampling point.

5. *Bioventing:* Treating contaminated soils by drawing oxygen through the soil to stimulate microbial growth and activity. It is needed when it becomes necessary to supply oxygen from air.
6. *Biofilters:* Use of microbial stripping columns to treat air emissions.
7. *Bioreactors:* A container/reactor used to treat liquid or slurries.
8. *Composting:* Aerobic, thermophilic treatment process in which contaminated material is mixed with a bulking agent.
9. *Land farming:* Solid phase treatment system for contaminated soils may be done *ex situ* or in a constructed soil treatment cell.

Microorganisms Involved in the Process of Bioremediation

Currently, a wide range of microorganisms (bacteria, archaebacteria, yeasts, fungi and algae) and plants are being studied for use in bioremediation processes (Table 8.1-8.3).

Microbes have been widely used in the process of environmental clean-up and are known as bioremediators. The process of bioremediation involve the use of microorganisms which are native to the contaminated sites by providing them sufficient nutrients and a few chemicals essential for their growth and development. This enables them to destroy the pollutants present in the contaminated sites (Chen *et al.* 2009, Kim *et al.* 2007). Amongst bacteria, *Bacillus* (Kim *et al.* 2007), *Pseudomonas* (Jayashree *et al.* 2012), and *Streptomyces* (Selatina *et al.* 2004) acts as a potent metal biosorbents. The potential of *Streptomyces* strain to retain trace elements from polluted waters has recently been confirmed by many workers. Some other common microorganisms used in the process of remediation (Table 8.1) are species of: *Achromobacter, Alcaligenes, Arthrobacter, Bacillus, Cinetobacter, Corynebacterium, Flavobacterium, Micrococcus, Mycobacterium, Norcardia, Pseudomonas, Vibrio, Rhodococcus and Sphingomonas* (Kim *et al.* 2007, Gupta *et al.* 2001, Jayashree *et al.* 2012, Nakajima *et al.* 2004). These microorganisms are used for the treatment of contaminated sites containing a wide variety of pollutants.

The removal of heavy metals cations from industrial waste water or recovery of metals from their solutions can be accomplished by methods that use microorganisms as cation sorbents (Babel *et al.* 2003). The mechanisms of metal binding to microbial biomass is divided into three types *(i)* intracellular accumulation (this process requires live cells); *(ii)* sorption or complex formation on cell surface (it takes place on both live and dead cells) and *(iii)* extracellular accumulation or precipitation (the process may require viable cells) (Kujan *et al.* 2005). The uptake of metal ion by living and dead cells consists of two modes. In the first mode metal ions binds to the surface of cell wall and extra cellular material whereas, the second mode involves the metal uptake into the cell across cell membrane and is referred as intracellular uptake, active uptake or bioaccumulation. Both living and dead

Table 8.1: Various bacterial and yeast species for bioremediation of toxic elements

Organisms	Genus/Species	Chemical/Toxic Element	References
Bacteria	*Arthrobacter sp.*	p-nitrophenol	Labana *et al*. 2005
	Bacillus sp.	Cu, Zn, Cd, Pb, Fe, Ni, Ag, Th, Ra and U	Kim *et al*. 2007 and Gupta *et al*. 2001
	Citrobacter sp.	U	Renninger *et al*. 2001
	Cupriavidus metallidurans	Zn and Cu	Grass *et al*. 2002
	Escherichia coli	Zn and V	Grass *et al*. 2002
	Escherichia hermannii	V and Zn	Hernandez *et al*. 1998
	Enterobacter cloacae	Pb, Cu, V and Cr	Hernandez *et al*. 1998
	Exiguobacterium aurantiacum	phenolics, heterocyclics and (PAHs)	Jeswani and Mukherji, 2012
	Geobacter Metallireducens	Fe	Lovely, 2002
	Micrococcus sp.	Th and U	Nakajima and Tsuruta, 2004
	Pseudomonas Aeruginosa	Cd, Pb, Fe, Cu, U, Ra, Ni, Ag,Zn, Th and Atrazine	Jayashree *et al*. 2012, pattus and Abdallah, 2000
	Ralstonia eutropha	2,4-Dichlorophenoxyacetic acid	Roane *et al*. 2001
	Streptomyces sp.	Cu, Zn, Cd, Pb, Fe, Ni, Ag, Th,Ra and U	Selatina *et al*. 2004
Archeabacteria Yeast	*Filo crenarchaeota*	Cd, Cu, Ni, and Zn	Sandaa. *et al*. 1999
	Candida utilis	Cd	Kujan *et al*. 2006
	Hansenula anomala	Cd	Watanabe *et al*. 2009
	Rhodotorula Mucilaginosa	Zn and Cd	Bin-hui *et al*. 2012
	Rhodotorula rubra	Hg	Ghosh *et al*. 2006
	Streptomyces sp.	Pb	Selatina *et al*. 2004
	Saccharomyces Cerevisiae	Cu, Zn, Cd, Pb, Fe, Ni, Ag, Th,Ra, U and Hg	Ghosh *et al*. 2006 and Bishnoi *et al*. 2005

cells shows first mode however, the second mode which is metabolism dependent occurs only in living cells. Metal uptake is also facilitated by the production of metal-binding proteins in living cells. Therefore, both living and dead cells are capable of metal adsorption. The use of dead biomass is preferred over living due to the absence of toxicity limitations, absence of growth media and nutrients requirements, and high capacity of binding metals (Bishnoi and Garima, 2005). In solutions the process of metal removal takes place by the formation of complex between the pollutants (metal) and the active groups on cell surface after interaction.

Yeasts are readily available source of biomass which shows the ability to resist under unfavorable environment. Many metals and metalloids can be accumulated by yeasts and some of them are essential for structural and catalytic functions, whereas others are of no metabolic importance (Chatterjee *et al.* 2011). Yeasts are also known for dye decolourization of food industry effluents mainly by three mechanisms such as: biosorption, bioaccumulation and biodegradation. The removing mechanisms of dyes color from industrial effluents, by yeast cells are either through absorbtion or adsorbtion at the cell surface (Donmez, 2002). The yeast species such as: *Candida, Clavispora, Debaryomyces, Leucosporidium, Pichia, Rhodosporidium, Rhodotorula, Sporidiobolus, Sporobolomyces, Stephanoascus, Trichosporon* and *Yarrowia* are used in bioremediation process and shows biodegrading properties (Csutak *et al.* 2010). Microbial biomass derived from yeasts, particularly *Candida utilis* has the ability to accumulate metal ions and radionuclides from the environment. A study by Kujan *et al.* 2006 also showed that *C. utilis* biomass can conveniently be used for cadmium biosorption from aqueous solutions.

There are some yeast like: *Rhodotorula mucilaginosa* which is efficient in bioadsorption of lead and are also known to accumulate free and complexed silver ions by metabolism dependent and independent processes (Gomes *et al.* 2002). A comparative study was made by Ksheminska *et al.* 2003 on the sensitivity of yeast *Pichia guilliermondii* to Cr (III) and Cr (VI) as well as on the uptake potential of Cr. The results indicated accumulation of Cr (III) and Cr (IV) by *Pichia* sp. and also showed increase in Cr tolerance by the addition of riboflavin.

Algae and Fungi

Algae and fungi plays important role in returning the environment to its original state altered by various contaminants (Table 8.2). The process of phycoremediation is defined as the use of algae to remove pollutants from the environment or to convert them into harmless form. Phycoremediation in a much broader sense is the use of micro or macroalgae for the removal or biotransformation of pollutants, including nutrients and xenobiotics from wastewater and CO_2 from air. Algae are highly adaptive and can grow autotrophically, heterotrophically or mixotrophically in any environment. In natural environments, algae play a major role in controlling metal concentration of lakes and oceans. It possess the ability to degrade or accumulate toxic heavy metals and organic pollutants such as: phenolics, hydrocarbons, pesticides and biphenyls from the environment, resulting in higher concentrations within themselves as compared to surrounding water (Shamsuddoha *et al.* 2006). Pollutant degrading mixotrophic algae are excellent agents for remediation and carbon sequestration (Subhaschandrabose *et al.* 2013). An alga fixes CO_2 and produce O_2 by the process of photosynthesis and increases BOD level in contaminated water along with the efficient removal of excess of nutrients (Fathi *et al.* 2013). Uptake of metals by living microalgae occurs in two steps. The first step is independent of cell metabolism and involves 'adsorption' onto the cell surface (physical adsorption) afterwards these ions are transported slowly into the cytoplasm known as chemisorptions (Vymazal, 1984). The second step is dependent on cell metabolism and involves absorption or intracellular uptake of heavy metals. Many studies have showed that various metals such as: Pb, Cu, Cd, Co, Hg, Zn, Mg, Ni and Ti are sequestered in polyphosphate bodies of algae and perform two functions *i.e.,* storage and detoxification of metals (Dwivedi, 2012). Due to its role in sequestration of heavy metals by algal cell wall, these are considered as an ideal source of multifunctional polymers (Seufferheld and Curzi., 2010). Algae are also known for effective removal of nitrogen from soil or water through the process of absorption and store it as biomass. As the time passes, the biomass decomposes and releases the nitrogen back into the soil (ammonia or urea) or atmosphere (N_2O), where it may be recycled or lost (Woodward *et al.* 2009). Algae plays important role in pH correction, sludge removal and TDs reduction, whereas in conventional treatment, separate methods or stages are required. Amongst algae, blue green algae or cyanobacteria are susceptible to various physical and chemical alterations of light, salinity, temperature and nutrient composition. Recently, there has been increasing worldwide interest in using cyanobacteria as an economic and low-maintenance remediation technology for contaminated and polluted sites. Cyanobacteria have been used efficiently for remediating dairy waste water by converting the dissolved nutrients into biomass. However, the beneficial application of cyanobacteria in bioremediation of contaminated waters, either natural aquatic environments or industrial effluents, still needs further research. The other algal species such as: *Aphanocapsa* sp., *Oscillatoria salina, Plectonema terebrans* and *Synechococcus* sp., develops mats in aquatic environments and have been successfully used in bioremediation of oil spills in different parts of the world [20,21,29]. Various species of algae such as: *Anabaena inaequalis, Chlorella sp., Stigeoclonium tenue, Synechococcus* sp. and *Westiellopsis prolifica* are resistant to heavy metals and thus used for the removal of heavy metals (Bajguz, 2011 and Kannan *et al.* 2012).

Another type of bioremediation is mycoremediation which uses fungal mycelium to decontaminate or filter the toxic waste from contaminated area. The fungal mycelia secrete various extracellular enzymes and acids that break down the lignin and cellulose. The key to mycoremediation is to determine the right fungal species to target a specific pollutant. Fungi (*Ligninolytic fungi*) such as: the white rot fungus *Phanaerochaete chrysosporium* and *Polyporus* sp., are promising candidates for bioremediation, as it shows the ability to degrade an extremely diverse range of persistent or toxic environmental pollutants such as: petroleum hydrocarbons, polycyclic aromatic hydrocarbons (PAHs), explosives, polychlorinated biphenyls (PCBs), and organochlorine pesticides (Wu and Yu, 2007). It has also been reported to degrade a wide variety of organo pollutants because of lignin-degrading or woodrotting enzymes. The extracellular enzymes secreted by white-rot fungi during lignin decay have been proposed as promising agents for oxidizing pollutants. *Cyathus bulleri*, a bird's nest ligninolytic fungus that colonizes with dead herbaceous stems, wood chips, dung, sticks and other woody debris are found ecologically suitable for lignin degradation. It produces a single laccase the internal peptides which bears similarity to enzyme laccases of several white rot fungi, the only difference lies in proportion of some basic and hydrophobic amino acids. Laccases are copper containing enzymes which catalyze the oxidation of a broad range of phenolic compounds and aromatic amines by using molecular oxygen as the electron acceptor (Garg *et al*. 2008). Many researchers have showed that the extracellular enzymes secreted by these fungi oxidizes woody plant material *i.e.*, lignin which shows structural similarity with PAHs (Levin *et al*. 2003). This process of degradation is called mineralization, and the end product is carbon dioxide (Mai *et al*. 2004). The mechanisms of degradation are not yet conclusively mapped but it is likely that intracellular and extracellular enzymes are responsible for oxidizing different pollutants under different conditions.

Phytoremediation is a fast remediation technique to clean contaminated sites. It has been accepted and utilized widely as an effective and environmental friendly green technology for permanent removal of pollutants (Chen *et al*. 2009). Phytoremediation has been defined as the use of green plants and their biomass to degrade or render harmless environmental contaminants. A large number of plant species have found to be efficient in phytoremediation of organic pollutants as mentioned in Table 8.3. Phytoremediation, when compared to physical and chemical remediation, shows several advantages as it helps: *(i)* in preserving the natural properties of soil; *(ii)* acquiring energy mainly from sunlight and *(iii)* maintaining high levels of microbial biomass in the rhizosphere (Huang *et al*. 2004). Although with these advantages, some plants show very low tolerance to soil

Table 8.2: Algae and fungi species capable of Bioremendiation

Organisms	Genus/Species	Toxic Chemicals/Elements	References
Algae	*Ascophyllum nodosum*	Pb, Cu and Cr	Gupta *et al*. 2001
	Anabaena inaequalis	Cr	Kannan *et al*. 2012
	Chlorella vulgaris	Cd, Ag, Cu, Th, Zn, Pb, Ni, Ra, Fe and U	Bajguz, 2011
	Cladophora glomerata	Cu, Pb, Cd, Cr, Ni, Fe, Zn, Mn, Sr and Cs	Vymazal, 1984
	Cyanobacteria	Pb, Hg and Cd	Rahman *et al*. 2011
	Nostoc sp.	Hg, Pb, Cd and Gamma-hexachlorocyclohexane	Rahman *et al*. 2011; Girish and Mohammad, 2013
	Oedogonium rivulare	Cr, Ni, Zn, Fe, Mn Cu, Pb, Cdand Co	Chatterjee *et al*. 2011
	Oscillatoria spp.	Cu, Pb, Cd and Co	Brhambhatt *et al*. 2012
	Sargassum spp.	Pb, U, Cd, Ni, Zn, Cu and Cr	Kuyucak and Volesky, 1989
	Scenedesmus obliquus	Cd and Zn	Harris and Ramelow, 2013
Fungi	*Aspergillus terreus*	Cr	Kumar *et al*. 2008 and Dias *et al*. 2002
	Aspergillus niger	Pb, Zn, Cd, Cr, Cu, Ni and Chlorpyrifos	Ahluwalia and Goyal, 2006
	Funalia trogii	Hg, Cd and Zn	Arica *et al*. 2004
	Ganoderma	Cr and Cu	Muraleedharan and Venkobachar, 1990
	Penicillium Chrysogenum	Pb, Fe, Ni, Ra, Th, U, Cu, Zn,Ag, and Cd	Chatterjee *et al*. 2011
	Phanerochaete Chrysosporium	2,4-dicholorophenol	Brhambhatt *et al*. 2012
	Pleurotus ostreatus	PAHs and Orange 3, 4-(4-nitrophenylazo) aniline	Kuyucak and Volesky, 1989
	Rhizopus sp	Cr	Harris and Ramelow, 1990

contaminants, which limits the degradation efficiency to an insufficient level for soil remediation. There are approximately 400 plant species form 45 different families which act as a hyperaccumalator plants. The major families include: *Brassicaceae, Fabaceae, Euphorbiaceae, Asteraceae, Lamiaceae* and *Scrophulariaceae.* There are various crops such as: *Astragalus racemosus, Haumaniastrum robertii, Ipomea alpine, Thlaspi caerulescens* and *Sebertia acuminate* showed the potential of accumulating Se, Co, Cu, Cd/Zn and Ni respectively (Lasat, 2002; Wuana and Okieimen, 2010).

A very few studies have been carried out on uptake, mobilization and transport of hazardous heavy metals (Pb, Cd, Cu, Zn, U, Sr and Cs) mechanisms. There are two approaches for phytoremediation of organic polluted soils based on the difference in remediative mechanism. *Firstly,* organic pollutants can be taken up directly by plants, resulting in the degradation of pollutants inside plants known as phytoextraction. *Secondly,* organic pollutants can be degraded by plant secreted enzymes or plant modified microbial community in rhizosphere called plant-assisted rhizoremediation (Alkorta and Garbisu, 2001; Gerhardt *et al.* 2009). It may be possible that some organic compounds are able to enter into plant cells by penetrating cell membrane. Certain plants are able to extract hazardous substances such as: arsenic, lead and uranium from soil and water. A study by McCutcheon and Schnoor (McCutcheon and Schnoor, 2003) indicates alpine pennycress (*Thlaspi caerulescence*), acts as hyperaccumulator of metals and are known for accumulating high levels of Cd and Zn from the environment. According to Kramer *et al.* 1996, it has been reported that *Alyssum lesbiacum acts* as a Ni hyperaccumulator and uses histidine, as an excellent Ni chelator, to acquire and transport Ni. The hyperaccumulator plants possess genes which regulate the amount of metal uptake from the soil by roots and deposit the metals at other locations within the plant. These genes govern various processes which increase the solubility of metals in the soil and help in the transport of proteins that translocate metals into root cells vacuoles thereby protects cell metabolism from metal toxicity. Thereafter, the metals enter the plant's vascular system and transported further to other parts of the plant and get deposited in leaf cells. Non-hyperaccumulator plants require addition of some chelated agents in soil to promote the uptake of heavy metals. The heavy metal tolerance mechanism ranges from exclusion, inclusion and accumulation by plants depending on species (Maiti *et al.* 2004). Willow (*Salix viminlais*) has a significant potential as a phytoextractor of Cd, Zn and Cu, as it shows high transport capacity of heavy metals from root to shoot (Salt *et al.* 1995). Another example of phytoremediation is *Pteridium esculentum* which extracts arsenic from soil at a much faster rate than other plants. Arsenic is stored in the fern's leaves at a much higher level than present in the soil, thus enabling effective environmental clean-up (Robinson *et al.* 2006). *Brassica juncea* was reported as a valuable plant for the removal of Se from soil. The volatilization of Se in the form of methyl selenate is a major mechanism of Se removal by plants (De Souza *et al.* 1999). Some plants can also remove Se from soil by accumulating nonvolatile methyl selenate derivatives in the foliage. Plants such as: *Medicago sativa, Zea mays, Tagetes patula* and *Helianthus* sp., are potential candidates for the phytoremediation of soils contaminated with PAEs, PAHs and uranium respectively (Brown *et al.* 1995; Fu *et al.* 1012).

Plant roots and shoots can be used to absorb and concentrate hazardous compounds, particularly heavy metals from aqueous solutions known as rhizofiltration. Hydroponically cultivated plants rapidly remove heavy metals from water and concentrate them in the roots and shoots. The process of rhizofiltration is effective in wetlands where contaminated water is allowed to come in contact with roots. The plant root exudates namely: organic acids, sugars and phenolics are commonly used as source of carbon and energy by soil microbes which show the ability to degrade various organic pollutants (Chaudhry *et al.* 2005). Plant roots not only secrete enzyme (laccase, nitrilase, dehalogenase and nitroreductase) degrading organic pollutants but also improve the degrading ability of microorganisms present in rhizosphere (Teng *et al.* 2010).

A large proportion of heavy metals remains sorbed to soil particles and to acquire these soil bound metals. phytoextracting plants play important role in the mobilization of metals into soil solution. The process of mobilization can be carried by various methods such as: metalchelating molecules that can be secreted into the rhizosphere to chelate and solubilize 'soil bound' metal (Raskin *et al.* 1997). *Secondly* the 'soil-bound' metal ions can be reduced by roots with the help of specific plasma membrane bound metal reductase, which increases metal availability (Welch *et al.* 1993). The plant roots can solubilize soil-bound toxic metals by acidifying their soil environment with protons extruded from roots. A similar mechanism has been observed for Fe mobilization in some Fe-deficient dicotyledonous plants (Crowley *et al.* 1991). The iron-chelating compounds, termed phytosiderophores, have been studied well in plants for *e.g.*, Mugineic and deoxymugeneic acids from barley and corn and avenic acid from oats. These phytosiderophores are released due to iron deficiency and help in mobilization of Cu, Zn and Mn from soil. Lastly, the roots can also employ rhizospheric organisms (mycorrhizal fungi or root-colonizing bacteria) in increasing the bioavailability of metals (Kinnersely, 1993).

Table 8.3: Plant species used for bioremediation

Organisms	Genus/Species	Toxic Chemicals/ Elements	References
Plants	*Ambrosia artemisifolia*	Pb	Wang *et al.* 2002
	Apocynum cannabinum	Pb	Wang *et al.* 2002
	Brassica juncea	Se, Pb and Cu	Wang *et al.* 2002
	Helianthus annus	As and Ur	Teng *et al.* 2010
	Medicago sativa	Benzopyrene, PAEs and PAHs	Fu *et al.* 2012
	Melastoma malabathricum	Al	Watanabe *et al.* 1998
	Nephrolepis exaltata	Hg	Chen *et al.* 2009
	Pteridium esculentum	As	Salt *et al.* 1995
	Pteris vitata	As, Hg, Cs and Sr	Robinson *et al.* 2006
	Salix viminlais	Cd, Zn and Cu	Choudhary *et al.* 2009
	Raphanus sativus	Cu	Robinson *et al.* 2006
	Thlaspi caerulescens	Cd and Zn	McCutheon and Schnoor., 2003

Essential Characteristics of Microbes for Bioremediation

1. Presence of microbes with the capacity to degrade the target compounds.
2. Substrate being accessible to the organism and capable of being used as energy and carbon source.
3. Presence of inducer to cause synthesis of specific enzymes for the target compounds.
4. Presence of an appropriate electron acceptor-donor system.
5. Ideal moisture and pH for microbial growth.
6. Nutrients for microbial growth and enzyme production.
7. Optimum temperature to support microbial activity.
8. Absence of toxic substance.
9. Microbes to degrade metabolic products.
10 Microbes to prevent transit of toxic intermediate products.
11. Ideal conditions to minimize competitive organisms for those conducting desired reactions.

Metabolic Process Involved in Bioremediation

Microbes that live virtually everywhere are the vital components for bioremediation. Microbial enzymes act as catalysts in degradation (catabolic) reactions that provide energy and material for synthesis of additional microbial cells. In general the biochemical process can be divided into two groups: fermentation and respiration.

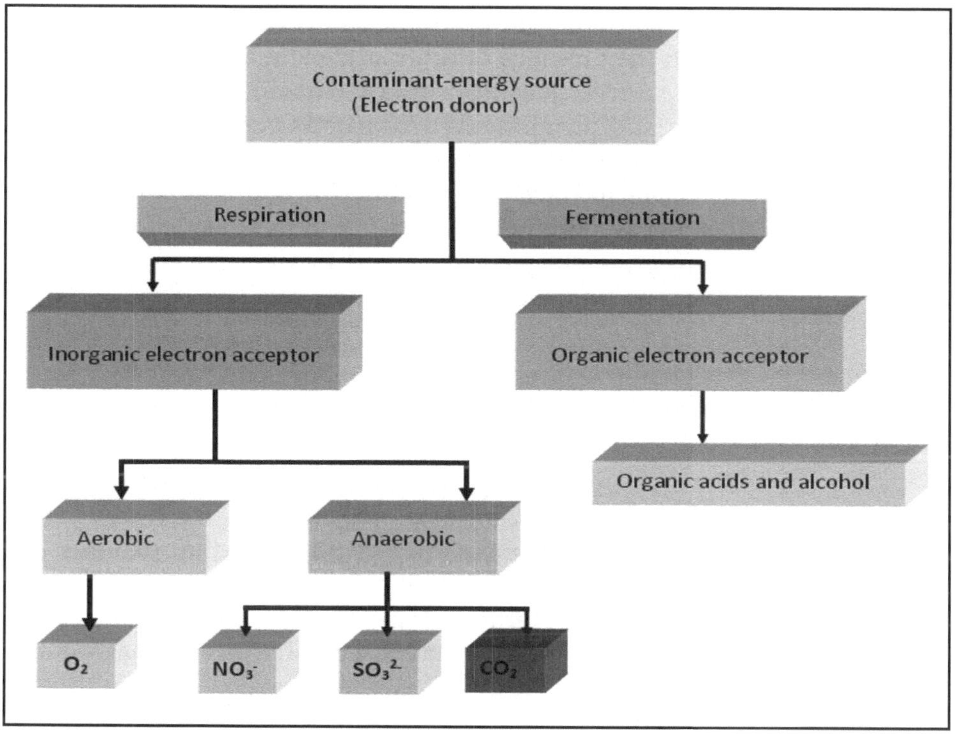

Fig. 8.1: **Different metabolic process involved in Bioremediation (Source: P. Rajendran and P. Gunasekaran, 2006).**

Different Metabolic Process Involved in Bioremediation

Fermentation metabolism is characterized by production of a mixture of end products with different levels of oxidation, such as: organic acids, alcohols, hydrogen and carbon dioxide.

Respiration is of two types:

1. *Aerobic:* When the molecular oxygen becomes the electron acceptor. Microbes use oxygen to oxidize part of the carbon in the contaminant to carbon dioxide and the rest of the carbon is used to produce new cell mass.
2. *Anaerobic:* When the respiration occurs in the absence of molecular oxygen. Nitrate (NO^{3-}), sulphate (SO_4^{2-}), iron (Fe^{3+}), manganese (Mn^{2+}), and even carbon dioxide serve as electron acceptors to degrade the contaminants. The by-products include nitrogen gas, hydrogen sulphide, reduced forms of metals depending on the electron acceptor.

Co-metabolism (synergistic transformation)

Microbes can transform contaminants even though the conversion reaction yields no benefit to the cell. The non-beneficial bioremediation is termed cometabolism/secondary utilization. It can be defined as degradation of a compound only in the presence of other organic material that serves as the primary energy source, *e.g.* Polynuclear aromatic hydrocarbons halogenated aliphatic and aromatic hydrocarbons and pesticides. A co-metabolite does not support the growth of the organism concerned and the products of transformation are accumulated stoichiometrically. The transformation does not require energy and it is a very slow process. Co-metabolism occurs since the enzymes produced by organism for metabolic activities of their major carbon source are not substrate specific and can act on other compounds.

Mechanisms of Bioremediation

Some of the technologies are fully developed and are being practiced as follows:

1. *Biosorption:* Biosorption is a property of certain types of inactive, dead microbial biomass to bind concentrated contaminants like, heavy metals from even very dilute aqueous solutions. Biomass that exhibits this property acts as a chemical substance (ion exchanger) of biological origin. The cell wall structure of certain algae, fungi, yeast and bacteria is responsible for this phenomenon, which is a passive process that requires no energy. Biosorption often results from the formation of metal-organic complexes with constituents of microbial cell walls, capsules, or extracellular polymers synthesized and excreted by the organisms. It may be resulted from the positively charged metallic cations being retained electrostatically by negatively charged functional groups in the walls, capsules or polymers. The mechanism of biosorption and the cell constituents involved in this process are usually unknown, although considerable research has been developed to trace the possible mechanisms. It involves mechanisms like ion exchange, chelation and complexation. Inorganic precipitation may occur by hydrolysis. Inorganic deposition occurs *via* adsorption by physical forces and ion entrapments in inner and intra-fibrillar capillaries and space of the structural polysaccharide network as a result of diffusion through cell walls and membranes (Vasudevan *et al.* 2001). Several active groups of cell constituents like acetamido group of chitin, structural polysaccharide of fungi, amine (amino and peptidoglycosides), sulphahydral and carboxyl groups in protein, phosphodiester (teichoic acids), phosphate, and hydroxyl in polysaccharides participate in biosorption (Vasudevan *et al.* 2001).
2. *Bioaccumulation:* The active mode of accumulation of contaminants by living cells is usually referred to as bioaccumulation. This process is metabolically dependent and can be significantly affected by the contaminants especially the metals. The use of living systems certainly

has applications in a selected recovery system. However, the toxicity and complexity of many wastes may limit the use of living system. There is little consensus regarding the actual mechanisms by which microorganisms actively perform precipitation, intracellular accumulation and oxidation or reduction. The concentration of a foreign substance within a biological system is dependent upon the rate of uptake, the duration of exposure and the rate at which it is being eliminated or reached upon by the system. The extent upto which a chemical shall be absorbed and bioaccumulated by an organism dependent on its solubility in fats or its lipophilicity.

3. *Precipitation:* Contaminants react with a product of microbial metabolism to yield water in soluble derivative. The removal of such precipitate constitutes remediation. Sulphides and phosphates are the common precipitates formed in microbes due to the production of H2S from sulphates and inorganic phosphates from organic phosphate compounds. The H2S/phosphates forms insoluble derivatives with a number of metallicions.
4. *Reductive halogenation:* This is potentially important in the detoxification of halogenated organic contaminants. The halogen atom (such as: chlorine) of the contaminant molecule is replaced by a hydrogen atom due to catalytic reaction of microbes. Two electrons are added, and the contaminant becomes less toxic and susceptible to further microbial decay than the parent compounds. In most cases this reaction does not generate energy but is an incidental reaction that may benefit the cell by eliminating the toxicity of the compound.
5. *Reduction:* Microbes can bring about the reduction of a wide array of inorganic anions and cations. Nitrate, sulphate and carbonate are the non-metallic anions that are reduced microbiologically. The reductions convert a higher oxidation state of the element to a lower one, *e.g.* Hg(II) to Hg(0), Fe(III) to Fe(II), Se(VI) to Se(0), Mn(IV) to Mn(II), and As(V) to As(III). The reduction changes the toxicity, water solubility and mobility of the element. In other words, one oxidation state is toxic but the reduced form has less or no toxicity at environmental conditions. An increase in water solubility and mobility can be exploited to bioremediate the insoluble form of an element in soil because the product of reduction would move out the solids into the water. A decrease in solubility of an element as a result of reduction can be used to remove it from surface to ground water. In some cases, the product of reduction is volatile, as in the reduction of nitrate to N2 or Hg(II) to Hg(0), and the loss of the element from soil or water is (as with nitrate) or could be (as with Hg) the basis for bioremediation (Alexander, 1977). The reduction reactions of microbes are catyalyzed enzymatically, but some result from the excretion by the organism of a reducing compound

that abiotically converts the ion or metabolic compound of a higher to a lower oxidation state. The enzyme-catalysed reactions serve as terminal electron acceptors permitting growth, much as O2 functions for aerobes, simple organic molecules for fermenting microbes, sulphate for *Desulfovibrio*, and nitrate for denitrifying bacteria and CO2 for methanogenic bacteria.

6. *Solubilization/Oxidation:* The oxidation reaction that has practical use is associated with the oxidation of sulphides. Fe (II) and elemental sulphur. Chemoautotrophic bacteria of the genus *Thiobacillus ferroxidans* use sulphides and Fe (II) as its energy source present in the ores and produce H_2SO_4 and Fe(III). The acidification process can be used in a beneficial way under a controlled or managed process known as bioleaching (Brierly, 1989).

Microbial Interaction for Optimization of Bioremediation

Microbes exhibit positive (commensalisms, synergism and mutualism) and negative (competition, amensalism, parasitism and predation) interactions that result in growth, survival and metabolism that are essential for bioremediation.

1. *Commensalisms:* Many contaminants are co-metabolized, a process in which microbes transform the contaminants without being able to use the energy derived from the metabolism to support growth. Co-metabolizing microbes may interact with other community members commensalistically, since co-metabolites serve as substrates for other microbes. Co-metabolism is the predominant mechanism for the transformation of many substrates, *e.g.* Polychlorinated biphenyls (PCBs). Analogue enrichment and cross-accumulated are the bioremedial approaches developed after understanding cometabolism.

In analogue enrichment, ecosystem may be enriched for co-metabolizing microbes by the addition of biodegradable compounds. In cross-accumulation, microbes acclimated to the biodegradation of a particular substrate can be acclimated to another contaminant that is structurally related. These approaches are advantageous since they can reduce the length of time between the first exposure to the contaminant and the onset of biodegradation.

2. *Synergism:* Microbes interacting syntrophically often supply the nutritional needs of each other. Syntrophism is common in anaerobic microbial communities, possibly due to the small enthalpy changes associated with most anaerobic bioconversions. The excretion of metabolic end products with high free-energy content creates a niche for other organisms to exploit and this can result in community succession. Microbial interaction can have a thermodynamic basis, as in anaerobic microbial consortia that transfer hydrogen. Interspecific hydrogen transfer forms the basis for syntrophic interactions, *e.g.*, metabolism of 3-chlorobenzoate.

3. *Competition:* Degradative microbes face competition with other organisms for nutritional and physical resources. Due to this competition, the expected bioconversion does not occur, even though the relevant degradative microbe is found in the environment. The dominance of one species over another can be due to its faster growth rate under the imposed selection pressure or its greater affinity for a substance, nutrient or physical resource. An understanding of the community structure is important for predicting the fate of contaminants in the environment and the remedial attempts.

Factors Affecting Bioremediation

The key element in any bioremediation process is the aerobic or anaerobic heterotrophs whose activity is affected by a number of physico-chemical environmental parameters namely: energy sources (electron donor), electron acceptors, pH, nutrients, temperature, moisture and inhibitory substances or metabolites. Boopathy (2000) has listed some important factors that may affect bioremediation (Rajendran and Gunasekaran, 2006).

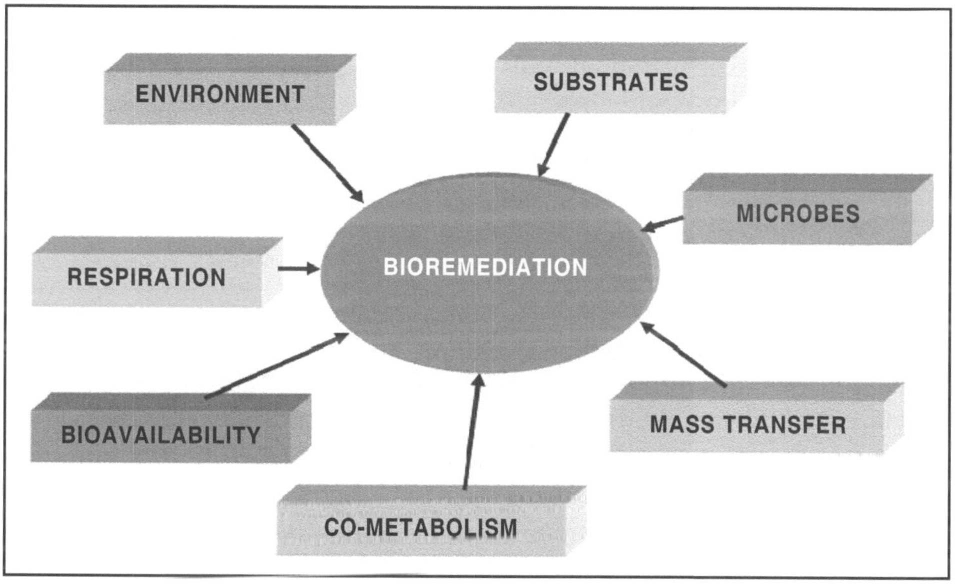

Fig. 8.2: **Factors affecting the process of bioremediation (*Source*: P. Rajendran and P. Gunasekaran (2006)**

Although the microorganisms are present in contaminated soil, they cannot necessarily be there in the numbers required for bioremediation of the site. Their growth and activity must be stimulated. Biostimulation usually involves the addition of nutrients and oxygen to help indigenous microorganisms. These nutrients are the basic building blocks of life and allow microbes to create the necessary enzymes to break down the contaminants. All of them will need nitrogen, phosphorous, and carbon. Carbon is the most basic element of living forms and is needed in greater quantities than other elements.

Microbial growth and activity are readily affected by pH, temperature, and moisture. Although microorganisms have been also isolated in extreme conditions, most of them grow optimally over a narrow range, so that it is important to achieve optimal conditions. If the soil has too much acid it is possible to rinse the pH by adding lime. Temperature affects biochemical reactions rates, and the rates of many of them double for each 10°C rise in temperature. Above a certain temperature, however, the cells die. Plastic covering can be used to enhance solar warming in late spring, summer, and autumn. Available water is essential for all the living organisms, and irrigation is needed to achieve the optimal moisture level. The amount of available oxygen will determine whether the system is aerobic or anaerobic. Hydrocarbons are readily degraded under aerobic conditions, whereas chlorinate compounds are degraded only in anaerobic ones. To increase the oxygen amount in the soil it is possible to till or sparge air. In some cases, hydrogen peroxide or magnesium peroxide can be introduced in the environment. Soil structure controls the effective delivery of air, water, and nutrients. To improve soil structure, materials such as: gypsum or organic matter can be applied. Low soil permeability can impede movement of water, nutrients, and oxygen; hence, soils with low permeability may not be appropriate for *in situ* clean-up techniques (Naik and Duraphe, 2012).

Limitations of Bioremediation

Bioremediation is an alternative method to incineration, catalytic destruction, adsorption, physical removal and the destruction of contaminants. Integration and proper utilization of natural or modified microbial capabilities with appropriate engineering designs provide suitable growth in the contaminated environments. However, the main constraints are:

1. Lack of sufficient knowledge based on accurately predicts pollution degradation rates and fates.
2. Designated sites as centers for bioremediation research and technology demonstration.

Though several microbes have been designed for bioremediation, the physical potential of microbial population to remediate environment of relevant size, homogeneity and variability has not been adequately tested.

Conclusion

Researches using bioremediation has shown great promise to date. Further researches in this field can result in the development of most efficient and less time consuming technologies. Also, further research is critical to investigate its application beyond the laboratory-scale and to develop the kinetics of degradation. Bioremediation is usually simple and less labor intensive. Also, Bioremediation is the most economical at the required efficiency when the soil to be treated is more. Although public attitudes toward bioremediation are generally favorable, the lack of knowledge about microorganisms and their natural role in the environment could affect the acceptability of their use. Before bioremediation techniques to be used widely, their efficacy and safety will have to be convincingly demonstrated and communicated to the public.

REFERENCES

Adriaens, P., Hickey, W.J. (1993). In Stone, D.L. (Ed), Biotechnology for the Treatment of Hazardous Waste. Lewis Publishers, Ann Arbor, pp. 97-120.

Ahluwalia SS, Goyal D. Microbial and Plant derived Biomass for Removal of Heavy Metals from Wastewater. *Bioresour Technol*. 2006; 98(12):2243-2257.

Alkorta I, Garbisu C. Phytoremediation of Organic Contaminants in Soils. *Bioresour Geomicrobiology Journal*. 8: 201-223.

Arýca M.Y., Bayramoglu G, Yýlmaz M, Genc O, Bektas S. Biosorption of Hg, Cd and Zn by Ca-alginate and Immobilized Wood Rotting Fungus *Funalia trogii*. *J. Hazard Mater*. 2004:109:191-199.

Babel S., Kurniawan TA. Low-cost Adsorbents for Heavy Metals uptake from Contaminated Water: A Review. *J. Hazard Mat*. 2003; 97:219-243.

Bajguz A. Suppression of *Chlorella vulgaris* Growth by cadmium, Lead, and Copper Stress and Its restoration by endogenous brassinolide. *Arch Environ Contam Toxicol*. 2011;60(3):406-416.

Bajguz A. Suppression of *Chlorella vulgaris* Growth by Cadmium, Lead, and Copper Stress and Its Restoration by Endogenous Brassinolide. *Arch Environ Contam Toxicol*. 2011; 60(3):406-416.

Bin-hui J., Qian-qian W., Li J., Yu Z., Hai-ning L. Study on Biosorption of Zn and Cd by a *Rhodotorula Mucilaginosa*. *Adv Biomed Eng Med Phys*. 2012; 6:185-190.

Boopathy R. (2000). Factors Limiting Bioremediation Technologies. *Bioresource Technol*. 74: 63-67.

Brahmbhatt NH., Patel RV., Jasrai RT. Bioremediation Potential of *Spirogyra* sp. And *Oscillatoria* sp. for cadmium. *Asian J Biochem Pharmal Res*. 2012; 2:102-107.

Brierley C.L. (1989). Bioremediation of Metal Contaminated Surface and Groundwater.

Chatterjee S., Gupta D., Roy P., Chatterjee NC., Saha P., Dutta, S. Study of a Lead Tolerant Yeast Strain BUSCY1 (MTCC9315). *Afr J Microbiol Res*. 2011; 5:5362-5372.

Chaudhry Q, Blom Zandstra M., Gupta S., Joner EJ. Utilising the Synergy between Plants and rhizosphere Microorganisms to Enhance breakdown of Organic Pollutants in the Environment. *Environ Sci Pollut R*. 2005;12:34-48.

Chen J., Shiyab S., Han FX, Monts DL, Waggoner CA. Bioaccumulation and Physiological Effects of mercury in *Pteris vittata* and *Nephrolepis exaltata*. *Ecotoxicol*. 2009;18:110-121.

Chen J., Shiyab S, Han FX, Monts DL, Waggoner CA. Bioaccumulation and Physiological Effects of Mercury in *Pteris vittata* and *Nephrolepis exaltata*. *Ecotoxicol*. 2009;18:110-121.

Choudhary S.P., Bhardwaj R., Gupta BD., Dutt P., Kanwar M., Arora M. Epibrassinolide Regulated Synthesis of Polyamines and auxins in *Raphanus sativus* L. seedlings under Cu metal stress. *Braz J. Plant Physiol*. 2009; 21:25-32.

Crowley DE, Wang YC, Reid CPP, Szaniszlo PJ. Mechanisms of Iron Acquisition.

Csutak O., Stoica I., Ghindea R., Ana-Maria T., Vassu T. Insights on yeast Bioremediation Processes. *Rom Biotech Lett*. 2010;15(2):5066-5071.

de Souza M.P., Chu D., Zhao M., Zayed A.M., Ruzin SE, Schichnes D., Terry N. Rhizosphere Bacteria Enhance Selenium Accumulation and Volatilization by Indian Mustard. *Plant Physiol*. 1999; 119(2): 565-573.

Dias M.A., Lacerda ICA, Pimentel PF, Castro HF, Rosa CA. Removal of Heavy Metals by an *Aspergillus terreus* strain immobilized in a polyurethane matrix. *Lett Appl Microbiol*. 2002; 34:46-50.

Donmez G. Bioaccumulation of the Reactive Textile Dyes by *Candida tropicalis* Growing in Molasses Medium. *Enzyme Microb Technol*. 2002; 20:363-366.

Dwivedi S. Bioremediation of Heavy Metal by Algae: Current and Future Perspective. *J. Adv Lab Res Biol*. 2012; 3(3):195-199.

Fathi AA, Azooz MM, Al-Fredan MA. Phycoremediation and the Potential of Sustainable Algal Biofuel Production using Wastewater. *Am J. Appl Sci*. 2013; 10(2):189-194.

Fu D., Teng Y., Luo Y., Tu C., Li S. Effects of alfalfa and organic Fertilizer on benzopyrene dissipation in an aged Contaminated Soil. *Environ Sci Pollut R*. 2012;19:1605-1611.

Fu D., Teng Y., Luo Y., Tu C., Li S. Effects of alfalfa and organic Fertilizer on benzopyrene Dissipation in an Aged Contaminated Soil. *Environ Sci Pollut R*. 2012; 19:1605-1611.

Garg S.N., Baranwal R.M., Mishra S.C., Chaudhuri T.K., Bisaria VS. Laccase of *Cyathus bulleri*: Structural, catalytic Characterization and Expression in *Escherichia coli* Biochim Biophys Acta. 2008; 1784:259-268.

Gerhardt K.E., Huang X.D., Glick B.R., Greenberg B.M. Phytoremediation and Rhizoremediation of Organic Soil Contaminants: – Potential and Challenges. *Plant Sci*. 2009; 176:20-30.

Ghosh S.K., Chaudhuri R., Gachhui R., Mandal A., Ghosh S. Effect of mercury and organo mercurials on cellular glucose Utilization: A Study using Resting mercury Resistant Yeast Cells. *J. Appl Microbiol*. 2006; 102:375-383.

Girish K., Mohammad K. Microbial Degradation of gammahexachlorocyclohexane (lindane). *Afr J. Microbiol Res*. 2013;7(17):1635-1643.

Gosavi K., Sammut J., Gifford S., Jankowski J. Macroalgal biomonitors of Trace Metal Contamination in Acid Sulfate Soil Aquaculture Ponds. *Sci Total Environ*. 2004;324:25-39.

Grass G., Wong MD, Rosen BP, Smith RL, Rensing C. ZupT is a Zn(II) uptake system.

Gupta V.K., Shrivastava A.K., Jain N. Biosorption of chromium (VI) from Aqueous Solutions by Green algae *Spirogyra* species. Water Res. 2001;35(17):4079-4085.

Gupta V.K., Shrivastava AK, Jain N. Biosorption of chromium (VI) from Aqueous Solutions by Green algae *Spirogyra* species. Water Res. 2001;35(17):4079-4085.

Gupta V.K., Shrivastava A.K., Jain N. Biosorption of chromium (VI) from Aqueous Solutions by Green algae *Spirogyra* Species. *Water Res*. 2001; 35(17):4079-4085.

Harris P.O., Ramelow G.J. Binding of Metal Ions by Particulate Biomass from *Chlorella vulgaris* and *Scenedesmus quadricauda*. *Environ Sci Technol*. 1990; 24(2):220-228.

Hernandez A., Mellado R.P., Martinez JL. Metal Accumulation and vanadium-induced Multidrug Resistance by Environmental Isolates of *Escherichia hermannii* and *Enterobacter cloacae*. *Appl Environ Microbiol*. 1998;64(11):4317-4320.

Huang XD, El-Alawi Y., Penrose D.M., Glick BR, Greenberg BM. A Multiprocess phytoremediation System for Removal of polycyclic Aromatic hydrocarbons from Contaminated Soils. *Environ Pollut.* 2004;130:465-476. in *Escherichia coli. J. Bacteriol.* 2002;184:864-866.

Jayashree R., Nithya S.E., Rajesh P.P., Krishnaraju M. Biodegradation Capability of Bacterial Species Isolated from oil Contaminated Soil. *J Academia Indust Res.* 2012; 1(3):140-143.

Jayashree R., Nithya S.E., Rajesh P.P., Krishnaraju M. Biodegradation Capability of Bacterial Species Isolated from Oil Contaminated Soil. *J. Academia Indust Res.* 2012;1(3):140-143.

Jeswani H., Mukherji S. Degradation of phenolics, nitrogen-heterocyclics and polynuclear Aromatic Hydrocarbons in a Rotating Biological Contactor. *Bioresour Technol.* 2012;111:12-20.

Kannan V., Vijayasanthi M., Chinnasamy M. Bioremediation of chromium in Tannery Effluent by Filamentous Cyanobacteria *Anabaena flos-aquae* West Kannan. *Int J. Environ Sci.* 2012; 2(4):2360-2366.

Kannan V., Vijayasanthi M., Chinnasamy M. Bioremediation of chromium in Tannery Effluent by filamentous Cyanobacteria *Anabaena flos-aquae* West Kannan. *Int J. Environ Sci.* 2012; 2(4):2360-2366.

Kim S.U., Cheong Y.H., Seo D.C., Hu JS, Heo JS, Cho JS. Characterisation of Heavy Metal Tolerance and Biosorption Capacity of bacterium strain CPB4 (*Bacillus* spp.). *Water Sci Technol.* 2007; 55(1):105-111.

Kim S.U., Cheong Y.H., Seo D.C., Hu JS, Heo JS, Cho JS. Characterisation of Heavy Metal Tolerance and Biosorption Capacity of Bacterium Strain CPB4 (*Bacillus* spp.). *Water Sci Technol.* 2007; 55(1):105-111.

Kim S.U., Cheong Y.H., Seo D.C., Hu JS, Heo JS, Cho JS. Characterisation of Heavy Metal Tolerance and Biosorption Capacity of Bacterium Strain CPB4 (*Bacillus* spp.). *Water Sci Technol.* 2007; 55(1):105-111.

Kinnersely A.M. The Role of Phytochelates in Plant Growth and Productivity. Plant Growth Regul. (1993); 12:207-217. Teng Y, Luo Y, Sun X, Tu C, Xu L. Influence of arbuscular mycorrhiza and Rhizobium on phytoremediation by alfalfa of an Agricultural Soil Contaminated with Weathered PCBs: A Field Study. *Int J. Phytorem.* 2010; 12:516-533.

Kramer U., Cotter-Howells J.D., Charnock J.M., Baker A., Smith A. Free histidine as a Metal chelator in Plants that Accumulate Nickel. *Nature.* 1996; 379:635-638.

Ksheminska H., Jaglarz A., Fedorovych D., Babyak L., Yanovych D., Kaszycki P, Koloczek H. Bioremediation of chromium by the yeast *Pichia guilliermondii* : Toxicity and Accumulation of Cr (III) and Cr (VI) and the influence of riboflavin on Cr tolerance. *Microbiol Res.* 2003;158(1):59-67.

Kujan P., Prell A., Safar H., Sobotka M., Rezanka T., Holler PP. Use of the Industrial Yeast *Candida utilis* for cadmium sorption. *Folia Microbiol.* 2006; 51:257-260.

Kumar R., Bishnoi N.R., Bishnoi G.K. Biosorption of chromium (VI) from Aqueous Solution and Electroplating Wastewater using Fungal Biomass. *J Chem Eng Data.* 2008; 135(3):202-208.

Kumari R, Kaur I, Bhatnagar AK. Enhancing Soil Health and Productivity of *Lycopersicon esculentum* Mill. using *Sargassum johnstonii* Setchell and Gardner as a Soil Conditioner and Fertilizer. *J. Appl Phycol.* 2013; 25(4):1225-1235.

Kuyucak N, Volesky B. Accumulation of cobalt by Marine Alga. *Biotechnol Bioeng.* 1989; 33(7):809-814.

Labana S., Singh O.V., Basu A., Pandey G., Jain RK. A Microcosm Study on Bioremediation of p-nitrophenol-contaminated Soil Using *Arthrobacter protophormiae* RKJ100. *Appl Microbiol Biotechnol.* 2005; 68(3):417-424.

Lasat MM. Phytoextraction of Toxic Metals: A Review of Biological Mechanisms. *J. Environ Qual.* 2002; 31:109-120.

Levin L, Viale A, Forchiassin A. Degradation of Organic Pollutants by the White rot basidiomycete *Trametes trogii*. *Int Biodeter Biodegr.* 2003;52(1):1-5.

Li Y, Li B. Study on Fungi-bacteria Consortium Bioremediation of Petroleum Contaminated Mangrove Sediments Amended with Mixed Biosurfactants. *Adv Mat Res.* 2011; 183:1163-1167.

Lovely DR. Dissimulatory Metal Reduction from early life to Bioremediation. ASM News. 2002; 68(5):231-237.

Machado M.D., Santos MSF, Gouveia C, Soares HMVM, Soares EV. Removal of Heavy Metal using a Brewer's Yeast strain of *Saccharomyces cerevisiae*: The flocculation as a Separation Process. *Bioresour Technol.* 2008; 99:2107-2115.

Madhavi Gaonkar Naik and Mohini D.D., (2012). Parameters affecting Bioremediation. *International Journal of Life Science and Pharma Research.* 2:3

Mai C., Schormann W., Majcherczyk A., Hutterman A. Degradation of acrylic copolymers by white rot fungi. *Appl Microbiol Biotechnol.* 2004;65:479-487.

McCutcheon SC, Schnoor JL. Phytoremediation Transformation and Control of Contaminants, pp. 987, Wiley-Interscience, New Jersey, USA; 2003.

Muraleedharan T.R., Venkobachar C. Mechanism of Biosorption of Copper (II) by *Ganoderma lucidum*. Biotechnol Bioeng. 1990;35:320-325.

Nakajima A, Tsuruta T. Competitive Biosorption of thorium and uranium by *Micrococcus luteus*. *J. Radioanal Nucl Chem.* 2004; 260:13-18.

Nakajima A., Tsuruta T. Competitive biosorption of thorium and uranium by *Micrococcus luteus*. *J. Radioanal Nucl Chem.* 2004; 260:13-18.

Nandal, M., Solanki, P., Rastogi, M. And Hooda, R., (2015). Bioremediation: A Sustainable Tool for Environmentak Management of Oily Sludge. *Nature, Environment and Pollution Technology*. 14(1):181-190. on baker's yeast. Bioresour. *Technol.* 89:281-87.

P. Rajendran, P. Gunasekaran (2006). Microbial Bioremediation. MJP Publishers. 29-61.

Pattus F., Abdallah M. Siderophores and Iron-transport in Microorganisms: Review. *J. Chin Chem Soc.* 2000; 47:1-20.

Rahman M.A., Soumya K.K., Tripathi A., Sundaram S., Singh S, Gupta A. Evaluation and Sensitivity of cyanobacteria, *Nostoc muscorum* and *Synechococcus* PCC 7942 for Heavy Metals Stress - A Step toward Biosensor. *Toxicol Environ Chem.* 2011; 93(10):1982-1990.

Raskin I., Smith R.D., Salt DE. Phytoremediation of Metals: using Plants to Remove Pollutants from the Environment. *Curr Opin Biotechnol.* 1997;8:221-226.

Renninger N., McMahon KD., Knop R., Nitsche H., Clark D.S., Keasling J.D. Uranyl Precipitation by Biomass from An Enhanced Biological Phosphorus Removal Reactor. *Biodegrad.* 2001; 12:401-410.

Roane T.M., Josephson K.L., Pepper IL. Dual-bioaugmentation Strategy to Enhance Remediation of Cocontaminated Soil. *Appl Environ Microbiol.* 2001; 67:3208-3215.

Robinson B., Kimb N., Marchetti M., Monid C., Schroeter L., Dijssel C., Milne G., Clothier B. Arsenic hyperaccumulation by Aquatic macrophytes in the Taupo Volcanic Zone, New Zealand. *Environ Exp Bot.* 2006; 58: 206-215.

Salt D.E., Blaylock M., Nanda Kumar PBA, Dushenkov V, Ensly BD, Chet I, Raskin I. Phytroremediation: A Novel Strategy for the Removal of Toxic Elements from Environment using Plants. *Biotechnol.* 1995; 13:468-475.

Sandaa R.A., Enger O., Torsvik V. Abundance and Diversity of archaea in Heavy-Metal Contaminated Soils. *Appl Environ Microbiol.* 1999; 65:3293-3297.

Selatnia A., Boukazoula A., Kechid B.N., Bakhti M.Z., Chergui A., Kerchich Y. Biosorption of Lead (II) from Aqueous Solution by a Bacterial Dead *Streptomyces rimosus* Biomass. *Biochem Eng J.* 2004; 19:127-135.

Selatnia A., Boukazoula A., Kechid B.N., Bakhti M.Z., Chergui A., Kerchich Y. Biosorption of lead (II) from Aqueous Solution by a Bacterial Dead *Streptomyces rimosus* biomass. *Biochem Eng J.* 2004; 19:127-135.

Selatnia A., Boukazoula A., Kechid B.N., Bakhti M.Z., Chergui A., Kerchich Y. Biosorption of Lead (II) from Aqueous Solution by a Bacterial Dead *Streptomyces rimosus* biomass. *Biochem Eng J.* 2004; 19:127-135.

Seufferheld M.J., Curzi M.J. Recent Discoveries on the Roles of polyphosphates in Plants. *Plant Mol Biol Rep.* 2010; 28:549-559.

Shamsuddoha A.S.M., Bulbul A, Huq SMI. Accumulation of arsenic in Green Algae and its Subsequent Transfer to the Soil-Plant System. *Bangladesh J Med Microbiology.* 2006; 22(2):148-151.

siderophores by microorganisms and plants. Plant Soil.1991;130:179-198.

Solanki, P., Yadvesh, Kumar, A. and Laura, J.S. (2014). Isolation and Assessment of Biodegradation Potential of Fungal Species Isolated from Sludge Contaminated Soil. *Intenational Journal of Current Microbiology and Applied Science.* 3(8): 197-204.

Subashchandrabose S.R., Ramakrishnan B., Megharaj M., Venkateswarlu K., Naidu R.R. Mixotrophic cyanobacteria and microalgae as distinctive Biological Agents for Organic Pollutant Degradation. *Environ Int.* 2013; 51:59-72.

Technol. 2001;79:273-276.

Teng Y, Luo Y, Sun X, Tu C, Xu L. Influence of arbuscular mycorrhiza and Rhizobium on phytoremediation by alfalfa of an Agricultural Soil Contaminated with weathered PCBs: A Field Study. *Int J. Phytorem.* 2010;12:516-533.

Vasudevan P., Padmavathy V, Dhingra SC (2001). Kinetics of Biosorption of Cadmium.

Vymazal J. Short-term uptake of Heavy Metals by periphyton Algae. *Hydrobiologia.* 1984; 119:171-179.

Wang J., Zhao Fang-Jie, Meharg AA, Raab A., Feldmann J., McGrath SP. Mechanisms of arsenic hyperaccumulation in *Pteris vittata.* Uptake kinetics, Interactions with phosphate, and arsenic Speciation. *Plant Physiol.* 2002; 130(3):1552-1561.

Watanabe T., Masaki K., Iwashita K., Fujii T., Iefuji H. Treatment and phosphorus Removal from High-concentration Organic Wastewater by the Yeast *Hansenula anomala* J224 PAWA. *Bioresour Technol.* 2009;100(5):1781-1785.

Watanabe T., Mitsuru O., Yoshihara T, Tadano T. Distribution and Chemical Speciation of aluminium in the Al Accumulator Plant, *Melastoma malabathricum L. Plant Soil* 1998; 201(2):165.

Welch R.M., Norvell W.A., Schaefer S.C., Shaff J.E., Kochian LV. Induction of iron (III) and Copper (II) reduction in pea (*Pisum sativum* L.) roots by Fe and Cu status: does the root-cell plasmalemma Fe(III)-chelate reductase perform a general role in regulating cation uptake?. Planta. 1993;190:555-561.

Woodward KB, Fellows CS, Conway CL, Hunter HM. Nitrate removal, denitrification and nitrous oxide Production in the riparian zone of an ephemeral Stream. *Soil Biol Biochem*. 2009;41:671-680.

Wuana RA, Okieimen FE. Phytoremediation potential of Maize (*Zea mays* L.): *A Review. Afr J Gen Agr*. 2010;6(4):275-287.

Page 138-156

MICROBIAL ENVIRONMENT AND BIOREMEDIATION
Edited by : Dr. Alka Chauhan; Dr. Ashok K. Rathoure & Dr. Raaz K Maheshwari
Edition : 2017
ISBN : 978-93-5056-856-9
Published by : Discovery Publishing House Pvt. Ltd., New Delhi (India)

9 Bioremediation
Principles and Strategies

Ashok K. Rathoure

INTRODUCTION

It is believed now that wastes are no longer treated as waste and they can be used as a valuable resource. Biomass can interact and confront with water and soil pollutants in both active (live) as well as passive (dead) way, thereby offering numerous opportunities of exploring them for environmental clean-up. With rapid increase in urban populations particularly in the developing world, there is a growing problem of how to manage organic waste and to find alternatives to landfill disposal particularly for domestic food waste and that from vegetable markets. According to the research team, it is an unfortunate fact of life that much of this waste is currently dumped on the outskirts of many towns and cities and is causing serious pollution, disease risk and general ecological harm. It also represents a considerable wasted resource, whereas the organic matter might be exploited usefully in growing food crops (Glazer and Nikaido, 2007).

Besides this, vast number of pollutants and waste materials containing heavy metals are also disposed into the environment per annum. Approximately 6×10^6 chemical compounds have been synthesized, with 1,000 new chemicals being synthesized annually. Almost 60,000 to 95,000 chemicals are in commercial use. According to Third World Network reports, more than one billion pounds (450 million kgms) of toxins are released globally in air and water. The contaminants causing ecological problems leading to imbalance in nature is of global concern.

DGM-Technical, Vardan EnviroNet, Gurgaon (Haryana), India.
E-mail: *asokumr@gmail.com*

Bioremediation is an option that offers the possibility to destroy or render harmless various contaminants using natural biological activity. As such, it uses relatively low-cost, low-technology techniques, which generally have a high public acceptance and can often be carried out on site (Vidali *et al.* 2001). Compared to other methods, bioremediation is a more promising and less expensive way for cleaning up contaminated soil and water (Kamaludeen *et al.* 2003). Bioremediation uses biological agents, mainly microorganisms, *e.g.*, yeast, fungi or bacteria to clean up contaminated soil and water (Strong *et al.* 2008). It results in the elimination, attenuation and/ or transformation of polluting or contaminating substances by the use of biological processes.

Principles of Bioremediation

Bioremediation is defined as the process whereby organic wastes are biologically degraded under controlled conditions to an innocuous state, or to levels below concentration limits established by regulatory authorities (Mueller *et al.* 1996). Most bioremediation systems are run under aerobic conditions, but running a system under anaerobic conditions may permit microbial organisms to degrade otherwise recalcitrant molecules. The microorganisms may be indigenous to a contaminated area or they may be isolated from elsewhere and brought to the contaminated site. Contaminant compounds are transformed by living organisms through reactions that take place as a part of their metabolic processes. Biodegradation of a compound is often a result of the actions of multiple organisms. When microorganisms are imported to a contaminated site to enhance degradation, the process is known as bio-augmentation. Since bioremediation mainly utilizes living organisms (plants) including: microbes (bacteria and fungi) that degrade or detoxify substances hazardous to human health and environment. Microorganisms secrete extracellular enzymes that attack the pollutants and convert them into harmless products. Therefore bioremediation can be effective only where environmental conditions permit microbial growth and activity; its application often involves the manipulation of environmental parameters to allow microbial growth and degradation to proceed at a faster rate. For degradation it is necessary that bacteria and the contaminants should be in contact. This is not easily achieved, as neither the microbes nor contaminants are uniformly spread in the soil. Some bacteria are mobile and exhibit a chemotactic response, sensing the contaminant and moving towards it. Other microbes such as: fungi grow in a filamentous form toward the contaminant. It is possible to enhance the mobilization of the contaminant utilizing some surfactants such as: sodium dodecyl sulphate (SDS) (Hetherington *et al.* 2006).

However, contaminants like chlorinated organic or high aromatic hydrocarbons are resistant to microbial attack and they are degraded either slowly or not at all. The main advantage of using bioremediation techniques is that they are more economical than the traditional methods of incineration and some pollutants can be treated on site thereby reducing exposure risks for clean-up personnel and potentially wider exposure as a result of transportation accidents. Since bioremediation is based on natural attenuation it is considered more acceptable than other technologies (Glazer and Nikaido, 2007). Besides this, earthworms can also be used to extract toxic heavy metals, including cadmium and lead, from solid waste from domestic refuse collection and waste from vegetable and flower markets. Three species of earthworm, *Eudrilus eugeniae, Eisenia fetida* and *Perionyx excavates* can be used to assist in the composting of urban waste and to extract heavy metals, cadmium, copper, lead, manganese, zinc, prior to subsequent processing. The process of vermicomposting in this way allows such waste materials to be remediated and the compost can be used subsequently in growing human food without the risk of accumulating heavy metals in crops (Kamarudheen *et al.* 2014).

Factors Affecting Bioremediation

The factors affecting bioremediation process include existence of a microbial population capable of degrading the pollutants; availability of contaminants to the microbial population; environment factors (soil type, temperature, pH and the presence of oxygen or other electron acceptors and nutrients).

Microbial Populations for Bioremediation Processes

Microbes are diverse in their habitat, they will adapt and grow at subzero temperatures, as well as extreme heat, desert conditions, in water, with an excess of oxygen, and in anaerobic conditions, with the presence of hazardous compounds or on any waste stream. Their main requirements are an energy source and a carbon source. Because of the adaptability of microbes they can be used to degrade or remediate environmental hazards. Aerobic bacteria recognized for their degradative abilities are: *Pseudomonas, Alcaligenes, Sphingomonas, Rhodococcus* and *Mycobacterium*. These microbes degrade pesticides and hydrocarbons, both alkanes and polyaromatic compounds as they use the contaminant as sole source of carbon and energy (Vidali, 2001; Prescott, 2002). Anaerobic bacteria are not as frequently used for degradation as aerobic bacteria but some of them are used for bioremediation of polychlorinated biphenyls (PCBs) in river sediments, dechlorination of the solvent trichloroethylene (TCE) and chloroform.

Ligninolytic fungi such as: the white rot fungus *Phanaerochaete chrysosporium* have the ability to degrade an extremely diverse range of persistent or toxic environmental pollutants. They utilize the substrates such as: straw, saw dust, or corn cobs. Methylotrophs grow by utilizing methane for carbon and energy. The initial enzyme in the pathway for aerobic degradation, methane monooxygenase, has a broad substrate range and is active against a wide range of compounds, including the chlorinated aliphatic trichloroethylene and 1,2-dichloroethane (Glazer and Nikaido, 2007).

Environmental factors for Bioremediation Processes

The growth and activity of the microorganisms must be stimulated to increase their population for bioremediation. It is achieved through 'bio-stimulation' that involves the addition of nutrients and oxygen to help indigenous microorganisms. These nutrients are the basic building blocks of life and allow microbes to create the necessary enzymes to break down the contaminants. All of them will need nitrogen, phosphorous and carbon for their growth (Prescott, 2002). Microbial growth and activity is affected by pH, temperature and moisture. Although microorganisms have also been isolated in extreme conditions, most of them grow optimally over a narrow range, so that it is important to achieve optimal conditions. Hydrocarbons are readily degraded under aerobic conditions, whereas chlorinated compounds are degraded only in anaerobic ones. To increase the oxygen amount in the soil it is possible to till or spurge air. In some cases, hydrogen peroxide or magnesium peroxide can be introduced in the environment. Soil structure can be improved by adding gypsum and organic matter (Prescott, 2002). Now-a-days, there are four main biological techniques used for treating soil and groundwater for stimulation of activity of indigenous microorganisms by the addition of nutrients, regulation of redox conditions, optimizing pH conditions; inoculation of the site by microorganisms with specific biotransforming abilities; application of immobilized enzymes; and use of plants (phytoremediation) to remove or transform pollutants (Vidali, 2001; Gupta, 2012). In the specific methods used for bioremediating contaminated soil and water, land-farming, composting, intrinsic bioremediation and slurry bioreactor are included.

Bioremediation Strategies

In-Situ Bioremediation

Bioventing encourages the *in-situ* biodegradation of POLs (petroleum-oil-lubricants) by providing oxygen to microorganisms in the soil. The system supplies oxygen by injecting air directly into the residual contamination. Bioventing uses low airflow rates to provide only enough oxygen to keep up microbial activity. Optimal flow rates maximize biodegradation as vapors move slowly through biologically active soil while minimizing volatilization of contaminants. A basic bioventing system includes a well and a blower, which pumps air through the well and into the soil (Lee *et al.* 2006).

Biopile treatment is a full-scale technology in which excavated soils are mixed with soil amendments, placed on a treatment area, and bioremediated using forced aeration. The contaminants are reduced to carbon dioxide and water. The basic biopile system includes a treatment bed, an aeration system, an irrigation/nutrient system and a leachate collection system. Moisture, heat, nutrients, oxygen, and pH are controlled to enhance biodegradation. The irrigation/nutrient system is buried under the soil to pass air and nutrients either by vacuum or positive pressure. The treatment time is typically 3 to 6 months (Wu *et al.* 2009).

Ex-Situ Bioremediation

These techniques mainly involve the excavation or removal of contaminated soil from ground. Land farming is a simple technique in which contaminated soil is excavated and spread over a prepared bed and periodically tilled until pollutants are degraded. The goal is to stimulate indigenous bio-degradative microorganisms and facilitate their aerobic degradation of contaminants. In general, the practice is limited to the treatment of superficial 10-35cm of soil. Composting is a process by which organic wastes are degraded by microorganisms, typically at elevated temperatures in the range of 55° to 65°C. The increased temperatures result from heat produced by microorganisms during the degradation of the organic material in the waste. In windrow composting, firstly, contaminated soils are excavated and screened to remove large rocks and debris (Blanca *et al.* 2007; 2008). The soil is transported to a composting pad with a temporary structure to provide containment and protection from weather extremes. Amendments (straw, alfalfa, manure, agricultural wastes and wood chips) are used for bulking agents and as a supplemental carbon source. Soil and amendments are layered into long piles, known as windrows. The windrow is thoroughly mixed by turning with a commercially available windrow turning machine. Moisture, pH, temperature and explosives concentration are monitored. At the completion of the composting period, the windrows are disassembled and the compost is taken to the final disposal area.

Biopiles are a hybrid of land-farming and composting. These are typically used for treatment of surface contamination with petroleum hydrocarbons. They are a refined version of land farming that tends to control physical losses of the contaminants by leaching and volatilization. Biopiles provide a favorable environment for indigenous aerobic and anaerobic microorganisms. Here engineered cells are used for construction of aerated compost piles (Fahnestock *et al.* 1998). Bioreactors/slurry reactors/aqueous reactors are used for *ex situ* treatment of contaminated soil and water. It involves the processing of contaminated solid material (soil, sediment, sludge) or water through an engineered containment system. Slurry bioreactor creates a three-phase (solid, liquid and gas) mixing condition to increase the bioremediation rate of soil bound and water-soluble pollutants as a water slurry of the contaminated soil and biomass (usually indigenous microorganisms) capable of degrading target contaminants. In general, the rate and extent of biodegradation are greater in a bioreactor system than *in situ* or in solid-phase systems because the contained environment is more manageable and hence more controllable and predictable.

The first patent for a biological remediation agent was registered in 1974, being a strain of *Pseudomonas putida* (Prescott *et al.* 2002) that was able to degrade petroleum. In 1991, about 70 microbial genera were reported to degrade petroleum compounds and almost an equal number has been added to the list in the successive two decades. These organisms belong to at least 11 different prokaryotic divisions (Glazer *et al.* 2007).

Novel Bioremediation Methods

Plasma Incineration

A novel method developed and used recently for treatment of wastes is plasma incineration or plasma assisted gasification. It uses plasma that causes the volatilization of solid waste materials under anaerobic conditions. The plasma generates a huge amount of energy which otherwise cannot be produced by nuclear fission/fusion. Under such extreme conditions, waste materials get decomposed and oxidized partially to harmless innocuous products like: carbon monoxide, hydrogen and water. During this process the organic matter of waste is converted into synthetic gas called *SynGas* while inorganic fraction is converted into an inert vitrified glass and thus no ash is left to be land-filled. The major advantages of this technology are that it reduces the production of exhaust gas and thus lessens the air pollution; toxic materials produced are entrapped and encapsulated thereby making easier and safer to handle; and finally equipment is compact so it takes a minimum space for large disposal wastes (Amin *et al.* 2012).

Pyrolysis Technology

Another recently developed method for bioremediation is Pyrolysis technology (developed by Energystics Technologies, Ltd). This method involves the use of electromagnetic waves (EM). Direct and concentrated electromagnetic waves are allowed to fall on solid, liquid or gaseous waste. This technology directly couples electromagnetic energy with a target material to produce heat. When EM waves fall on the target, it absorbs energy producing temperature which is above the melting or vaporization temperature of target waste material. Such a high temperature causes the disassociation of strong molecular bonds in waste materials. This technology requires only a relatively small energy input because the technology does not utilize conductive medium. In order to demonstrate the effect of this technology on animal tissues, pyrolysis of beef carcass was done which resulted in complete dematerialization of the tissue leaving no residues or smoke. The major advantages of Pyrolysis technology are that it produces instantaneous but controllable heating and releases no harmful emissions (Shepera, 2004 and Jones *et al.* 2004).

Conditioning

Conditioning is done to enhance the characteristics of bio-solids for their further processing. There are many conditioning technologies like:

ultrasonic degradation, chemical degradation, enzyme addition, electro-coagulation and biological cell destruction. These processes modify the inorganic and organic characteristics of waste which is critical to other processes (Hetherington *et al.* 2006).

Ultrasonic Degradation

This is the first step of the conditioning process. Solid wastes are subjected to acoustic waves to attain extremely high temperatures and pressures within biosolids. This result in the complete destruction of microbial cells due to shear stresses produced as a result of explosion of gas bubbles. This process is adjustable to high frequency and low frequency waves. The major advantages of this technique is that it causes an increase in rate of cell disruption, decrease in anaerobic digestion time, thereby reducing sludge quantity and increases the biogas production (Hetherington *et al.* 2006).

Chemical Cell Destruction

This process ensures disruption of the cell membrane of microorganisms in waste activated sludge process for the improved efficiency of anaerobic digestion and amount of biogas. The waste material is treated with caustic soda for about one hour. This causes the weakening of cell membrane of microorganisms and also decreases the viscosity of solution. For industrial scale treatment, Microsludge TM (Biocell) is used for this purpose. It uses industrial-scale high pressure homogenizer which causes a sudden and enormous pressure drop responsible for causing lysis of microbial cell in the sludge. This sludge is then liquefied, mixed with primary sludge followed by: anaerobic digestion to produce biosolids and biogas (Hetherington *et al.* 2006).

Enzyme Conditioning

Enzyme conditioning is done with the help of microbes (both aerobic and anaerobic) that produces specialized enzymes (usually an enzyme mixture with specific nutrients like: humic acids, amino acids) which degrade organic materials converting them into carbon dioxide and water. This method increases the dewaterability of biosolids and also reduces odours during digestion process (Hetherington *et al.* 2006).

Electro-coagulation

This is the recently developed method where electric current is used to increase the rate of anaerobic digestion of waste material. The electric current so produced dissolves an anode (sacrificial anode) and releases chemically reactive aluminum into the wastewater stream.

The positively charged aluminum ions attract very fine negatively charged ions and particles towards them resulting in agglomeration. As a result, the agglomerated particles increase in size and settle down due to their increased weight (Hetherington *et al.* 2006; Amin *et al.* 2012).

Biological Cell Destruction

This process involves the use of a chemical agent that possesses strong oxidation properties. The agent weakens the cell wall of bacteria. These processed bacteria are then returned back to the activated sludge process where they decompose into carbon dioxide and water.

Thermophilic Fermentation

This method utilizes the microorganisms to increase the rate of digestion process at high temperatures. Thus sewage sludge and other waste residuals are converted into a fertilizer grade product. Another technology called ThermoMaster™ process has been developed in which auto-heated aerobic digestion is operated at a relatively short residence time (30 hours) to maximize the production of single-cell protein using an influent waste material as a substrate. The solids thus obtained are dried and pelletized (Hetherington *et al.* 2006; Amin *et al.* 2012).

Anaerobic Digestion

The first phase consists of volatile fatty acid digester where digestion takes place at around 35°C. In the next phase, the temperature is further increased in a thermophilic range of 50-56°C where further digestion takes place under anaerobic conditions. In the final phase, the heating is slowed down till temperature reaches around 35°C.

Recent advancements in technology have led to the use of ozone treatment for anaerobic digestion. The biosolids are first subjected to anaerobic digestion and then are passed into a reaction tank where they are exposed to low levels of ozone. Studies have shown that only 0.06g of ozone per gram of dissolved solids is sufficient to destroy the biological activity of digested biosolids. The ozone treated waste material is then sent to thickening tank followed and back to digester in which both ozone treated and non-ozone treated waste materials are mixed. After this, waste material is either sent for dewatering or for ozone treatment (Vranitsky and Lahnsteiner, 2002).

Electro Dewatering of Waste Material

Conventional dewatering technologies, such as: centrifuges, belt filter presses, and rotary vacuum filters, are not effective methods for treating sewage sludge with high water content. Alternatively, waste material is subjected to direct current (DC) which in the initial stage causes particles to migrate to the oppositely charged electrode (electrophoresis). Due to electro-osmosis, cake formation occurs as ions migrate to the oppositely charged electrode. This technology is suitable for use in combination with conventional filtration (Kim *et al.* 2014).

Electroacoustic Dewatering

This is another method of dewatering waste where both electric field and ultrasound waves are used to increase the efficiency of dewatering.

Electric field is used for electrophoresis and electro-osmosis whereas acoustic waves (sound waves) are used in maintaining electrical continuity throughout the waste material. The main advantage of using acoustic waves is that they decrease specific energy consumption, increases the filtration rate and helps to keep cathode clean (Hetherington *et al.* 2006).

Mechanical Freeze Thaw

In this process, the sludge is frozen followed by crushing and thawing under natural conditions. During freezing, the chemical bonds in the sludge are altered thus making removal of water easier.

The treated sludge is then subjected to conventional sludge dewatering equipment (Amin *et al.* 2012).

Hydrothermal Oxidation

This technology is also known as 'Supercritical water oxidation'. In this process, the water is heated and pressurized above the critical point at 374°C and 3,191 pounds per square inch (psi). Consequently, the solubility of organic substances and oxygen into water is significantly increased. The main advantage of this technology is that it decomposes organic matter completely and produces a high quality effluent (Amin *et al.* 2012).

Drying of Waste Material

Drying is done to remove the water from the waste residues collected from both domestic, industrial and agriculture waste. This reduces weight and volume with high solid percentage. Drying can be through direct or indirect heating. The different methods of drying are discussed below:

Belt Drying

It involves the use of two or more slow moving belts that are arranged in series. The air is supplied around the belts. The dewatered sludge is spread in the form of a thin layer on a belt to increase the surface area (Amin *et al.* 2012).

Direct Microwave Heating

This process involves the use of high-efficiency multi-mode microwave system which is specifically designed to remove moisture. It removes water and pathogens from dewatered sludge. This process is highly automated and can dry waste materials having an initial moisture content of 85 per cent to a final moisture content of 10 per cent. This technology has an added advantage that it has the capacity of about 100 per cent pathogen without any change in its nutrient content (Amin *et al.* 2012).

Flash Drying

This method can dry waste material to upto 90 per cent or more solids. Sludge containing water is fed into a centrifuge machine where dewatering takes place and its solid content reach upto 25 per cent concentration. This material is then discharged into thermal stage as a fine-grained spray. Once the particles of solid waste enter thermal cyclone chamber, they get dried up instantly. These dried particles are then taken out of the chamber in a fraction of second, with the help of sweep gas. The sweep gas, drawn through ventilator fan is reheated in hot gas generator before re-entering into dryer loop (Amin *et al*. 2012).

Fluidized Bed Dryer

After the wet cake is formed, it is passed through the fluidized bed dryer where it comes into contact with already dried granules. Indirect heating is then applied by means of tubular heat exchangers that are immersed in fluidized layer of solids. The major advantages of this technology are that it can dry the sewage material upto 90 per cent solid content (Amin *et al*. 2012).

Chemical Drying

This process involves the drying of solids through chemical reaction. The dewatered waste material is allowed to react with ammonium salts or anhydrous ammonia and concentrated organic acids like: sulphuric acid and phosphoric acid. The reaction of ammonia with organic acids generates heat and during this reaction sulphates and phosphates are produced. The heat produced from the reaction is utilized for drying of waste materials. During this process, hard granular materials are produced that can be mixed with plant nutrients to raise their nutritive value (Amin *et al*. 2012).

Bioremediation by Genetic Engineering

Biotechnological technique like genetic engineering can be used for improving bioremediation of heavy metals and organic pollutants. Transgenic plants and associated bacteria can be used to create genetically modified organisms for bioremediation by over-expressing the genes responsible for their metal-binding proteins or peptides that in turn enhance their heavy metal accumulation and/or tolerance. Furthermore transgenic algae and microorganisms mutated with bioluminescence genes can be used in bio-monitoring of organic and inorganic pollution. There are several approaches for the construction of GEMs for bioremediation application. First approach is the identification of organisms suitable for modification with the relevant genes, *e.g*., aquatic microbes can be used to develop GEMs for bioremediation of aquatic sources. The use of such organisms would avoid the supplementation of nutrients to the inoculated environment, thereby reducing the costs incurred and maintenance required. Scientists have developed *Anabaena sp*. and Nostoc *ellipsosporum* by the insertion of linA (from *P. paucimobilus*) and fcbABC (from *Arthrobacter globiformis*) respectively (Kulshreshtha, 2013). The second approach is the pathway construction, extension and regulation. GEMs have developed by improving existing catabolic pathways or to extend these pathways to degrade some more compounds which are not possible to degrade by using wild strain. The complete catabolic pathway may be encoded by a single microorganism, or by a consortium of microorganisms, each performing one or more of the stages of bioremediation of xenobiotics. In this way, constructed GEMs possess the degradation capabilities of different microbial communities due to the alteration of gene sequences which further improve the efficiency and efficacy of the catabolic pathways (Kulshreshtha, 2013).

Third approach is modification of enzyme specificity and affinity, *e.g., E. coli* strain is genetically modified to express a hybrid gene cluster for the degradation of trichloroethylene (TCE). Fourth approach is bioprocess development, monitoring, and control, and bioaffinity, bioreporter, sensor applications for chemical sensing, toxicity reduction, and end point analysis. Bioluminescence can be easily detected and do not require expensive devices, exogenous addition of chemicals or co-factors. Further, GEMs possess chemical sensors that allow the monitoring of contaminant bioavailability rather than just contaminant presence. Bioluminescence producing GEMs also help us to understand the spread of microbes in the polluted area and end point of the bioremediation (Kulshreshtha, 2013).

In a recent study, a *Pseudomonas putida* strain was genetically engineered for 1,2,3-trichloropropane bioremediation. 1,2,3-Trichloropropane (TCP) is a toxic compound that is recalcitrant to biodegradation in the environment. Attempts to isolate TCP-degrading organisms using enrichment cultivation have failed. Finally, the dehalogenase gene (dhaA31) was cloned and was introduced into the genome of strain MC4 using a transposon delivery system. Growth of the resulting engineered bacterium, *P. putida* MC4-5222, on TCP was observed, and all organic chlorine was released as chloride. The results demonstrated the successful use of a laboratory-evolved dehalogenase and genetic engineering to produce an effective, plasmid-free, and stable whole-cell biocatalyst for the aerobic bioremediation of a recalcitrant chlorinated hydrocarbon (Samin *et al.* 2014). Transgenic *Chlamydomonas* cells express metallothionin, a metal binding protein. These cells grow at normal rates in the presence of lethal concentrations of cadmium accumulating five-fold more cadmium compared to wild type cells. Mixotrophy in cyanobacteria and microalgae can provide many competitive advantages over bacteria and fungi in degrading persistent organic pollutants (POPs) (Subashchandrabose *et al.* 2013).

Bioremediation using Earthworms (Vermiculture)

Earthworms could be used to extract toxic heavy metals, including cadmium and lead, from solid waste from domestic refuse collection and waste from vegetable and flower markets.

Three species of earthworm, *Eudrilus eugeniae, Eisenia fetida* and *Perionyx excavates* are used to assist in the composting of urban waste and to extract heavy metals, cadmium, copper, lead, manganese, zinc, prior to subsequent processing. The process of vermicomposting in this way allows such waste materials to be remediated and the compost can then be used in growing human food without the risk of accumulating heavy metals in crops. Studies have shown that up to three-quarters of the various heavy metals can be removed by the worms from solid waste. The *E. eugeniae* species is the most effective worm at remediating solid waste and producing rich compost. Research has shown that the heavy metal content of such waste can be reduced to levels significantly below the permissible safe limits. The mechanism involved is because of worm's digestive system that is capable of detaching heavy metal ions from the complex aggregates between the ions and humic substances in the waste during the process of rotting. Various enzyme-driven processes leads to assimilation of the metal ions by the worms so that they are locked up in the organism's tissues rather than being released back into the compost as worm casts. The separation of dead worms from compost is a relatively straightforward process allowing the heavy metal to be removed from the organic waste (Science Daily, 2012).

In a recent research, phenol bioremediation potential of Earthworms was studied. Earthworms were maintained under proper growth conditions. Different concentrations of phenol ranging from 10ppm to 50ppm were taken for the assays. All the bioremediation assays were done in the soil with phenol dispersed in water and remediation rates were observed for 24 hours, 48 hours, 72 hours, 96 hours and 120 hours. The initial concentration of phenol was increased eventually and the rate of bioremediation was estimated using 4-amino anti-pyrine method. The phenol degradation activity of the gut microflora of the earthworm along with the soil microflora was also observed on a formulated media. The amount of phenol bioremediated was found higher in case of earthworm and not the microflora solely. It was found to be 30 ppm in 48 hours when the initial concentration was 50 ppm (Kamarudheen *et al.* 2014). In another study, the earthworms' capacity to remediate the quality of soils polluted with heavy metals (Zn, Cu, Mn, Pb) as a result of using the swine residual water in agriculture (50 m^3 ha^{-1}) was distinguished. The study has been conducted in a Chernozem (FAO System), in a culture of *Zea mays* L. The collected data consisted of soil analyses and tissue analyses to establish the heavy metal uptake by earthworm species. Determination of the heavy metal contents of soil has been realized on two depth intervals: 0-10 cm and respectively 10-20 cm, through the method of flame atomic absorption spectrometry. Earthworm extraction was done using formaldehyde according to the methodology in force at six months since the residual water has been applied on soil. Both for earthworm number and earthworm weight there were significant differences (<0.05) between the values recorded in controls and treatments, *i.e.*, the earthworm number considerably increased in the variants fertilized with swine residual water and also the earthworm weight, which confirm the earthworm preference for the organic matter provided by the residual water. Also there were significant differences (<0.05) between the three analyzed earthworm species regarding the accumulation process of the investigated microelements and, among them, *Lumbricus rubellus* showed in its tissues the lowest concentration of microelements and *Allolobophora rosea* the highest concentrations. There were also much lower concentrations of the studied microelements in the earthworm tissues as compared with the adjacent soil in all analyzed species, and among them there was recorded the lowest content of heavy metals in *Lumbricus castaneus*. This aspect and also the fact that this species has been the best represented as numeric abundance in the experimental soil confirm the good capacity of this species to tolerate the presence of the heavy metals in soil and to metabolize them with the soil ingestion within the feeding process. The results of this study support the idea claiming the earthworms' bioremediator potential of the soils polluted with heavy metals, as a possibility to restore their quality by maintaining in appropriate levels the earthworm populations in the agricultural lands. These findings also come to sustain the specialization of this role on earthworm species (Iordache and Borza, 2012).

Duckweeds for Phytoremediation

Effective wastewater treatments through conventional methods that rely on heavy aeration are expensive to install and operate. Duckweeds are capable of recovering or extracting nutrients or pollutants and are an excellent candidate for bio-remediation of wastewaters. Such plants grow very fast, utilizing wastewater nutrients and also yield cost effective protein-rich biomass as a by-product. Duckweeds being tiny surface floating plants are easy to harvest and have an appreciable amount of protein (15%-45% dry mass basis) and a lower fiber (7%-14% dry mass basis) content. Besides nutrient extraction, duckweeds have been found to reduce total suspended solids, biochemical oxygen demand (BOD), and chemical oxygen demand in wastewater significantly. Depending on the initial concentrations of nutrients, duckweed-covered systems can remove nitrate at daily rates of 120-590 mg $NO_3^- m^{-2}$ (73%-97% of initial concentration) and phosphate at 14-74 mg $PO_4 m^{-2}$ (63%-99% of initial concentration). Removal efficiencies within 3 days of 96 per cent and 99 per cent have been reported for BOD and ammonia. Besides several genera of duckweeds (*Spirodela, Lemna, Wolffia*), other surface-floating aquatic plants like water hyacinth (*Eichhornia*) are well known for their phyto-remediation qualities (Gupta and Prakash, 2014). Duckweed culture is an eco-friendly approach of phyto-remediation which will not only help in free-of-cost extraction of nutrients in the form of protein-rich biomass but also bio-remediate the ponds, lakes, and other water bodies and make them a more suitable water resource for aquaculture. Wastewater-duckweed-carp poly-culture makes the perfect integrated package for pollution control and re-use of recovered nutrients. Moreover, in view of increased pressure on land over the years for production of food and fodder (due to ever increasing population, urbanization, industrialization, etc.), utilization of an alternate resource for the purpose makes sense. In this direction, duckweed culture holds ample scope not only for high quality food production through aquaculture but also releasing pressure on the underground water resources (Gupta and Prakash, 2014).

Mushrooms and Bioremediation

Spent mushroom compost is generated as waste after the harvesting of mushroom crop. Recently, it is proposed to call it as 'post mushroom substrate' because it is not really spent and has many uses. The composition of spent mushroom substrate varies depending on the type of mushroom to be cultivated and substrate used. It is proved as an excellent source of humus, although much of its nitrogen content has been used up by the growing mushrooms. It remains a good source of general nutrients (N, P, K along with trace elements) which makes it well suited for supporting plant growth (Svoboda *et al.* 2002). Mushrooms are found to possess the two basic abilities of biodegradation and bioaccumulation for the bioremediation of waste. Biodegradation ability of mushrooms is due to the presence of many enzymes involved in the degradation of pollutants and solid waste residues though the extent and safe level is unknown. Moreover, mushrooms are known for the bioaccumulation of pollutants or heavy metals from the habitat in which they are growing. Mushroom possesses a very effective mechanism that enables them to take up some trace elements from the substrate. Heavy metal accumulation ability of mushroom has been studied by the number of authors (Kala and Svoboda, 2000; Svoboda *et al.* 2002; Kulshreshtha and Sharma, 2014).

Bioremediation of Plastic and Rubber by Endophytic Fungi

The massive and rapid accumulation of plastic and rubber waste is a problem that cannot be ignored. While there has been an enormous boom in synthetic polymer production, methods of treating these materials after disposal have not been able to keep up. Since several types of plastic and rubber contain the same chemical bonds that are found in natural plant polymers, specific attention is given to the ability of endophytes, organisms that grow symbiotically inside plants, to degrade synthetic plastic and rubber. The endophytic fungus *Pestalotiopsis microspore* has previously been identified in the degradation of the plastic polyester polyurethane. This fungus secretes a small enzyme that is responsible for plastic degradation (Legaspi and Elaine, 2014).

Bioremediation through Microbes: Growth Parameters

Most bioremediation systems work under aerobic conditions, but recalcitrant molecules are degraded by microbial organisms only under anaerobic conditions. Bioremediation depends on various parameters: nature of pollutants, soil structure, pH, moisture content and hydrogeology, nutritional state, microbial diversity of the site, temperature and oxidation-reduction (redox-potential) (Dua *et al.* 2002). In bioremediation processes, microorganisms use the contaminants as nutrient or energy sources (Tang *et al.* 2007). Bioremediation activity through microbes is stimulated by supplementing nutrients (nitrogen and phosphorus), electron acceptors (oxygen), and substrates (methane, phenol, and toluene), or by introducing microorganisms with desired catalytic capabilities (Ma *et al*. 2007; Baldwin *et al*. 2008). Plant and soil microbes develop a rhizospheric zone which is also used as a tool for accelerating the rate of degradation or to remove contaminants. In addition to this, aromatic compounds are persistent environmental pollutants that are widely distributed in the biosphere due to anthropogenic activities. These compounds are highly toxic to living beings; therefore, many of them have been listed as priority pollutants by Environmental Protection Agency. Microbial degradation has emerged as an effective technology to remove these compounds from environment. Many microbial enzymes such as: oxygenases, dehalogenases, reductases, hydroxylases and dehydrogenases are involved in the degradation of these environmental pollutants. Among them, oxygenases are the key enzymes for aerobic biodegradation of aromatic compounds because they are involved in the initial reaction of degradation and also catalyze the ring cleavage of the aromatic compounds which is the essential step for the complete mineralization of these compounds (Arora *et al*. 2009). Oxygenases catalyze insertion of one or two oxygen atoms into the substrates. Two classes of oxygenases have been identified based on number of oxygen atom used in the oxidation: mono-oxygenases and dioxygenases. Monooxygenases incorporate one atom of the oxygen into the substrate whereas dioxygenases add both atoms of the oxygen (Arora *et al*. 2009).

Pros and cons of Bioremediation

Bioremediation is a natural process and is therefore perceived by the public as an acceptable waste treatment process for contaminated material such as: soil. The residues for the treatment are usually harmless products and include carbon dioxide, water and cell biomass. Theoretically, bioremediation is useful for the complete destruction of a wide variety of contaminants. Many compounds that are legally considered to be hazardous can be transformed to harmless products. This eliminates the chance of future liability associated with treatment and disposal of contaminated material. In bioremediation, there is no need of transferring contaminants from one environmental medium to another and the complete destruction of target pollutants is possible. Bioremediation can also be carried out on site, without causing a major disruption of normal activities. This also eliminates the need to transport quantities of waste off site and the potential threats to human health and the environment that can arise during transportation. Bioremediation can prove less expensive than other technologies that are used for clean-up of hazardous waste (Dua *et al*. 2002).

The major con of bioremediation is that the process is limited to those compounds that are biodegradable. Not all compounds are susceptible to rapid and complete degradation. There are some concerns that the products of biodegradation may be more persistent or toxic than the parent compound. Biodegradation process is a natural phenomenon and is highly specific. There are major site factors required for complete biodegradation that include the presence of metabolically capable microbial populations, suitable environmental growth conditions, and appropriate levels of nutrients and contaminants. Biodegradation is often difficult to extrapolate from bench and pilot-scale studies to full-scale field operations. Research is needed to develop and engineer bioremediation technologies that are appropriate for sites with complex mixtures of contaminants that are not evenly dispersed in the environment. Contaminants may be present as solids, liquids, and gases. Bioremediation often takes longer than other treatment options, such as: excavation and removal of soil or incineration. Regulatory uncertainty remains regarding acceptable performance criteria for bioremediation. There is no accepted definition of "clean", evaluating performance of bioremediation is difficult, and there are no acceptable endpoints for bioremediation treatments (Dua *et al*. 2002).

Conclusion

Environmental pollution affects quality of life and environmental ecosystem. Since decades, many attempts are being done to reduce environmental pollution. Among these attempts bioremediation is one of the good remedial techniques. Bioremediation technique involves the use of microorganisms to reduce the toxicity of harmful wastes and heavy metals from contaminated wastes water. Some other methods of bioremediation are by using earthworms (vermiculture), duckweeds and mushrooms, thermophilic fermentation or by genetically engineered microbes including endophytic fungi for biodegrading plastic wastes. Recently bioremediation is used in combination with other physical and chemical methods such as: plasma incineration, pyrolysis, conditioning, electro-coagulation, electroacoustic dewatering, mechanical freeze thaw, hydrothermal oxidation, flash drying, microwave heating, fluidized bed dryer, and chemical drying. Bioremediation can thus be proved as a problem-solving approach in the field of solid waste by detoxifying wastes. Due to its cost effectiveness and lesser environmental impact, it offers an attractive and more conventional clean-up technology.

REFERENCES

Arora, P.K.; Kumar, M.; Chauhan, A.; Raghava, G.P. and Jain, R.K. (2009). OxDBase: A Database of Oxygenases Involved in Biodegradation. BMC Res Notes 2: 67.

Baldwin, B.R.; Peacock, A.D.; Park, M; Ogles, D.M; Istok, J.D.; McKinley, J.P.; Resch, C.T. and White, D.C. (2008). Multilevel Samplers as Microcosms to Assess Microbial Response to Biostimulation. *Ground Water*, 46: 295-304.

Blanca, A-L.; Angus, J.B.; Katarina, S.; Joe, Lopez-Real, Nicholas, J.R. (2007). The Influence of different Temperature Programmes on the Bioremediation of Polycyclic Aromatic hydrocarbons (PAHs) in a coal-tar Contaminated Soil by in-vessel Composting. *Journal of Hazardous Materials*, 14: 340-347.

Blanca, A-L.; Spanova, K.; Beck, A.J. and Russell, N.J. (2008). Microbial Community Structure Changes during Bioremediation of PAHs in an aged coal-tar Contaminated soil by in-vessel Composting, *International Biodeterioration and Biodegradation*, 61: 357-364.

Dua, M.; Sethunathan, N. and Johri, A.K. (2002). Biotechnology Bioremediation Success and Limitations. *Applied Microbiology and Biotechnology*, 59:143-152.

Fahnestock, F.M.V.; Wickramanayake, G.B.; Kratzke, K.J. and Major. W.R. (1998). *Biopile Design, Operation, and Maintenance Handbook for Treating Hydrocarbon Contaminated Soil*, Battelle Press, Columbus, OH.

Glazer, A.N. and Nikaido, H. (2007). Microbial Biotechnology: Fundamentals of Applied Microbiology, 8: 510-528.

Kamaludeen, SPBK.; Arunkumar, K.R.; Avudainayagam, S. and Ramasamy, K. (2003). Bioremediation of chromium Contaminated Environments. *Indian Journal of Experimental Biology*, 41: 972-985.

Lee, T.H.; Byun, I.G.; Kim, Y.O.; Hwang, I.S. and Park, T.J. (2006). Monitoring Biodegradation of Diesel Fuel in Bioventing Processes using in situ Respiration Rate. *Water Science and Technology*, 53(4-5):263-72.

Ma, X.; Novak, P.J.; Ferguson, J., Sadowsky, M.; LaPara, T.M., Semmens, M.J. and Hozalski, R.M. (2007). The Impact of H2 Addition on Dechorinating Microbial Communities. *Bioremediation Journal*, 11: 45-55.

Prescott, L.M.; Harley, J.P. and Klein, D.A. (2002). Microbiology. Fundamentals of Applied Microbiology, 2: 1012-1014.

Strong, P.J. and Burgess, J.E. (2008). Treatment Methods for Wine-related ad Distillery Wastewaters: A Review. *Bioremediation Journal*, 12: 70-87.

Tang, C.Y.; Criddle, QS Fu CS. and Leckie, J.O. (2007). Effect of flux (transmembrane pressure) and Membranes Properties on Fouling and Rejection of Reverse osmosis and nanofiltration membranes Treating perfluorooctane sulfonate containing Wastewater. *Environmental Science and Technology*, 41:2008-2014.

Vidali, M. (2001). Bioremediation: An Overview. *Pure Applied Chemistry*, 73:1163-1172.

Wu, T. and Crapper, M. (2009). Simulation of Biopile Processes using a hydraulics Approach, *Journal of Hazardous Material*, 171(1-3):1103-11.

Inderscience Publishers. "Bioremediation of Toxic Metals using Worms: Earthworms soak up Heavy Metal." Science Daily, 16 August 2012. www.sciencedaily.com/releases/2012/08/120816133420.htm

Gupta C. (2012). Role of Bioremediation in Environment Management. In: Environment and Biotechnology (Prasad, R. (ed.) and Arvind Kumar) LAP LAMBERT Academic Publishing GmbH and Co., Germany, 110-130.

M. Hetherington, M. Moore, R. Pepperman, T. G. Shea, L. Stone, R. Reimers and P. Rom, "Emerging Technologies for Biosolids Management," *Office of Wastewater Management U.S. Environmental Protection Agency Washington, D.C.*, pp. 1-1-9-4, 2006

Amin T., Chhabra P, Bhat SV. Recent Advancements in Food Waste Management. *International Journal of Advancements in Research and Technology*, September-2012, 1(4): 1-9.

Shepera TJ. "Personal Communication to A. Nutsch Regarding Energy"eam™ Technology: Thomas J. Sheperak (President and CEO, Energystics Technologies, Ltd.)," 2004.

Jones DD, Hawkins S and Ess DR. "Carcass Disposal: A Comprehensive Review," in *Non-Traditional and Novel Technologies*, 2004, pp. 1-38.

Riggle, D. (1989). Revival time for Composting Food Industry Wastes. BioCycle, 29, 35-37.

Grobe, K. (1994). Composter links up with Food Processor. BioCycle, 34, 40, 42-43.

Schaub, S.M., and Leonard, J.J. (1996). Composting: An Alternative Waste Management Option for Food Processing Industries. *Trends in Food Science and Technology*, 7, 263-268.

Nakata, B. (1994). Recycling by-products on California vineyards. BioCycle, 34, 61.

Vranitsky R. and Lahnsteiner, J. Sewage sludge Disintegration using ozone – A Method of Enhancing the anaerobicstabilization of sewage sludge," *Proceedings of the European Biosolids and Organic Residuals Workshop, Conference and Exhibition*, 2002.

Kim S, Kim J and Chung J. (2014) Improved Waste-activated Sludge Dewatering using sludge/oil emulsion, ultrasonic and Microwave Technologies. *Water SA* 40(4): 677-685.

Hetherington M., Moore M., Pepperman R., Shea T.G., Stone L., Reimers R. and Rom P. Emerging Technologies for Biosolids Management. *Office of Wastewater Management U.S. Environmental Protection Agency Washington, D.C.* pp. 1-1-9-4, 2006.

Kulshreshtha S, Sharma K (2014). Perspectives of Bioremediation through Mushroom Cultivation. *J. Bioremed Biodeg* 5: e154. doi: 10.4172/2155-6199.1000e154.

Kala P, Svoboda L (2000). A Review of Trace Element Concentrations in Edible Mushrooms. *Food Chemistry* 69: 273-281.

Svoboda L, Kalač L, Špička J, Janoušková J (2002). Leaching of Cadmium, Lead and Mercury from Fresh and dL rerently preserved edible mushroom, *Xerocomus badius*, during soaking and boiling. Food Chemistry 79: 41-45.

Legaspi, Elaine M. Bioremediation of Plastic and Rubber by Endophytic Fungi EPA Grant Number: F13A30122, Yale University, Project Period: 2014 - 2016.

Gupta, C., and Prakash, D. (2014). Duckweed: An Effective tool for Phytoremediation. *Toxicological and Environmental Chemistry (Taylor and Francis)* DOI:10.1080/02772248.2013.879309

Dua, M.; Sethunathan, N. and Johri, A.K. (2002). Biotechnology Bioremediation Success and Imitations. *Applied Microbiology and Biotechnology*, 59:143-152.

Tang, C.Y.; Criddle, QS Fu CS. and Leckie, J.O. (2007). Effect of flux (transmembrane pressure) and Membranes Properties on Fouling and Rejection of Reverse osmosis and nanofiltration Membranes Treating Perfluorooctane sulfonate containing Wastewater. *Environmental Science and Technology*, 41:2008-2014.

Ma, X.; Novak, P.J.; Ferguson, J., Sadowsky, M.; LaPara, T.M., Semmens, M.J. and Hozalski, R.M. (2007). The Impact of H2 Addition on Dechorinating Microbial Communities. *Bioremediation Journal*, 11: 45-55.

Baldwin, B.R.; Peacock, A.D.; Park, M.; Ogles, D.M.; Istok, J.D.; McKinley, J.P.; Resch, C.T. and White, D.C. (2008). Multilevel Samplers as Microcosms to Assess Microbial Response to Biostimulation. *Ground Water*, 46: 295-304.

Arora, P.K.; Kumar, M.; Chauhan, A.; Raghava, G.P. and Jain, R.K. (2009). OxDBase: A Database of Oxygenases Involved in Biodegradation. BMC Res Notes 2: 67.

Iordache M. and Borza I. The Bioremediation Potential of Earthworms (Oligochaeta: Lumbricidae) in A Soil Polluted with Heavy Metals. *Journal of Food, Agriculture and Environment (JFAE)*, 2012, Vol. 10, Issue 2, pp. 1183-1186.

Kamarudheen N, George C, Bose I, Sathiavelu M and Sathiavelu A. Earthworm Mediated Bioremediation of phenol. *Asian Journal of Microbiology, Biotechnology and Environmental Sciences*, 16(2), 2014; 449-453.

Samin G., Pavlova M., Arif MI, Postema CP., Damborsky J., Janssen DB A Pseudomonas putida strain genetically engineered for 1,2,3-trichloropropane bioremediation. *Appl. Environ Microbiol*. 2014; 80(17):5467-76.

Kulshreshtha S. (2013). Genetically Engineered Microorganisms: A Problem-Solving Approach for Bioremediation. *J. Bioremed Biodeg* 4: e133.

Subashchandrabose S.R., Ramakrishnan B., Megharaj M., Venkateswarlu K., Naidu R. Mixotrophic cyanobacteria and Microalgae as Distinctive Biological Agents for organic Pollutant Degradation. *Environ Int*. 2013; 51:59-72.

Index